Conflict and Harmony
in Multi-Ethnic Societies

Major Concepts in Politics and Political Theory

Garrett Ward Sheldon
General Editor

Vol. 9

PETER LANG
New York • Washington, D.C./Baltimore
Bern • Frankfurt am Main • Berlin • Vienna • Paris

Walter Morris-Hale

Conflict and Harmony in Multi-Ethnic Societies

An International Perspective

PETER LANG
New York • Washington, D.C./Baltimore
Bern • Frankfurt am Main • Berlin • Vienna • Paris

Library of Congress Cataloging-in-Publication Data

Morris-Hale, Walter.
Conflict and harmony in multi-ethnic societies:
an international perspective/ Walter Morris-Hale.
p. cm. — (Major concepts in politics and political theory; vol. 9)
Includes bibliographical references (p.   ) and index.
1. Political stability. 2. Ethnic relations—Political aspects. 3. Pluralism
(Social sciences). 4. Trust (Psychology). 5. Comparative government.
I. Title. II. Series.
JC330.2.M67   323.1'1—dc20   95-16666
ISBN 0-8204-2837-X
ISSN 1059-3535

Die Deutsche Bibliothek-CIP-Einheitsaufnahme

Morris-Hale, Walter:
Conflict and harmony in multi-ethnic societies: an international perspective/
Walter Morris-Hale.–New York; Washington, D.C./Baltimore; Bern; Frankfurt
am Main; Berlin; Vienna; Paris: Lang.
(Major concepts in politics and political theory; Vol. 9)
ISBN 0-8204-2837-X
NE: GT

Cover design by James F. Brisson.

The paper in this book meets the guidelines for permanence and durability
of the Committee on Production Guidelines for Book Longevity
of the Council of Library Resources.

Printed in the United States of America.

Dedication

To Vivian-Larzette: my mother, my best friend, my muse.

Acknowledgements

I should like to thank the Smith College students, who have taken my African courses and South African seminar, as well as my Plural Societies courses over the past twenty-five years.

I should also like to express my deep appreciation to Ellen Dibble, class of 1968, who typed the many early drafts of this manuscript, Anna Fedyshyn, class of 1995, who prepared the final camera-ready manuscript, and Amy Brown, class of 1989, who drew the maps.

Table of Contents

List of Maps

List of Tables

For it is not always when things are going from bad to worse that revolutions break out. On the contrary, it oftener happens that when a people which has put up with an oppressive rule over a long period without protest suddenly finds the government relaxing its pressure, it takes up arms against it. . . . The most perilous moment for a bad government is one when it seeks to mend its ways. . . . Patiently endured so long as it seemed beyond redress, a grievance comes to appear intolerable once the possibility of removing it crosses men's minds. For the mere fact that certain abuses have been remedied draws attention to the others and they now appear more galling; people may suffer less, but their sensibility is exacerbated.

—Alexis de Tocqueville,
L'Ancien Régime et La Révolution

Preface

The aim of this study is twofold. First, to illustrate the role of British colonial policies and the legacies of those policies, in Britain's former colonies and dependent territories, in perpetrating and exacerbating ethnic animosity in the politics of independent states. Second, to illustrate that ethnic animosity on politics is not confined to nation-building, developing states, but is endemic in many industrial and post-industrial, developed nations as well. Thus, this study is a challenge to the assumption of such writers as Robert Milne, Donald Horowitz, John Furnivall, and Larry Diamond et al.[1] Their assumption is summarized in Furnivall's statement that in the tropics, i.e., in developing states, ethnic groups live side by side but do not integrate, except in the world of commerce, while in developed nations, such as the United States, ethnic groups meet on equal terms as a consequence of their tradition of western culture.

The central question in this study is: If you change people's "behavior," by law of edict, but not their "attitudes," by conviction, have you solved or resolved the problem of ethnic animosity in politics or merely papered it over from where it may emerge, in violence, at a more unpropitious moment? Thus, the primary effort of students of ethnic politics must be to formulate means that will alter behavior, in the short term, while, at the same time, to elicit means for inducing changes in attitudes, in the long term, in order to achieve a meaningful resolution to ethnic animosity and ethnic conflict in politics. It is a principal assumption of this study that education and economics are key factors in ameliorating ethnic discord in local and national politics.

In this study, ethnicity is viewed as a major factor in the politics of developed nations, those with a so-called western cultural tradition, and nation-building, developing states, those with a tradition of the colonial experience. Often, in an ambiguous usage, ethnicity is taken to mean "race" or "tribe," but much is omitted in this uncertain usage. In this study, ethnicity is used to encompass—separately, collectively, or in any combination of two or more characteristics—race, religion, language, culture, or group identity. As employed in current social science literature, ethnicity is a term in search of an unmistakable meaning.

Notes

1. Robert Stephen Milne, *Politics in Ethnically Bipolar States* (Vancouver, Canada: University of British Columbia Press, 1981); Donald L. Horowitz, *Ethnic Groups in Conflict* (Berkeley, CA: University of California Press, 1985); John Furnivall, *Colonial Policy and Practice* (Cambridge, England: Cambridge University Press, 1948); and Larry Diamond, Juan Linz, and Seymour Martin Lipset, eds., *Democracy in Developing Countries: Africa* (Boulder, CO: Lynne Rienner Publishers, 1988).

Introduction

Trust is the most essential ingredient in human relationships whether between individuals, groups, or states. The unspoken question is, "Can I trust you not to betray me?"

This is a study of comparative politics in multi-ethnic societies. As a consequence of their differences in historical experiences, social cohesion, political, economic, and psychological development, each of the countries in the seven case studies—Switzerland, Britain, Northern Ireland, Canada, Malaysia, Nigeria, and South Africa—is at a different stage in its internal political integration and its domestic level of mutual trust. These differences are the most distinguishing characteristics among them and, in turn, have profoundly influenced the development of their political integration and the sense of trust among the diverse ethnicities in their populations. Political integration and mutual trust are so intimately interwoven as to constitute the singular, most ambitious goal of any political community. Yet, the most difficult domestic problem that each country has had to face results from their ethnic diversity. The key to their future is the attainment of political unity, stability, and continuity, despite their ethnic diversity. Success of this awesome task can only be achieved through political integration, mutual trust, and enlightened leadership.

The contention of this study is also that ethnic disharmonies are less likely to be extreme, that is, violent in a political community that has a significant number of voluntary associations, because citizens who belong to numerous and diverse associations will be exposed to a variety of divergent points of view, and such exposure helps to produce a willingness to compromise that is conducive to stable government and an integrated society. Being exposed to a variety of divergent points of view, citizens come to appreciate that social, economic, and political issues have more than one side: some contacts incline them to favor one course of action, while others influence them in opposite directions, thereby making conflicting points of view less threatening. In resolving these competing points of view, citizens come to adopt a more reasoned stance on public issues, while leaders of ethnic groups, aware that their followers are subject to myriad, competing pressures, tone down their demands on government and on rival ethnic groups. The resulting compromises mean the clash of interests is less vehement; social and political tensions are less strident; and ethnic groups are more willing to trust their ethnic opposites and less likely to respond violently to their success. This is the rationale behind the concept, the notion, of cross-cutting pressures, that is, multiple associations that subject the individual to conflicting pressures.

A similar rationale is inherent in James Madison's *Federalist Paper Ten,* with its advocacy of enlightened self-interest and multiple associations, with a citizen's associations overlapping rather than coinciding. If they are cumulative, that is, if they only bring the citizen into contact with others having the same view he already holds, they will reinforce his biases, his discriminations, and his prejudices, in sum, his fears, thereby exacerbating rather than ameliorating ethnic disharmonies by encouraging extremism and violence. The true objective is to produce citizens who are strong individuals, who associate freely with different groups, but who come together for the common cause of the entire political community: its stability and continuity.

In the eighteenth century, when the thirteen American colonies sought to sever their relationship with Britain in order to attain psychological satisfaction, political integration, and political success by creating an independent state and building a united nation, they came to the conclusion that these goals were unattainable without a violent effort. But once that violent episode was over, the sense of national unity was threatened by the presence of *factions*, which would later produce an horrendous civil war. James Madison defined factions as, "A number of citizens, whether amounting to [a] majority or minority of the whole, who are united and actuated by some common impulse of passion, or of interest, adverse to the rights of other citizens, or to the permanent and aggregate interests of the community."[1] Madison believed that factions were rooted in the nature of man:

So strong is this propensity of mankind, to fall into mutual animosities, that where no substantial occasion presents itself, the most frivolous and fanciful distinctions have been sufficient to kindle their unfriendly passions, and excite their most violent conflicts. But the most common and durable source of factions, has been the various and unequal distribution of property. Those who hold, and those who are without property, have ever formed distinct interests in society.[2]

Madison believed that although the causes of factions were rooted in man's nature, the effects of factions could and should be controlled. Ethnicity, too, is a form of factions that cannot be eliminated, but whose effects can and should be controlled. For Madison, if a faction consisted of a minority, it could be constrained by the republican principle of majority rule; if a faction consisted of the majority, the republic's principal resource was an informed, enlightened, and vigilant citizenry: one that was diverse in its interests. So too with ethnic disharmonies, a solution can be found in the concept of pluralism, that is, diverse interests and multiple associations.

To associate with others is a natural phenomenon of the human experience. In the fifth century B.C., Aristotle remarked that to survive alone, one must be either a god or a beast.[3] Nevertheless, Aristotle distinguished between types of associations:

Every form of friendship involves association. But kinship and comradeship may be distinguished as peculiar forms [because they depend peculiarly on natural feeling and innate sympathy]. The form of friendship which unites fellow citizens—or fellow tribesmen, or fellow voyagers—is more in the nature of pure association, since it seems to rest on a sort of compact. . . . All associations are in the nature of parts of the political association. Men journey together with a view to some particular advantage, and by way of providing some particular thing needed for the purposes of life; and similarly the political association seems to have come together originally, and to continue in existence, for the sake of the *general* advantage which it brings.[4]

In the modern world, this natural need for association has become more pressing, as societal relationships have become more complex and impersonal. In this context, ethnic associations have been grasped, sometimes tenaciously, as a familiar and reassuring anchor in the modern world of turbulence and uncertainty.

And yet, ethnicity is one of the least precise terms in the lexicon of current social science usage.[5] In fact, ethnicity is an ambiguous term in search of a precise definition, although Nathan Glazer has written,

> The term ethnic refers to a social group which consciously shares some aspects of a common culture and is defined primarily by descent. It is part of a family of terms by similar or related meaning, such as "minority group," "race," and "nation"; and it is not often easy to make sharp distinctions between them.[6]

In this study, ethnicity will refer singularly and collectively to an individual's or group's race, religion, language, or culture. In this context, ethnicity has both an individual and a group significance. In terms of its individual significance, ethnic affiliation gives a person a sense of belonging, a sense of security. In terms of its group significance, members consider themselves a fellowship which is distinguishable from other fellowships by dint of their ethnic alliance and characteristics. For example, a group's ethnic bond may be shared culture, and that culture may be a pattern of fundamental beliefs and values, such as the differentiation between right and wrong. Thus, the group's culture becomes the recognition of the distinctiveness of its standards of behavior, and prizing those standards to the extent that members feel most comfortable and secure when among others who share those standards.

All human beings are cultural beings, but not all human beings consider their membership in an ethnic group their only or their most significant mark of distinction, whether it relates to race, religion, or language. This means that ethnicity is but one kind of bond among individuals and groups. Other bonds are ties relating to age, gender, class, occupation, region, and street gang affiliation, while, in terms of political association, the most significant bond is that of citizenship. Each of these non-ethnic bonds assumes varying degrees of significance, as conditions of social, economic, and political change develop which, in turn, produces new membership in multiple, non-ethnic associations. Nevertheless, individuals of other ethnic groups are tempted to label members of a particular ethnic group, and then, to categorize them according to how they perceive those individuals fulfilling their categorization. In other words, to stereotype them. Ethnicity, however, depends upon self-identification and not merely upon others categorizations and stereotypes, although the ways in which individuals and groups define themselves is partly in response to how others perceive them.

A distinguishing characteristic of ethnic affiliation is that members share clusters of beliefs and values. Rarely, however, will a single ethnic attribute or feature sustain an ethnic group's solidarity. For instance, in the United States, Catholics are an ethnic group with considerable power in voting on social issues. American Catholics, however, do not constitute a monolithic ethnic voting group, because, in America, Catholicism is professed by ethnic groups of diverse racial and language backgrounds, for example, there are white Catholics, black Catholics, Korean, Japanese, and Spanish-speaking Catholics. By contrast, in Northern Ireland, Catholics do constitute a monolithic ethnic voting group, because in Northern Ireland, religious ethnicity is interwoven with all other aspects of how the group perceives itself and how it is perceived by others. This means that, in Northern Ireland—where mutual trust is absent—Catholic and Protestant affiliations shape all allegiances, all associations, all expectations, and all fears, although both groups are English-speaking Europeans.

American Catholics have not succumbed to a similar fate, because, in America, that nation's Constitution—as written, interpreted, and implemented—has engendered a sense of trust among ethnic groups, and, as important, the concept of cross-cutting pressures is operative. Its operation is most effective where group associations are not merely ethnic but pluralistic, that is, where they are voluntary, multiple, and overlapping rather than coinciding in the cement of *primordial attachments*.

As a concept, primordial attachment is closely associated with Clifford Geertz, who has written,

By a primordial attachment is meant one that stems from the "given"—or, more precisely, as culture is inevitably involved in such matters, the assumed "givens"—of social existence: immediate contiguity and kin connection mainly, but beyond them the giveness that stems from being born in a particular religious community, speaking a particular language, or even a dialect of a language, and following particular social practices. These congruities of blood, speech, custom,

and so on, are seen to have an ineffable, and at times, overpowering coerciveness
in and of themselves. One is bound to one's kinsman, one's neighbor, one's fellow
believer, *ipso facto*:   as the result not merely of personal affection, practical
necessity, common interest, or incurred obligation, but at least, in great part, by
virtue of some unaccountable absolute import attributed to the tie itself.[7]

Geertz maintains that a primary task of developing states is to
subordinate primordial attachments to the necessity of building a strong
and stable nation-state, because, although the nation-state is the legal
basis for sovereignty, ethnic allegiances may compete with the state for
loyalty, challenge it for power and legitimacy, and, ultimately, weaken its
authority.   Nonetheless, the aim should not be to eradicate primordial
attachments, which, in any case, is quite unlikely, but rather to channel
those sentiments in directions that would assist the state in its nation-
building projects. This, however, is no easy task because the desire to
channel primordial sentiments towards positive state ends is made more
difficult by the modernization process itself.   That is, as a country
modernizes, as it produces more goods and services, as it attains a higher
standard of living for its citizens, and as the quality of life, generally,
improves for its citizens, so too does the competition for the country's
economic, social, and political rewards.   In such circumstances, the
devotion to primordial attachments, that is, to ethnic loyalties, tends to
become greater in its intensity, not less.   In Northern Ireland, this
monolithic loyalty is the result of the country's history and *political
culture*.

The concept of political culture assumes that each individual will, in
his own historical context, learn and incorporate into his own dynamic
personality the knowledge and feelings about his own political system.
This means that the political culture of a political system is limited but
given firm structure by the factors of an individual's dynamic personality.
That is, each generation receives its political culture from the previous
one, accepting or rejecting what came before, as a generation and as an
individual. This process of socialization follows the laws that govern the
development of the individual's personality and his acceptance or
rejection of the political system's general culture. In essence, a political
system's political culture consists of the values, beliefs, customs, and

symbols that define the situation in which political actions take place. Political culture, therefore, encompasses both the political ideas and the operating norms of a political system. However, as in all human creations, ethnic group's perceptions and their political culture are subject to change, for change is the only constant in nature. This means that the fundamental nature of an ethnic group's common culture and its associational expression still permit a surprising degree of adaptation, without surrender to complete assimilation. For instance, in the United States, an ethnic group may become Americanized and yet survive as an identifiable ethnic entity. Sometimes this survival can be traced to the ethnic group's tenacity in withstanding subtle, and not so subtle, obstacles put forward by other ethnic groups in a *multi-ethnic society.*

Today, most of the world's states are multi-ethnic societies, and most of them include ethnic minorities which account for more than 20% of their populations. Such multi-ethnic societies tend to be politically divided in their domestic affairs, and, if their populations are also stratified, the risk of violent confrontation is imminent. Stratification simply means that within a political system different levels of class, caste, status, and privilege have developed. In South Africa, the political system is highly stratified with privileged whites at the top of a pyramidal structure, deprived Africans at the bottom, and assimilated coloreds and Asians somewhere in between. Now, consider what happens when a country with South Africa's stratification profile begins to modernize: more children begin to attend modern schools and this experience, together with the effects of advertising, the mass media, and the general exposure to modernization, begins to exercise a powerful demonstration effect. Demonstration effect is the sum of the effects modern practices, propaganda, and living conditions have on the habits and aspirations of people who were previously unfamiliar with them. Prominent among these effects are a rise in economic demands for goods and services and a rise in political demands for more rights and greater opportunities. This is a crucial stage in any country's development, for now the deprived, depressed, and disadvantaged begin to want to move up in the pyramidal structure, both economically and politically. In political science, this phenomenon is referred to as the Revolution of Rising Expectations.

Modernizing propaganda, as well as politicians, modern education, and the mass media, encourage groups and individuals not to take their stratified positions as God-given—something akin to Plato's system of metals—but as somehow the result of their own efforts. In other words, one's place in the pyramidal structure should be achieved and should not be ascribed or predetermined.

Talented, ambitious, and energetic young people now want to move up and feel resentful and frustrated, if they cannot, for, when they try to move up, they bump their heads on the feet of the ethnic group occupying the next higher level on the stage of success and stratification. In these circumstances, ethnic groups tend to be clannish, that is, mutually exclusive. The ensuing ethnic struggle is an expression of underlying social conflicts, and the intensity of such conflicts grows with the extent of economic inequality. For instance, lack of employment and gross inequality of opportunity are two main factors that intensify social conflict between ethnic groups. A multi-ethnic society with gross inequality and deep stratification is inherently unstable and, therefore, susceptible to chronic incidences of violence.

One method for alleviating instability and developing national cohesion and political integration has been through the deliberate actions of elite leaders. The method has been extremely successful in Switzerland and has been termed the *consociational model of democracy*. The political scientist who has devoted the most effort in the development of a theory for the consociational model is a Dutchman named Arend Lijphart,[8] although the American political scientist David Apter may have been the first to use the term, which he did in 1961 in a book entitled *The Political Kingdom in Uganda*.[9]

Basically, the consociational model of government by a coalition of elite leaders, is designed to turn a political system with a fragmented and stratified political structure into a stable democracy. Lijphart contends that a successful consociational model requires several interwoven essentials. First, the elite leaders of each group must have the ability to satisfy the divergent needs and demands of their group. Second, they must be willing and able to work together in a common effort. Third, the collective leadership must be committed to the maintenance of the political system and the development of its political cohesion. Other essentials are based on the assumption that the collective leadership recognizes the consequences of continued ethnic fragmentation and stratification, which could lead to violence and, ultimately, to the system's political disintegration. Malaysia illustrates the consociational model in action and its weaknesses after several years of resounding success.

In Switzerland, for over 140 years, a variation of the consociational model has been a sterling success, long before the term consociational model of democracy came into usage. More importantly, in Switzerland, the concept of cross-cutting pressures can be demonstrated, in practice, for within its tiny borders live an amalgam of ethnic groups—German, French, Italian, and Romansh-speakers, as well as Catholic, Protestant, and Jewish adherents—who do so in tolerance, in public tranquility, and in mutual trust. The Swiss model is not perfect, but it works perfectly well under human circumstances. On the other hand, in Canada, the dichotomization of the English-speaking Protestants and the French-speaking Catholics has not produced a similar accommodation, because, in Canada, the concept of cross-cutting pressures is inoperative and mutual trust is absent, leading to violent ethnic conflicts but not yet to civil war as in Nigeria.

Switzerland is the only polity in this analysis that was never a dependency in the British Empire. Thus, some lessons may be learned from the Swiss experience of ethnic accommodation that could be beneficial to developed nations and nation-building states the world over, as these states approach the twenty-first century and ethnic conflicts consume the energy, the attention, and the lives of their citizens as well as those of their political leaders. Despite its ethnic diversity, why has Switzerland known such peace, security, and prosperity for a century and a half, while the rest of the world has wasted its human resources in violent ethnic confrontations of the civil war, genocide, ethnic cleansing, and holocaust variety?

Multi-ethnic societies have been conceived of in numerous ways with the attachment to primordial "givens" being only one. After the Second World War, John Sydenham Furnivall, a British scholar with many years of academic and administrative experiences in both British and Dutch colonies in the Far East, conceived of them as *plural societies*, and he did so in conjunction with two hypotheses. First, Furnivall said of plural societies,

> They mix but do not combine. Each group holds by its own religion, its own culture and language, its own ideas and ways. As individuals they meet, but only in the market-place, in buying and selling. There is a plural society, with different sections of the community living side by side, but separately, within the same political unit. Even in the economic sphere there is a division of labour along racial lines.[10]

Secondly, Furnivall made a dynamic distinction between the plural society and the mixed society:

> Outside the tropics society may have plural features, notably in South Africa, Canada and the United States, and also in lands where the Jew has not been fully assimilated into social life. . . . But in general these mixed populations have at least a common tradition of western culture, and, despite a different racial origin, they meet on equal terms and their relations are not confined solely to the economic sphere. There is a society with plural features, but not a plural society.[11]

Furnivall concluded that when compared with Western democracies, colonial dependencies had fundamentally different social organization, which were based on race. Therefore, he applied the term plural society to describe a medley of ethnically diverse peoples held together, politically, by dint of the colonial power's will. These colonial dependencies were dominated by Western democracies, which imposed their ideas, their systems, and their institutions upon those that already existed and were indigenous. This produced a forced union not only of political systems but of peoples who were at different levels of modernization as well as possessing different values about the meaning of human existence. In political analysis, one refers to such a forced union as a dyarchy, two political systems existing simultaneously with one superimposed upon the other. British rule in Malaya and Nigeria was a prime example of such anomalies with the resulting form of administration called Indirect Rule and with ethnically diverse peoples living side by side, but in segregated communities. Furnivall characterized this segregation as the result of social cleavage, cultural diversity, and mutual avoidance. He suggests that, lacking any shared social experiences, peoples in plural societies tended to become not only socially isolated but, in some instances, socially decivilized.

Economic factors played a dominant role in Furnivall's equation. Plural societies arose where economic factors were exempt from control by social will and this was a phenomenon found only in the tropical dependencies and not in the mixed societies of Western democracies, because only in the plural societies had economic factors been set loose to reorganize the social order, without the consent of social will. Economic factors acted as determinants—creating and maintaining the plural society in circumstances of social cleavage, cultural diversity, and mutual avoidance—under the domination of a colonial power. As a consequence, political integration was not natural, not voluntary, but was imposed by the dominant will of the colonial power and its exploitative economic system.

There were obvious flaws in Furnivall's otherwise provocative assessments. First, Furnivall failed to emphasize that the colonial policy of "Divide and Rule" not only perpetuated but exacerbated the condition of exclusive communalism. Second, he failed to emphasize that diverse ethnic peoples, under colonial domination, were enormously susceptible to primordial attachments and that these attachments played a powerful role in alienating them from all but their communal associates.

Third, in the three countries he used to illustrate his theory of mixed populations with plural features, but were not deemed to be plural societies, Furnivall ignored the indigenous African majority in South Africa, the indigenous minorities in Canada, and the indigenous minorities and descendants of slaves in the United States as well as the decivilizing consequences of imposed or self-segregation on these disinherited and disadvantaged peoples. This oversight was deliberate. Before the end of the Second World War, most Western scholars viewed those countries in terms of their immigrant white groups, because they were the dominant factor in their social, economic, political, and psychological life. Canada held a very special place in the British Empire, for, along with Australia, New Zealand, and South Africa, it was one of the four white dominions to whom the British granted internal self-rule. Furthermore, after the loss of the thirteen American colonies, Canada was the last British bastion of white supremacy on the North American continent. Therefore, in Canada, the emphasis was on the competition between the English and French-speaking Canadians; in South Africa the emphasis was on the competition between the Boers and the English-speaking South Africans; and in the United States the emphasis was placed on the competition among a medley of immigrant groups of European descent. However, since the Second World War and the decolonization that followed, the emphasis in social science research and analysis has shifted from the descendants of European immigrants to the indigenous peoples and to others who have been referred to as the wretched of the earth. Nevertheless, descendants of European immigrants remain, in each of these three countries, the dominant political and economic power and, therefore, cannot be ignored, as is borne out in this analysis. Moreover, the contention of this study is that Furnivall's differentiation between plural societies and mixed populations was not only an oversimplification but that it obscured the similarities between developed nations and nation-building states, in the post-colonial era, especially with regards to their ethnic relationships. Therefore, the purpose of this study is to examine ethnic relations in both developed nations and nation-building states to discern their origin, intensity, and manageability.

Nation-building is not a finished product but a continuous, evolutionary process, which occurs in two sequences. First, there is the *creation of the state*, the settlement of its territorial boundaries, and the organization of its political institutions. Second, there is the *development of the nation*, the expansion of the individual's perception from ethnic loyalty to national loyalty, and the confirmation of the citizen's duties, rights, and responsibilities in conjunction with ethnic and associational duties, rights, and responsibilities. Most former colonial dependencies have accomplished the first sequence but have had grave difficulties in accomplishing the second, and this is because nation-building is an extremely slow, arduous, and complex process, which is made more vexing by the desire of most citizens and some leaders to live in a *democratic environment.*

Democracy, however, is difficult to operate, successfully, when the citizenry are apathetic with regards to public affairs and public policy or when they have little or no experience in a modern participatory form of government. Furthermore, a democracy requires not only a passion for liberty but also a passion to preserve the conditions in which liberty thrives. This means citizens must possess enough of the common goals, and the means for attaining them, to sustain the nation-state against the fierce conflicts of factions and special interests. Put succinctly, *democracy is the most delicate and most difficult form of government.* It rests upon rather precarious conditions, because for representative institutions to function, successfully, a wide agreement on fundamental principles and values and a willingness to compromise on less important issues is necessary. Moreover, as enlightened leadership is so vital to the success of the whole process, one is reminded by Madison that "enlightened statesmen will not always be at the helm."[12]

Finally, a primary contention of this study is that although ethnic conflicts seem to be endemic, whether one analyzes developed nations on nation-building states, upon closer examination one sees that the real culprit may be economic inequality. What James Madison pointed out two centuries ago is worth repeating: "The most common and durable source of factions has been the various and unequal distribution of property. Those who hold and those who are without property have ever formed distinct interests in society."[13] The contention of this study is not, however, that by seeing ethnic conflicts as reflections of economic inequality one can solve all of the problems between ethnic groups. Some ethnic controversies may have become so deep-seated and intractable as to withstand any solution short of secession, that is, separation into distinct political entities, as may be the case in some recently independent states in Eastern Europe such as Yugoslavia. Nevertheless, by identifying economic inequality as a conspicuous cause of ethnic conflicts, one can deal with a tangible and adjustable factor in the political equation. Taken alone, ethnicity is infinitely more difficult, if not impossible, to accommodate. If, however, the problem can be viewed as one involving economic inequality, a solution is possible, given the limits of a country's economic resources, and its citizens' will to reverse chronic economic disparities. In the final analysis, what are essential for any viable solution to ethnic disharmonies in multi-ethnic societies is the presence of cross-cutting pressures through multiple associations, mutual trust among the citizenry, and a leadership that is not only enlightened but dynamic.

Notes

1. Marvin Meyers, editor, *The Mind of the Founder: Sources of the Political Thought of James Madison* (Hanover, NH, by University Press of New England for Brandeis University Press, 1981), 89.

2. Madison, *Federalist Paper Ten, Ibid.*, 90.

3. Ernest Barker, *The Politics of Aristotle* (New York: Oxford University Press, 1958), 6.

4. Ibid., 2.

5. "Ethnicity seems to be a new term . . . it does not appear in the 1933 edition of the *Oxford English Dictionary*, and only makes its appearance in the 1972 *Supplement*, where the first usage recorded is that of David Riesman in 1953. It is included in *Webster's Third New International*, 1961, but did not find its way into the *Random House Dictionary of the English Language* of 1966, nor the *American Heritage Dictionary of the English Language*, 1969. It did, however, make the 1973 edition of the *American Heritage Dictionary*, where it is defined as: 1. The condition of belonging to a particular ethnic group; 2. Ethnic pride." Nathan Glazer and Daniel Patrick Moynihan, "Why Ethnicity?" *Commentary* (October 1974): 33.

6. Nathan Glazer, "Ethnicity: A World Phenomenon," *Encounter* (London) (1975): 1.

7. Clifford Geertz, *Old Societies and New States* (New York: The Free Press, 1963), 109.

8. Arend Lijphart, "Consociational Democracy," *World Politics* 21 (January 1969), and Arend Lijphart, *Democracy in Plural Societies* (New Haven: Yale University Press, 1977).

9. David Apter, *The Political Kingdom in Uganda* (Princeton: Princeton University Press, 1967), 24-25.

10. John Furnivall, *Colonial Policy and Practice* (Cambridge, England: Cambridge University Press, 1948), 304.

11. Ibid., 305.

12. Madison, *Federalist Paper Ten*, 91.

13. Ibid., 90.

Chapter One
Switzerland: A Paradigm

In Carol Reed's classic motion picture, *The Third Man*, Orson Welles portrays the despicable scoundrel, Harry Lime. Lime's villainy is that in war-ravaged, post-Second World War Vienna, he sells on the black market much needed and scarce penicillin that has been stolen from Allied military hospitals. Lime's crime, however, does not end there; with water he dilutes the penicillin in order to increase his profits. This highly unsafe concoction is used in unsuspecting Viennese civilian hospitals on children, many with meningitis. Some die, while others are debilitated for life. In the end, Harry Lime, like a rat, is cornered in the sewers of Vienna and destroyed. Midway through the film, Orson Welles, in his wine-mellow voice, says to his friend Joseph Cotton, by way of justifying his actions, that Italy, under the Borgias, spread terror, violence, and fratricide, but produced the Renaissance, while Switzerland, with brotherly love and 500 years of democracy, only produced the cuckoo-clock. Movie audiences usually give this punch-line a hearty laugh, while the Swiss hang their heads in resignation. They are accustomed to such put-downs, which insinuate plodding mediocrity. Nevertheless,

in a world torn asunder by racial strife and ethnic conflicts Switzerland is often cited as a model case of cultural coexistence, a nation which has managed to weld four different language groups and two major religions into a stable and harmonious unity.[1]

What Switzerland has attained is the envy of the world. A small nation with few natural resources other than its hard-working people, its abundant forests, and its jetting water power, Switzerland has consistent economic growth and development, as well as a much heralded democracy. The nation is stable, cohesive, and politically integrated.

Local autonomy is reconciled with the need for central government control. Ethnic extremism is rare. Citizens are free to participate actively in government and in the making of laws by which they are governed,

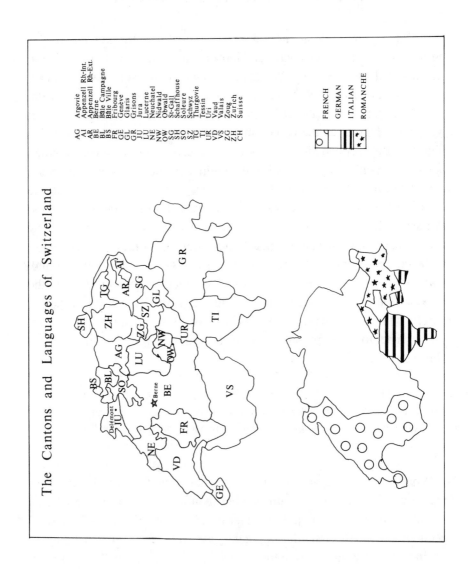

The Cantons and Languages of Switzerland

AG Argovie
AI Appenzell Rh-Int.
AR Appenzell Rh-Ext.
BE Berne
BL Bâle Campagne
BS Bâle Ville
FR Fribourg
GE Genève
GL Glaris
GR Grisons
JU Jura
LU Lucerne
NE Neuchatel
NW Nidwald
OW Obwald
SG St-Gall
SH Schaffhouse
SO Soleure
SZ Schwyz
TG Thurgovie
TI Tessin
UR Uri
VD Vaud
VS Valais
ZG Zoug
ZH Zurich
CH Suisse

FRENCH
GERMAN
ITALIAN
ROMANCHE

through their vote and through that most unique device of direct democracy, the referendum. Put succinctly, in Switzerland the possibility of dictatorship by the one, the few, or the many is extremely remote. This accomplishment was not easy, but an arduous task that, sometimes, seemed a hopeless endeavor. Nevertheless, the Swiss took seven hundred years to construct the nation they enjoy today.

On August 1, 1991, the Swiss celebrated their 700th anniversary of democracy, which began, in 1291, when men from the mountain cantons of Uri, Schwyz, and Unterwalden met in the meadows of Rütli, along the banks of Lake Lucerne, and pledged their allegiance to aid, support, and protect their traditional civil rights and system of laws from the menace of encroachment by the powerful Hapsburg dynasty. From this nucleus grew, first, a loose confederation of autonomous cantons that evolved into a federation, unifying a Swiss nation of over 6½ million citizens, 26 cantons, and more than 3,000 communes.

Since 1848, with one exception—the Jura Crisis—Switzerland has avoided the debilitating repercussions of ethnic animosity, which seemingly is concomitant with multi-ethnic, plural societies, by allotting substantial cultural and communal responsibilities to the regional governments, the cantons. In fact, the Swiss Constitution gives to the cantons all powers not specifically delegated to the federal government, as does the Tenth Amendment of the American Constitution. Therefore, the Swiss cantons are often compared with the American states. However, as they have more autonomy, more responsibility, and more real power than the American states, this comparison is superficial. The closest relatives to the Swiss cantons are the Canadian provinces. For instance, in the Canadian crisis over Quebec nationalism, so in the Swiss crisis over Jurassian separatism, the problem arose, was fought, and was finally resolved within the confines of the canton of Berne, of which the Northern and Southern Jura were integral parts. Only at the last minute did the rest of the Swiss citizens become directly involved and participate in a national referendum to decide whether the Northern Jura should become a separate canton. They said yes! In other words, ethnic pride is assuaged, at the cantonal not the federal level. The Swiss federal government does not play God.

The communes represent the third level of political allegiance and participation for the Swiss citizen: the federal or national, the cantonal or regional, the communal or local; and most Swiss feel a more binding loyalty to their commune of birth than native New Yorkers do to the Bronx.

There are 3,061 communes in the Confederation today, each run by a local authority, many of which, like the cantons, enjoy a high degree of independence. It is at this local level that Swiss democracy is most direct. By participating in the local Commune Assembly . . . and by voting, the citizens themselves elect their communal or municipal authorities and run their own affairs. . . . The administrative autonomy of the communes and cantons allow every citizen to participate intensively in public life and in the way his community is run.[2]

In Switzerland, no central authority supervises children's education, which is significant because education is often a primary cause of ethnic discord in multi-ethnic, plural societies. Education is entirely within the purview of the cantonal and communal authorities who supervise, disseminate, and finance the education of their children.

Furthermore, the security of law and order are within the domain of cantonal and communal government responsibility, as no national police force exists, although the federal government has jurisdiction over the country's national militia,[3] which may be called to cantonal assistance, but only at the behest of the cantonal government. "As Mr. Furgler [the then Federal Minister of Justice] has argued, the Swiss citizen-soldier is not trained to handle demonstrations and riots, and the use of the army for public order can be counter-productive."[4]

Finally, the Swiss federal government may not even raise federal taxes without the consent of the cantons, that is, without a national referendum involving the citizens of all cantons. However, as the federal government has been forced, by necessity, to take on more responsibility in such areas as economic planning, resource allocation, and environmental control, especially after the dire years of food shortages and unemployment that accompanied the First World War, its powers have increased, while those of the cantons have been diminished. Nevertheless, the cantons are still the most potent single factor in the Swiss political and social arena: they remain the *locus operandi* for ethnic assuagement.

Until 1979, 25 Swiss cantons existed: 19 were full cantons, while 6 were termed half cantons. Over the centuries, in cantons with incompatible parts a schism developed—sometimes over religion but more often over politics and power. The discordant factions were separated, thereby creating the half cantons. For instance, in 1432, the canton of Anterwalder was divided into Obwalder (the Upper) and Nidwalder (the Lower) because of their political incompatibility. In 1592, the Protestant Reformation was the cause of Appenzell being divided into Appenzell Outer-Rhodes, which became Protestant and Appenzell Inner-Rhodes, which remained Catholic. "Basel was divided into two half-cantons in 1833, when the former rural subjects of the city refused to remain under the same political roof as their former urban masters,"[5] thereby creating Basel Town and Basel Country, with the crosier on their bishop's staff turned in opposite directions on their respective cantonal flags for subtle distinction. Nonetheless, in cantons where ethnic minorities continued to reside, the majority usually tolerated their presence, especially where the theory of cross-cutting pressures was operative, that is, where language loyalty and religious affiliation did not coincide but overlapped thus causing a psychological dilemma that had to be resolved on the basis of something other than ethnicity. In 1979, with the birth of the Jura canton, the number of cantons increased, but the change was in complete accord with Swiss political culture, that is, Swiss tradition, Swiss tolerance, and Swiss patience.

The official name of the Swiss state is Confédération Helvétique, but that name is misleading because modern Switzerland is a federation not a confederation. The term Helvétique comes from the name Helvetian attributed to German tribes that migrated from the Rhine River to settle between the Alps and Jura Mountains more than 2,000 years ago. Adding to the confusion in nomenclature, the Swiss Constitution is entitled the *Federal Constitution of the Swiss Confederation* and begins with the words "With the intent of strengthening the alliance of the Confederation [Switzerland] has adopted the following Federal Constitution." The term confederation is a reminder of the 18th century, when the cantonal members of the alliance were totally dominant, but today, with a strong central government, Switzerland fulfills all the qualifications of a federation.

Karl Deutsch identifies four characteristics which distinguish a federation from a confederation, and, in each instance, they verify Switzerland's status as a federation.[6] First, in the area of its organization, its bureaucracy, its budget, the military forces at its command, and its constitutional jurisdiction, the central government of a federation has greater authority than does the coordinating mechanism of a confederation. Moreover, in each of these areas, the central government of a federation is more powerful than any of its component parts. In a confederation, however, the centralized functions and institutions are weaker than those of the strongest members making up the alliance and, sometimes, are totally nonexistent. Second, while the central government of a federation touches the lives of all citizens directly, the coordinating mechanism of a confederation touches them indirectly, through the regional government. In other words, a confederation can affect the lives of its constituents only to the extent that regional government will permit. Third, in a confederation, members may secede from the alliance simply by the decision and actions of the regional government to do so, whereas, in a federation, secession is unconstitutional without the compliance of the central government. Fourth, within the sphere of its jurisdiction, the laws of a federation prevail over those of its regional components, and the regional governments are constitutionally obligated to obey and carry them out. However, in a confederation, the laws of decisions of the coordinating authority of the alliance are biding only if the regional government chooses to acquiesce.

Today, Switzerland is a federation, but it has not always been. Switzerland, as did the United States, evolved from a loose collection of self-interested, though like-minded, confreres to become a solid union representing the interests of one, indivisible republic. While the Americans took just over 5 years, from 1782 to 1787, to accomplish this transformation, the Swiss took over 500 years, but, in the process, Switzerland became "the most practical, the most hard-headed, the most enduring democracy in the world."[7]   An American diplomat said, succinctly, "Certainly no other nation today can equal the Swiss achievement of finding advantage in adversity, of maintaining unity in a diverse and varied society, and of adapting to the complexities of modern life while clinging tenaciously to historic values and traditions."[8]

Swiss Constitutional Changes

From its inception, in 1291, through its successive stages of development, Switzerland remained, until the end of the 18th century, a loose alliance of independent cantons bound together for mutual protection and self-interest.   The alliance had neither an effective legislature, nor a potent executive, nor a common body of laws. Each canton created its own laws and was its own master. The mutual interests of the members of this alliance were discussed in an assembly called a Diet, which was a diplomatic congress, not a parliament, without any decision-making powers other than those conferred upon it by the cantonal governments. To this assembly each canton sent a delegation of two instructed representatives, who were responsible only to their cantonal governments. This Diet met not regularly but periodically. In fact, from 1663 to 1776, it did not meet at all, because the political climate was too saturated with divisive issues.

During this period of its political development, Switzerland was not a nation but rather a frontier region, a formidable fortress hidden behind the imposing Alps and Jura mountains. Swiss fighting men, who had become famous as fierce and efficient mercenaries, were a formidable military force, which stimulated, among Swiss leaders, major foreign policy ambitions. But once those ambitions were substituted for internal cohesion and political integration, Switzerland would, eventually, become a nation.

By the end of the 18th century, the Swiss Confederation was moribund and frequently convulsed by Civil War. It had "no constitution, no central government, no national army, not even a capital city."[9] Its members were all sovereign cantons joined together merely by their own free will and particular, centrifugal interests.

In 1798, the confederation changed beyond recognition, as the result of an invading French army brandishing its weapons and its revolutionary ideas of liberty, equality, and fraternity. For the next four decades, either under direct French tutelage or indirect French influence, the Swiss instituted a series of constitutional changes that were intended to make the state more just, liberal, and democratic at both the national and cantonal levels. The first were contained in the Helvetic Constitution of 1798, Switzerland's first written constitution, which proclaimed the state a republic—indivisible with one powerful central government—which was the exact opposite of what the confederation had been. However, the Helvetic Republic, created by Napoleon, proved to be inefficient and inoperative; "The transition to a centralized state was too abrupt, too much at variance with all Swiss traditions to last."[10] Nevertheless, between 1798 and 1803, countless amendments were considered, before the idea of a Swiss republic was abandoned. In 1803, the Helvetic Constitution was replaced by the Mediation Constitution, which was drawn up by the Swiss, in Paris, under the watchful eye of Napoleon, who decided he had erred in trying to turn the moribund confederation into a republic but not in attempting to make it a viable political entity. Therefore, the Mediation Constitution restored to the cantons virtually all their former independence.

The French Revolution of 1830 sent ripples of warning throughout Switzerland and its reinstated cantonal governments to either liberalize their basic laws or face the prospect of civil war. As a consequence, between 1830 and 1833, ten cantons—all urban, Protestant, and German-speaking—liberalized their constitutions by instituting such measures as freedom of the press, equality before the law, and universal adult suffrage for men.

Swiss Neutrality

However, before the Revolution of 1830, at the Congress of Vienna of 1814-1815, the victorious powers, i.e., Prince Metternich, sought to ostracize the rambunctious, imperialistic-minded French by surrounding France with strong allies, such as the canton of Berne, who could serve as a buffer to those ambitions. Moreover, the Congress granted Switzerland the status of permanent neutrality. These were, seemingly, two contradictory objectives. Nevertheless, in the western world, only Austria has a similar status of permanent neutrality guaranteed by international treaty. In 1955, Austria's perpetual neutrality was one of the conditions stipulated by Britain, France, the Soviet Union, and the United States for removing their occupying armies from the land of the vanquished House of Hapsburg and the subdued Austrian republic. Otherwise, according to international law, neutrality, as a legal status, only exists in times of war. For instance, the neutrality that Sweden grants itself in peacetime is without legal validity, because it has not been sanctioned and guaranteed as a permanent status by international treaty. In other words, Sweden could go to war anytime it wished but not Austria and Switzerland.

In 1919, the Treaty of Versailles reaffirmed Switzerland's status of perpetual neutrality. Therefore, the Swiss accepted membership in the League of Nations, but only after the League's Council agreed that Switzerland would not be obliged to take part in any military sanctions, which member states were legally obligated to do under the terms of the League's Covenant and its system of collective security. As war and the demise of the League grew imminent and measures of collective security seemed ineffective, and perhaps dangerous, the cautious Swiss persuaded the League that they should be relieved from even having to participate in economic sanctions. As a consequence of its inter-war experiences with the League and collective security, Switzerland has staunchly refused to join the United Nations, although it has a Permanent Observer in New York. Moreover, Switzerland is an active member of several international organizations that are affiliated with the U.N., such as the International Labor Organization (ILO) and the World Health Organization (WHO), both of which have their headquarters in Geneva, Switzerland. However, the Swiss have not joined the World Bank or the International Monetary Fund, the two primary economic institutions of the United Nations.

Ostensibly, the Swiss have never joined the United Nations because they fear that the U.N.'s system of collective security would jeopardize their status of neutrality, which is the cornerstone of their national security. The Swiss reasoning is this: as the U.N. Charter gives the Security Council the enforcement power to implement its decisions by calling upon member states to participate in military, as well as economic, sanctions, Switzerland could be drawn into an armed conflict, such as the 1991 Desert Storm campaign, that could jeopardize its foreign relations with other states. Therefore, the Swiss have rejected the United Nations form of political integration.

In 1982, however, the Federal Council, the national executive, proposed to the Federal Assembly, the national legislature, that Switzerland become a full member of the United Nations. The Federal Assembly approved the proposal and only a positive response from the Swiss electorate in a national referendum stood in the way of fulfillment. However, the Swiss people still oppose full membership in the United Nations. For instance, in October 1983, in a radio survey, 45% of the Swiss polled were against membership, 39% were in favor, while the rest were undecided. Therefore, although the national executive and legislative bodies of the Swiss federation favored full membership in the United Nations, they were reticent about setting a date for the required national referendum for fear that their proposal would be rejected by the Swiss electorate, which would not be the first time that the Swiss electorate had acted on its own. For instance, in 1959, when the national electorate was composed entirely of men, it rejected the strong recommendation of the Federal Council and Federal Assembly to grant women their right to vote in national elections.

Finally, in March of 1986, the Swiss electorate voted on the issue of Swiss membership in the United Nations and delivered one of the most devastating referendum defeats of a Federal government-sponsored proposal in Swiss history. The final tally was 1,591,428 votes against joining the United Nations, or 75.7%, to 511,548 votes for joining the U.N.: a margin of 3 to 1 against. The turnout of 50% of the eligible voters exceeded the 35% average for such referenda and underscored the emotional and hard-fought nature of the campaign.

Not one of the Swiss cantons produced a margin in favor of the proposal. Even in Geneva, which is the European headquarters of the United Nations and 18 of its specialized agencies, only 30.2% of the electorate were in favor of the proposal to join the United Nations as a full member. Voter rejection seemed largely due to fears that joining the U.N. would compromise the nation's neutrality, involve its citizen-army in unwanted U.N. peacekeeping operations, and endanger the viability of institutions such as the International Committee of the Red Cross, which the Swiss organized. The rejection also amounted to a "no confidence vote" by the politically astute Swiss electorate on the very nature of the United Nations, which many Swiss perceived, at the time, to be dominated by the Soviet Bloc and Third World countries as a forum of worthless and often futile politicking.

Thus, on the international scene, permanent neutrality is to the Swiss what religious and language tolerance are on the national scene. Both are the touchstones of the nation's pursuit of external and internal peaceful coexistence.

Swiss Women

Until 1971, an anachronistic monstrosity was that Swiss women were denied their right as citizens to vote, except at the regional level in some French-speaking cantons. Not until March 1971 did Switzerland cease to be the penultimate bastion in the Western world where only males had the right to vote and to hold federal positions at the highest levels. By their reactionary behavior, Swiss men were linked with those of certain Arab countries who denied female citizens this basic, democratic right. After 1971, only tiny Liechtenstein stubbornly refused to grant women this basic right of citizenship in the Western world. Finally, in 1984, the men of Liechtenstein consented in a referendum to grant their female citizens their right to vote.

Earlier, in June 1981, the Swiss electorate approved a constitutional amendment that extended the guarantee of equality between the sexes. This guarantee included equality in education, in jobs, and in the home. The amendment appeared to provide a basis for efforts to end sexual discrimination in the remaining areas of Switzerland where women were not allowed to vote in cantonal or communal elections, for the amendment expanded the article in the Constitution that says, "All Swiss are equal under the law." The new amendment was explicit in stating that both women and men are entitled to equal rights. In the national referendum that approved the constitutional amendment, the vote was 797,679 in favor and 525,950 against. Seventeen of the 26 cantons recorded a favorable vote, with the strongest opposition coming from the reactionary, mountain regions of central Switzerland. Not surprisingly, women in some of those regions were not even allowed to participate in local affairs. For instance, the all-male electorate in Appenzell Outer-Rhodes, one of Switzerland's least populous cantons, with a population of about 13,500, stubbornly maintained a tradition which went back beyond the creation of the Alliance in 1291, of repeatedly denying women any say in local affairs. As late as April 1982, by a margin of 4 to 1, they voted against women voting in cantonal or communal elections. Finally, in 1990, they relented, and women gained their right to participate in local affairs. In the same year, the Swiss Federal Court took action and ruled that Swiss women in Appenzell Inner Rhodes had the right to participate in cantonal elections, and, by extension, the ruling also applied to Appenzell Outer Rhodes.

Language and Religion

At the end of the 18th century, language was not a divisive factor in Switzerland's political integration, until the predominantly French-speaking Jura region was attached to the German-speaking canton of Berne at the Congress of Vienna in 1815. On the other hand, religion in Europe had been a symbol of discordant nationalism and the cause of barbarous blood-letting since 1517, when Martin Luther posted his 95 theses to the church door at Wittenberg, and the Protestant Reformation began.

Language

Throughout the history of the Confederation, German was the dominant language.

Until the end of the 18th century, Switzerland was a purely Germanic country, ruling over and allied with some French and Italian-speaking neighbors. The written language in which all official documents were drafted was literary German. The spoken tongue was a German dialect, or rather, as every canton and even every region had its own, a variety of German dialects. These "patois" were sufficiently alike to be universally understood in all cantons, but sufficiently different from the more literary forms of German spoken beyond the Rhine to be a real obstacle in familiar intercourse and thereby an effective protection against foreign influence. In fact, this Germanic pre-revolutionary Switzerland had more to fear from French than from German foreign influence.[11]

Until the Constitution of 1848, German was the Confederation's only official language. In 1848, an article was adopted that simply stated: "The three main languages of Switzerland, German, French, and Italian, are the national languages of the Union."[12] Even with the entrance of French-speaking people into the Confederation, most ordinary Swiss still spoke a German dialect, although the aristocracy spoke French, as the language of culture, as it set them apart from the peasants.

Today, among the indigenous Swiss, 65% speak German, 18% French, 10% Italian, and 1% Romansh. Only in the Grison canton is Romansh, a form of Latin, spoken. In 1938, by a national referendum, which amended the Swiss Constitution, Romansh was added as a fourth "national" language but not as an "official" language. This meant that although Romansh could be used in an official capacity at the cantonal and communal levels, it could not be used at the national level in federal affairs, where the official languages remain German, French, and Italian. The raising of Romansh to the status of a national language was the Swiss attempt to thwart the growing irredentist menace of the Italian fascists and their designs on Italian and Romansh-speaking localities in Switzerland.

Religion

For more than 300 years, disputes over religious affiliation almost tore the already fragile Swiss Confederation to shreds: "After the Reformation, the cantons being their own masters, the Protestant states tolerated only Protestants as citizens and the Catholic states only Catholics."[13] The last serious conflict, with religious overtones, was a skirmish, in 1847, called the Sonderbund War that lasted about three weeks.[14] While the Sonderbund War had religious overtones—with seven rural, conservative, Catholic cantons rebelling against Protestant hegemony—what they were actually resisting was the ascendancy of 19th century ideas of social, economic, and political liberalism that were emanating from the more progressive, urban, Protestant cantons. "One of the main purposes of the federal Constitution set up in 1848 and amended in 1874 was to break down . . . barriers, to create a truly Swiss citizenship and to guarantee certain fundamental rights to all Swiss of all creeds throughout the whole country."[15]

In conjunction with the Sonderbund crisis was the expulsion from Switzerland of the Jesuits, the Roman Catholic church's most potent response to the Protestant Reformation. In 1577, the Jesuit Order, founded by Ignatius de Loyola in 1534,[16] had established a seminary in Switzerland. By 1845, in Lucerne, the Jesuits had gained control over education and opposed such liberal objectives as freedom of the press and political equality. The Jesuits were despised and distrusted by the protestant members of the Confederation. So much so that not until 1973, when the Swiss electorate, by referendum, amended that section of the 1848 Constitution which had banished them, were they allowed to return.

After 1848, religious animosity ceased to be an impediment to Swiss political integration, with two possible exceptions: the crisis provoked by the Vatican's pronouncement, in 1870, of the Pope's infallibility and the Jura Crisis a hundred years later.

The dogma of papal infallibility, which should be studied in conjunction with the rise of 19th century nationalism in Italy, declared that, when the Pope spoke *ex cathedra* on matters of faith and morals, meaning with authority from the Seat of His Authority, the throne of St. Peter's, his pronouncements were infallible by virtue of his supreme apostolic powers. Some Swiss Catholics, referred to as "old Catholics," rebelled against this dogma and other papal pronouncements of the period, which set off a schism within the Roman Catholic sect itself.

The Jura Crisis

The Jura Crisis began in 1814-1815, at the Congress of Vienna, when the victorious allies succumbed to the persuasions of Prince Metternich of Austria and ceded the Jura region to the canton of Berne, as compensation for the loss of lands that had once been subject to Berne's rule but were now sovereign members of the Swiss Confederation, and, just as important, the Jura region was to serve as a buffer against any future French aggressive tendencies.

The ethnic composition of the Jura was "typically Swiss" and would change very little in the next one hundred and fifty years. In 1970, the Jurassians were predominantly French-speaking (69%) and mainly Catholic (63%). At the time, the region was divided into seven administrative districts, but only six of them were involved in the crisis. The seventh, Laufen, was Catholic but, like Berne, was German-speaking. The three districts that made up the Northern Jura were Delémont, Porrentruy, and Franches-Montagnes: all were French-speaking, Catholic, and impovrished, the three districts that made up the southern Jura were Moutier, Courtelary, and La Neuveville: all were French-speaking, but, like Berne, Protestant and prosperous. "Sixty percent of the South Jura communes are industrialized as compared with 10% of the North Jura ones."[17]

Ostensibly, for language regions, the North wanted to separate from Berne and establish an independent canton, while the South, for economic reasons, wanted to stay with Berne, the source of its prosperity. "The northerners are our Celts, lively and open, intelligent and progressive, fascinated by words and politics. The southerners are more like the Bernese, hard-working and conservative, interested in business and money."[18]

Although the crisis had been smoldering for over 130 years, one incident was enough to set a course that would lead to the birth of a new canton, the Northern Jura. What happened was this:

In 1947 a routine shuffle of portfolios occurred in the cantonal executive. A Jurassian member was nominated unanimously by the cantonal executive council to become Director of Public Works and Railways, but his appointment was blocked by the legislative assembly on the ground that a post of such importance should go to a German-speaking councillor. This incident caused a storm of protest leading to the formation of a central committee to safe-guard interests of the Jura and to study the question of autonomy.[19]

The Canton of Berne tried to assuage the northerners' ethnic pride, but to no avail. Axiomatically, a crucial moment occurs in a country's political integration when those who believe that, in the past as in the present, they have been oppressed and denied their rights begin to achieve some of their goals; then their demands become more strident, as they develop a thirst for even greater concessions and accommodations, for nothing seems to assuage their ethnic pride.

Two corollaries to this axiom are: if their demands are not met, social unrest in the form of ethnic violence may likely ensue, even perhaps a civil war; if their demands are granted, regional autonomy may become even more appealing, and perhaps, even the creation of a separate political entity, that is, a new state, a new province, or a new canton.

Significantly, in 30 years of violent confrontation—all within the confines of the Canton of Berne—the total number of fatalities directly related to this highly explosive and emotional struggle was a single death, a Jurassian separatist shot by a pro-Berne farmer, and this despite all adult Swiss males possessing a firearm, their army rifle.

The Jura Crisis was resolved by the famous Swiss referendum mill churning steadily but surely on, through three decades. By this slow, methodical, democratic process, the bankers, the farmers, the clock-makers of Switzerland resolved an emotional impasse that had threatened to disrupt the stability of their political integration. The Jura Crisis was contained within the confines of the Canton of Berne with the rest of the Swiss electorate becoming directly involved only at the last moment in the national referendum to determine whether a new canton should be born, and they said yes.

The Jura Crisis began over language loyalty with religious affiliation added later as a unifying symbol among northern Catholics. In fact, the crisis was over economic advantage versus ethnic pride. In the North, ethnic pride could not be assuaged, therefore, autonomy was granted. In the South, however, economic self-interest took precedence over ethnic pride. Today, the Swiss are deeply relieved to no longer hear the ticking of a time-bomb, in the Jura, which threatened the security and stability of political integration in their multi-ethnic nation. Instead, the loudest sound coming from the Jura region is the ticking of the watches and cuckoo-clocks, which the Jurassians produce so efficiently and in such abundance.

Summary

The Swiss have been able to manage their language and religious pluralism because, fortunately, these two aspects of their ethnicity generally overlap rather than coincide; that is, the process of cross-cutting loyalties operates effectively. For instance, in 1936, Professor Rappard reported,

> Today, 57.3 percent of the population are Protestant and 41 percent are Catholic. The Protestants outnumber the Catholics in twelve cantons, of which nine are German and three French-speaking. The Catholics, on the other hand, outnumber the Protestants in ten cantons, of which seven are German, two are French and one is Italian-speaking. Furthermore, in most of the Protestant cantons there are strong Catholic minorities, whereas in eight out of the ten Catholic cantons, the Catholics represent over 80 percent of the total population. This geographical and statistical distribution of the two rival faiths, even if it has not always prevented oppression, obviously makes for mutual toleration.[20]

In 1968, Kurt Mayer reported similar findings and presented the following table:

Table I
Percentage Distribution of Swiss Citizens by
Mother Tongue and Religious Affiliation, 1960

Mother Tongue	Protestant	Roman Catholic	Old Catholic	Jewish	Other or None
German	61.3%	37.2%	0.7%	0.2%	0.6%
French	53.7%	44.4%	0.3%	0.3%	1.3%
Italian	4.6%	93.6%	0.2%	0.1%	1.5%
Romansh	34.6%	64.8%	0.3%	-	0.3%
Total	57.1%	41.3%	0.6%	0.2%	0.8%

First and perhaps foremost is the fact that the linguistic boundaries do not coincide with but cut across the religious boundaries in most cases and therefore serve to offset one another. As Table I shows, three of the four language groups are religiously mixed to a high degree. Of the German-speaking Swiss close to two-thirds are Protestants while more than one-third are Roman Catholics. With the Romansh-speakers, the proportions are reversed, while the French-speaking Swiss are more evenly split: 54 percent are Protestants and 44 percent are Roman Catholics. Only the Italian-speaking Swiss are religiously homogeneous: 94 percent of them are Catholics.[21]

In 1970, 55% of the Swiss resident population were Protestants and 43% were Catholics. Ten years later, 44.3% were Protestants and 47.6% were Catholics. The presence of large numbers of foreign workers, especially from the Catholic countries of Italy and Spain, caused this shift in religious affiliation statistics. As for language, these figures have remained fairly constant, as is borne out in Table II.

Table II
Language Percentages, Including Resident Aliens[22]

Mother Tongue	1960	1970	1980
German	69.3%	64.9%	65.0%
French	18.9%	18.1%	18.4%
Italian	9.5%	11.9%	9.8%
Romansh	0.9%	0.8%	0.8%
Others	1.4%	4.3%	6.0%

James Madison would have applauded the Swiss solution for diffusing factions, in accordance with his ideas as stipulated in the religious clauses of the First Amendment of the American Constitution, and for diluting the effects of factions, in accordance with his "republican remedy for the diseases most incident to republican government," as stated in *Federalist Ten.*

Today, religious rivalry has given way to mutual toleration and in contemporary Switzerland religious pluralism is considered an integral element of the national equilibrium . . . that both German-speaking Swiss and French-speaking Swiss are religiously divided creates a political framework of great complexity in which the linguistic and religious minorities can combine to form a majority. This constitutes a system of checks and balances which prevents permanent freezing of the front lines when either religious or linguistic issues arise.[23]

Switzerland, through a process of cross-cutting loyalties, has been able to maintain more than a modicum of harmony, unity, and stability, i.e., political integration. The nation's history, traditions, tolerance, and patience have allowed and even encouraged diverse cultural underpinning to coexist. Swiss political integration is the success story of modern multi-ethnic societies, but the ability of the Swiss to tolerate ethnic diversity depends on strict decentralization to a degree that most modernizing states probably feel they cannot afford. Furthermore, in the past, infrequent movement between cantons and the relative constancy of ethnic proportions created a safety cushion. For instance, until the adoption of the Constitution of 1848, permanent migration from one canton to another was forbidden, thereby preserving ethnic territorial integrity. However, as modernization's priorities gave primary to the maximum use of human resources, this rigid stance became impractical. Nevertheless, intercantonal mobility on a permanent basis is still infrequent in comparison with interstate migration in the United States. Furthermore, children of families migrating to a new canton are obliged to use the local language in school. Consequently, German, French, and Italian language frontiers have remained sharply defined even after more than a century of legalized migration. For instance, the 1960 census showed that in all German-speaking cantons, from 94% to 99% of the Swiss population had German as their mother tongue, in French-speaking cantons the percentages were between 82% and 87%, while in Ticino 88% had Italian as their mother tongue. Although Switzerland is one of the most dramatically multi-ethnic countries in the world, each of its territorial subunits is remarkably homogeneous.[24] Modernization and immigration, however, are altering that homogeneity.

Prosperity and growing European integration are upsetting the integrative conditions inside Switzerland by attracting new immigrants from other countries, mainly from Mediterranean and Adriatic Europe. Today, Switzerland has the highest percentage of foreign workers of any country in Europe. They have not always gotten on well with their hosts. Ironically, the French Huguenot immigrants, escaping from religious persecution and the revocation of the Edict of Nantes in the 17th century, brought with them expertise in such industries as textiles and watch-making which are today the basis of Swiss prosperity.

Economic progress has added a new outside dimension to Switzerland's political integration. Nevertheless, the nation's tradition of reaching decisions by consensus bodes well for the future, for it has produced a stable, responsive, and enlightened country where drastic extremes of wealth and poverty are virtually unknown.   Against such extremes Madison warned America in *Federalist Ten.*

Notes

1. Kurt Mayer, "The Jura Problem: Ethnic Conflict in Switzerland." *Social Research* 3, no. 5 (Winter 1968):707.

2. Swiss Federal Government, *Switzerland: People, State, Economy, Culture* (Berne, Switzerland, 1991), 37.

3. "Most Swiss have a gun at home, but the country has one of the lowest crime rates in the world. Ownership of weapons is widespread because all Swiss men [between the ages of 20 and 50] have to undergo annual military training and must take the army rifle and ammunition home after the training course. They are the only soldiers in the world to do so." *New York Times*, 31 May 1977.

4. *New York Times*, 3 December 1978.

5. Professor William Rappard, *The Government of Switzerland* (New York: Van Nostrand, 1936), 33.

6. Karl Deutsch, *Politics and Government: How People Decide Their Fate*, 2nd ed. (Boston: Houghton Mifflin, 1974), 211-212.

7. Herbert Kubly, *Switzerland* (Time, Inc., 1964), 10.

8. Ibid., 7.

9. Mayer, 711.

10. Mayer, 712.

11. Rappard, 6, 7.

12. Ibid., 8.

13. Ibid., 11, 12.

14. The Sonderbund Alliance consisted of Uri, Zug, Schwyz, Unterwalden, Fribourg, Valais, and Lucerne.

15. Rappard, 12.

16. Some sources give the date as 1540.

17. Michel Bassand, "The Jura Problem," *Journal of Peace Research*, Special Issue: "Peach Research in Switzerland" 12, no. 2 (1975): 147.

18. Keith Richardson, "Swiss Passions Make a Rift in Alps," *London Sunday Times*, 24 September 1978.

19. Mayer, 732.

20. Rappard, 11.

21. Mayer, 715.

22. *The Europa Year Book 1984: A World Survey* (London: Europa Publications, 1984), 1:827.

23. Mayer, 715, 716.

24. Appendix A.

Chapter Two
Britain: The Mother Country,
The Place of Refuge

England in Ireland

In the view of the British historian Arnold Toynbee, with the end of European colonialism, after the Second World War, the non-Western majority of the human race again laid siege to fortress Europe, after an interval of almost 500 years. According to Toynbee, not since 1492, when Ferdinand and Isabella of Spain had expelled the Moors and thus terminated their hegemony in the Iberian peninsula, had Europe been threatened by an invasion of non-Europeans: the immigrants from former colonial territories. During the interim, European colonialism had been on the offensive in an attempt to place the whole world under its dominant rule, with the rest of the world coming to think of Europeans as habitual aggressors.

Whatever the validity of such an interpretation of history, European colonialism undeniably became a hated symbol of centuries of Western aggression, expansion, and racial domination.

To understand the phenomenon of this European adventure, and the multi-ethnic, plural societies that it spawned, one must look, first, at the English colonization of Ireland during the second half of the 16th century, because Ireland was the model, the prototype, for all subsequent British colonial adventures in places as disparate as Malaya, Nigeria, Canada, and South Africa. But before England could expand beyond her own borders, there had to be somewhere to expand, and Ireland was the ideal location.

> Ireland, though undeniably of major importance in the expansion, was significantly unlike the other areas which drew England's attention overseas. The differences are obvious . . . the proximity, the long familiarity, the inhabitants, and the trading relationship are only the most conspicuous ways in which Ireland differed sharply from colonial sites in America and elsewhere.[1]

However, as a Christian people, the English had to fortify themselves with a moral justification for the subjugation and exploitation of another European people, especially as the Irish were also Christian and civilized. Or were they?

In the 16th century, to the European ethno-centric mind, to be European meant to be Christian and to be Christian meant to be civilized. Therefore, the English could not, without compunction, subjugate and exploit the Irish, unless, they could satisfy themselves that the Irish were neither Christian nor civilized. This would then make any action taken against them morally justifiable, as it would be action not only against a savage but against an infidel as well. The premise for this rationale was that only through contact with Christians could the savage be brought to civilization and salvation.

For centuries, before the Elizabethan era, European intellectuals had been fascinated with savagery, but not among themselves.

> They were incurious concerning the manners and customs of nearby European barbarians or savages. They preferred to deal with the cultures of classical peoples, or to follow classical models of cultural description. . . . Even as late as the thirteenth century, Bartholomew of England, whose ambitious encyclopedia became widely known, found little he wanted to say about the cultures of the contemporary peoples of Europe. There was scant interest in the manners of the barbarians of Northern and Western Europe as reported so graphically by Caesar. . . . Medieval man was indifferent to the ideas and behavior of the nearby European barbarian or savage—probably because medieval man was so often the very savage the ancients had seen fit either to eulogize or belittle. The commentator preferred to dwell upon the savagery of antiquity. He was carried away by reports, gleaned from the classics, of the existence of human monsters. These creatures haunted the minds of Europeans. They could not be exorcised, but appeared and reappeared for centuries, in the work of would-be scientists, in the sermons of the clergy, and in poetry and drama.[2]

Since the voyages of Columbus to the New World, Europeans had become very curious about peoples whom they thought of as savages, such as the Indians in the New World, many of whom had been brought to Europe as exhibits.[3] These European intellectuals asked themselves: were these peoples like themselves? What made them different? What did this difference mean? The conclusion they came to was that these peoples were not like themselves. They were primitive savages living in the state of nature without laws, without religion, without culture. In short, they were uncivilized beasts who engaged in the most uncivilized practice of all, cannibalism. These European intellectuals never asked themselves whether to kill a man over a few square miles of Spain, or Poland, or Sweden, or England was more logical than to do so in order to survive starvation.

Ironically, the discoverer of the New World was more objective and more tolerant of non-European cultures than were the adventurers and intellectuals who were his contemporaries.

His initial response to the peoples of the New World . . . was less medieval than that of Sir Walter Raleigh, who reported on the people of Guiana a century later. Though the mind of Christopher Columbus may have been, as many now think, an inextricable mixture of ambition, cold scientific curiosity, and medieval credulity. . . the most significant of his contributions to the history of ethnological ideas were his realistic, down-to-earth judgements of the Caribs and their culture. . . . More important yet, were his simple descriptions of the customs and the appearance of the island peoples, to which were added the unequivocal statement that, so far as he knew, there were *no human monstrosities* such as thronged the pages of medieval cosmographies and travel tales. The whole population was said to be very well informed. Even those called cannibals were physically normal men, except that they wore their hair long like women. Living at a time when most men's minds were swamped by religious and superstitious extravagances and deprived of good education, this sailor approached ethnological phenomena with an amount of tolerance and critical detachment unusual in his day—and possibly also in ours.[4]

Columbus was more tolerant than most Europeans who lived centuries after him, who had much more scientific knowledge to guide them but who, unlike Columbus, never encountered them in their own cultural milieu, but, nevertheless, pronounced non-European cultures as barbaric or non-existent. To the European intellectuals, the non-Europeans were primitive savages whose lives were governed not by reason, like their own, but by insatiable passions. For instance, in 1651, Thomas Hobbes wrote that the life of the primitive savage in the state of nature was "solitary, poore, nasty, brutish, and short."[5] Moreover, although Hobbes never set foot in America, he used the American Indians to confirm his

ethno-centric bias that "The savage people in many places of America
. . . have no government at all; and live at this day in that brutish
manner, as I said before."[6] Later, in 1689, John Locke also wrote about
the non-Europeans in his imaginary state of nature, but he envisaged them
as rational primitives without laws: "Where there is no Law, there is no
Freedom. . . .[7] Wherever there are any number of men, however
associated, that have no such decisive power to appeal to, there they are
still in the State of Nature."[8] In 1859, John Stuart Mill, one of the
pillars of Western liberalism, combined the ideas of Hobbes and those of
Locke with Machiavelli's famous dictum that the end justifies the means,
and came to this conclusion,

> We may leave out of consideration those backward states of society in which the
> race itself may be considered as in its nonage. . . . Despotism is a legitimate mode
> of government in dealing with barbarians, provided the end be their improvement,
> and the means justified by actually effecting that end. Liberty, as a principle has
> no application to any state of things anterior to the time when mankind had
> become capable of being improved by free and equal discussion. Until then, there
> is nothing for them but implicit obedience to an Akbar or a Charlemagne, if they
> are so fortunate as to find one.[9]

A basic tenet of British colonial policy, which also came to be used as
a stratagem by other European powers, was to convince themselves,
outsiders, and often the peoples they colonized that the indigenous
inhabitants of the Americas, as well as those of Sub-Saharan Africa, were
primitive savages living in the state of nature. However, in Ireland the
English first tried out and refined this conjuring act. The intellectual
sleight of hand for the English was to make their conception of the
primitive savage first applicable to the Irish Catholics and then to
non-Europeans, such as those in the Americas and in Africa. The agility
and dexterity with which the English went about this feat boggles the
mind.

> The questions that we must pose are how at the mid-sixteenth century, the Irish,
> a people with whom the English had always had some familiarity, came to be
> regarded as uncivilized, and what justifications were used for indiscriminate slaying
> and expropriation.[10]

In 1595, Edmund Spenser[11] (1552?-1599), the first major English poet since Chaucer (1340?-1400), wrote *A View of the Present State of Ireland*, in which he repeated in prose views he had expressed in poetry, in 1590, in *The Faerie Queen*,[12] which he dedicated to Elizabeth Tudor and in which he said of the Irish, "they often made beastliness, excess, and irrationality a theme."[13]

Spenser added,

> They are all papist by their profession, but in the same so blindly and brutishly informed, for the most part, that you would rather think them atheists or infidels. . . . Not one in a hundred knows any ground of religion and article of his faith, but can perhaps say his "Our Father" or his "Hail Mary": without any knowledge or understanding of what one word means.[14]

Of the Irish and their Catholic clergy, Spenser wrote,

> The general fault comes not of any late abuse either of the people or their priests, who can teach no better than they know . . . it is certain that religion was generally corrupted with their popish triumph. Therefore, what other could they learn than such trash as was taught them, and drink of that cup of fornication with which the purple harlot had then made all nations drunk. . . . Since they drank not of the pure spring of life but only tasted of such troubled waters as were brought unto them, the drugs thereof have brought great contagion in their souls, which daily increases and being augmented with their own lewd lives and filthy conversation, has now bred in them this general disease, that cannot, but only with very strong purging, be cleansed and carried away.[15]

As for the future of the Irish Catholics and their clergy, Spenser concludes,

> For the sin or ignorance of the priest shall not excuse the people, nor the authority of their great pastor, Peter's successor, shall not excuse the priest, but they all shall die in their sins, for they have all erred and gone out of the way together.[16]

William Shakespeare (1564-1616), in *The Tempest*, epitomizes the English intellectual's view of the primitive savage. Shakespeare begins by having his enlightened hero, Prospero, who has perfected the art of magic, acknowledge his reliance upon Caliban, the primitive savage, by saying, "He does make our fire, fetch our wood, and serves in offices that profit us."[17] Then, Caliban laments, "This island's mine . . . which thou tak'st from me. When thou cam'st first, thou strok'st me and made much

of me . . . and then I lov'd thee . . . curs'ed be I that did so!"[18]
Shakespeare's Prospero denounces Caliban in language which is
remarkably similar to that used by Spenser to denounce the Irish
Catholics:

> Abhorred slave, which any print of goodness wilt not take, being capable of all ill!
> I pitied thee, took pains to make thee speak, taught thee each hour one thing or
> other: when thou didst not, savage, know thine own meaning, but wouldst gabble
> like a thing most brutish, I endow'd thy purposes with words that made them
> known. But thy vile race . . .[19]

It is important that one distinguishes between the *Old English* of
pre-Elizabethan times and the *New English* settlers of the later centuries.
The *Old English* settled in Ireland when religion was neither a problem
nor a question—virtually all the inhabitants of Ireland were
Catholics—although the *Old English* believed that the Irish practice of
Catholicism was not what it should be owing to certain inherent Irish
vices attributable to Gaelic customs and traditions:

> That the Irish were Christian was never doubted by the Normans or their
> successors, but it was always recognized that Christianity in Gaelic Ireland did not
> fully conform to Roman liturgical practice, and that many pre-Christian traditions
> and customs were only slightly veneered by Christianity. Criticism of unorthodox
> practices were frequent but deviance of this nature was not uncommon in medieval
> Europe, and two systems—an episcopal church on English lines in the Pale and
> environs, and an Irish-speaking, loosely structured church in Gaelic
> areas—continued to tolerate each other's presence.[20]

The substantive difference between the *Old English* and the Gaelic
Irish was mainly over secular matters, such as land, rather than difference
of religious belief, for both were Christian. However, the *New English*,
who were English and Scottish settlers transplanted to Ireland in the 16th
and 17th centuries, abhorred all things Irish, especially the Irish practice
of religion. These new immigrants made no attempts to assimilate Irish
culture but rather gloried in their English and Scottish heritage, most
especially in their new Protestant religion. Today, mainly the descendants
of the *New English* and the Gaelic Irish live alongside one another in
Northern Ireland.

In the 16th century, English intellectuals acknowledged that a people
could be civilized and not be Christian: this they recognized in the
civilization of the Roman Empire and that of the Arabs, their Muslim

adversaries during the Crusades. However, for a people to be Christian and not civilized was to them unconscionable. Therefore, their aim was to *prove* that Irish Catholics were anything but Christian, thereby rendering them uncivilized.

English adventurers came to Ireland with preconceived ideas about the primitive savage which were gleaned from writings dating back to Herodotus,[21] the Greek historian of the 5th century B.C., and the observations, but more likely merely the opinions, of travelers, explorers, and Christian missionaries.[22]　What the English adventurers saw in Gaelic Ireland was the wish-fulfillment of horror stories they had heard dating back to antiquity.

> By declaring the Irish to be pagan . . . the English were decreeing that they were culpable since their heathenism was owing not to a lack of opportunity but rather to the fact that their system of government was antithetical to Christianity. Once it was established that the Irish were pagans, the first logical step had been taken toward declaring them barbarians. The English were able to pursue their argument further when they witnessed the appearance of the native Irish, their habits, customs, and agricultural methods.[23]

The Irish peasants were a pastoral people often having no fixed abode and often moving from place to place in search of food and water for themselves and their livestock. Anthropologists refer to this behavior as transhumance migration. In English eyes, the absence of a stationary habitat was *proof* of Irish primitivism. But, this was not all:

> The Irish were also declared to be exceedingly licentious. Incest was said to be common among them, and Gaelic chieftains were accused of debauching the wives and daughters of their tenants. The Irish appeared therefore not only as pagan but also as barbaric.[24]

Thus, the English, in their own minds, had established a moral justification for subjugating the Irish Catholics. They paid lip-service to converting the Irish from their sinful and backward ways to a chaste and enlightened Christianity, but "They made no effort to accomplish this end, contending that conversion was impossible as long as the Irish persisted in their barbarous way of life."[25]

The English, in the late 16th century, convinced themselves that not only were the Irish socially inferior but that the English were culturally and morally superior, thereby giving themselves a moral justification for later actions. In time, this moral justification became a moral imperative.

As they perpetrated this myth, the English grew in pride and self-confidence, while the Irish, until the end of the 19th century and the Gaelic cultural revival in written and spoken literature, were psychologically and physically subdued into a class of hewers of wood and drawers of water.

> The retention of such a myth in the face of adversity must, however, be taken as indicating the colonists' insecurity: he needed to think of himself as setting out on a crusade, bringing the *gentle government* of the English to the oppressed. If he was to admit that the oppressed did not exist or were not anxious to avail themselves of English justice, then the colonists' raison d'etre was called in question.[26]

The humiliation this demeaning servitude meant to the Irish sense of self-worth angers Irishmen today, for they see that the English took not only their land but tried, as well, to take away their dignity.

In other lands, the English were to perpetuate the myth of their cultural and moral superiority, but, in those countries, the ethnic factor was race rather than religion: "Both Indians and blacks, like the Irish, were accused of being idle, lazy, dirty, and licentious, but few serious efforts were made to draw any of them from their supposed state of degeneracy."[27] In Ireland, however, race or pigmentation was not a visible factor. The Irish and English were both island peoples, pale in complexion, descendent from common ancestors, Adam and Noah, according to Scriptures. In addition, the concept of race in the 16th century had not evolved to the sophisticated yet murky level that it has today.

> The problem of pigmentation, already a very old one at the time of the Renaissance, was stilled somewhat as an element in intergroup relations by the confident Europocentric theory that variations in complexcion was ascribable to difference in length of exposure of originally white skin to the rays of the sun. The popularity of this theory helped to keep the Negro and other darker-skinned peoples theoretically in the family of Adam, thus upholding their dignity as human beings. . . . In these earlier days, the word *race*, in its many linguistic forms and cultural applications, held little meaning.[28]

Not until 1735, and the publication of *A General System of Nature* by the Swedish botanist Carl Linné,[29] did a specific classification of human beings into superior and inferior beings would give Europeans a clear conscience about their sense of inherent superiority over non-Europeans and amongst themselves. However, in Ireland, the aim of the English was not merely to demean the Irish but to crush them utterly. That the Irish sense of self-worth survived in spite of the English onslaught is a tribute to the human spirit and its tenacity. It is also one of the high points and cultural miracles in the annals of Western history.

Migrants and Immigrants in Britain

The first of July 1962 marked the end of an era. The great West Indian migration to Britain was over. It began with a hurricane and ended in a whirlwind. The hurricane which struck Jamaica in the summer of 1951 was one of the contributory factors which sparked off the great migratory movement of Commonwealth citizens from the British Caribbean territories to their "Mother Country." This was the first large-scale entry of coloured people into Britain—for many natives of the British Isles it provided their first real encounter with people of another colour. . . . The curtain came down with dramatic suddenness at midnight on 30 June 1962 when the Commonwealth Immigration Act became law.[30]

In any enquiry into the political integration and disintegration of multi-ethnic, plural societies, one country's name crops up more often than any other. That country was instrumental in turning Canada, Malaysia, Nigeria, South Africa, and Northern Ireland into the multi-ethnic, plural societies that exist today. That country, of course, was Britain, upon whose Empire the sun never set. Where, in country after country, the British established themselves as the Guardians, the Philosopher-Kings, with one-quarter of the human race moved about as adroitly as one moves pawns on a chessboard.

Appropriately, therefore, we begin our analysis with the effects of ethnicity on Britain itself, to see how she, who gave birth to so many multi-ethnic, plural societies abroad, has fared when her progeny's offsprings have come home to Mother England, especially immigrants from the Commonwealth.[31]

Until the end of the Second World War, John Furnivall would have described Britain, not as a plural society nor even as a mixed society, but as a homogeneous society:

The plural society has a great variety of forms, but in some form or other it is the distinctive character of modern tropical economy. Outside the tropics society may have plural features, notably in South Africa, Canada and the United States, and also in lands where the Jew has not been fully assimilated into social life; in other countries also there are mixed populations with particularist tendencies. But, in general, these mixed populations have at least a common tradition of western culture, and, despite a different racial origin, they meet on equal terms and their relations are not confined solely to the economic sphere. There is a society with plural features, but not a plural society. . . . In a homogeneous society the tension is alleviated by their common citizenship, but in a plural society there is a corresponding cleavage along racial lines.[32]

Since the Second World War, British homogeneity has been seriously challenged, as race and immigration have combined to make ethnicity a major issue in British domestic politics.

Prior to the Second World War, immigrants[33] to Britain were overwhelmingly whites, who came mainly from Ireland and the four British Dominions of Canada, Australia, New Zealand, and South Africa. Since the Second World War, there has been a large influx of immigrants of different colors from Asia, Africa, the Middle East, the Mediterranean, and the Caribbean, immigrants of color from the outposts of the defunct British Empire. Collectively, the British refer to these immigrants as *coloureds*, a term which many Africans and West Indians regard with disdain.[34]

For centuries, small numbers of such immigrants settled in Britain permanently. Slaves and ex-slaves, as well as Chinese and Indian sailors of the 17th, 18th, and 19th centuries, came to Britain and were absorbed, effortlessly, into the British cultural landscape. Many took British wives and mistresses and settled in the port areas of cities such as London, Cardiff, and Liverpool. They formed small, isolated communities, which were *visible* only to a very small segment of the native British population.

Prior to the Second World War, the remainder of the non-white population was composed of a handful of students and professionals, who came from the outposts of the British Empire for study, for business, or for short holidays.

Thus, prior to the Second World War, despite the British Empire and colonial history, the overwhelming majority of the indigenous British population was not accustomed to seeing or having physical contact with non-white people. In fact, in a 1951 national survey conducted by the British Central Office of Information, more than 50% of the indigenous British population had never met a non-white person in their lives. Of those who had, the great majority had done so, not in Britain but overseas, when serving in the armed forces or in the colonial service, and, even among these, very few had ever had any real social contact with non-whites.

The British Crisis and Debate over Commonwealth Immigration

With the Second World War, that momentous catalyst of historical change in the 20th century, Britain began to experience the largest and most diversified influx of migrants and immigrants in its history. This was due to Britain's full employment economy and the country's chronic lack of skilled and unskilled workers. At the time, these migrants and immigrants were recruited by public service organizations and entrepreneurs to come to Britain, and they were encouraged to do so by the British government. For example, in 1961, during the debate in the British House of Commons over the Conservative Government's proposed Commonwealth Immigration Bill, many Members of Parliament (MPs) expressed their views on the relationship between Commonwealth immigration and Britain's full employment economy.[35] R. A. Butler,[36] the Home Secretary, when introducing the Government's Bill for its Second Reading, said,

> We all know that throughout the continuous evolution of the Commonwealth, citizens of member-States have always been free to come here and stay here as long as they like. This has been a cherished tradition of the Mother Country. . . . We know how valuable the immigrants have been. . . . In particular, our hospitals and public transport system would be in difficulties were it not for the services of immigrant workers. I pay a tribute to the courteous and efficient way in which so many of them serve us in our hospitals, buses and railways, restaurants and other branches of essential services.[37]

Charles Royle, the Labor MP for Salford, West, also paid tribute to the importance of immigrant workers to Britain's transportation system:

> In 1960, 236,000 people from the Commonwealth started work in this country. In London Transport at the moment there is an overall staff deficiency of 4,500, 2,000 bus drivers, 1,000 conductors, 200 booking clerks and guards. Two hundred and fifty thousand scheduled miles per week—5 percent—are being lost. Underground journeys are being cut by 200 a week.[38]

Mr. Royle also quoted from a letter in *The Times of London* on October 23, 1961, from Field Marshall Claude Auchinleck which said, "During the years . . . we were building the Empire we depended very largely on *coloured* manpower to fight battles for us. This manpower was drawn from different parts of the world but chiefly from India."[39]

Nigel Fisher, the Labor MP for Surbiton, stated succinctly, "There is no unemployment problem in Britain today and we all know it."[40] He went on to say, "The average West Indian immigrant gets a job within three weeks of his arrival and most of them do so within one week."[41] Finally, with information that must have raised a few eyebrows, the MP for Surbiton announced to the House, "We are told that the British Army is seeking coloured Commonwealth recruits to help to get its strength up to the figure of 165,000 men. So lack of employment is not a valid reason for [this] Bill."[42]

Hugh Gaitskell, the Leader of the Labor Party, summed up the Opposition's views on the relationship between Commonwealth immigration and British employment:

Does he [R. A. Butler, the Home Secretary] really imagine that there is a serious danger of unemployment? . . . Everyone knows that we have a far smaller rate of unemployment than we ever had with a smaller population before the war. . . . there is no danger here. As I have said, the movement of immigration is closely related to the movement of unfilled vacancies. If we were to run into a recession, we should find the immigration drying up extremely quickly.[43]

Foremost among the pre-war migrants and immigrants to Britain were the Irish who, along with other British subjects and citizens of the Republic of Ireland, were allowed unrestricted entry into Britain. The constant wave of Irish migrants and immigrants might seem strange—even after Southern Ireland was separated from Britain[44]—given that, throughout the 19th and much of the 20th centuries, Irish Catholics met with a hostility more vicious and more demeaning than anything experienced before or since by any migrants or immigrants to Britain. Ireland, however, was desperately poor, and its people sought a better life wherever they could, even in Britain.

For a long time the population of England and Wales was roughly double the population of Ireland. . . . In 1841, the population of England and Wales was just under 16 million and the population of Ireland was 8,200,000—nearly double that of Scotland. In 1851, the population of England and Wales was up to 18 million while Ireland's was down to 6,500,000. In 1901, the population of England and Wales was 32,500,000, while Ireland's was down to 4,500,000. In the last census, 1961, the population of England and Wales was given as 51¼ million, while that

of Ireland—and all these figures include Northern Ireland as well as Eire—was
down to 4,300,000.

Do the Irishmen want to leave home? I know of no one who is more moved by
emotion about his home and the traditions of his country than Irishmen. But the
Irish have had to leave home because there was no source of livelihood for them.
That is why they come here. They would much prefer to live in their own
homes.[45]

Second, among pre-war migrants and immigrants to Britain, were
continental Europeans who fell into two categories. One consisted of
refugees and exiles of whom the Poles were the most numerous. The
other consisted of selected migrants mainly from Germany, Austria,
Spain, and Italy. These continental migrants entered Britain under the
strict control of the British Ministry of Labor whose Minister told the
House of Commons, "Aliens may come in only if they have a job to go
to for which a British worker is not available."[46] These alien migrants
came to Britain to fill jobs in the undermanned industries or to undertake
specialized assignments. After their sojourn in Britain, many of them
returned to the continent.

Alien migrants, who are not the subject of this analysis, fall into a
category different from that of Commonwealth immigrants, although
Britain's entry into the European Community may cause some confusion.
Nevertheless, in 1961, the Home Secretary told the House of Commons,

We have long been familiar with the control of the immigration of aliens: it has
been controlled in modern times since 1905. An alien is not allowed to stay in this
country unless he makes a case, first, for admission and then for permanent
residence in this country. Under this system about 16,000 aliens a year settle here
as permanent residents.[47]

Before, during, and after the Second World War, the peoples of color,
who immigrated to Britain, were not alien migrants but came from British
dependencies within the Empire and from newly independent countries
within the Commonwealth. Most of them come from the West Indies.
In 1958, Jamaica joined the West Indian Federation along with nine other
British possessions in the Caribbean. Three years later, however, Jamaica
withdrew and in August of 1962 attained its political independence, as
did other members of the Federation, subsequently. But until then, as
Hugh Gaitskell, Leader of the Labor Opposition, told the House of
Commons in 1961,

They are still our Colonies. We are responsible for them, and they think of themselves, as anybody who has been there knows, as British people. Oh, yes, they do. It is rather moving. I found when I was there that they look on us as the Mother Country in a very real sense . . . as they have a right to—because of their history . . . a history of British merchants collecting their ancestors from Africa as slaves and taking them over there and treating them in a way, I think, none of us would approve of.[48]

Clement Davies, the Labor MP for Montgomery, reiterated Gaitskell's sentiments.

We owe a deeper obligation to these people than to almost any other part of the Commonwealth. Our ancestors took people by force from the West coast and East coast, but in the main from the West coast, of Africa and, under the most cruel conditions trans-shipped them to the West Indies, where their descendants now live. We thus owe the West Indians a special obligation.[49]

Unlike the continental European sojourners, but like the Irish immigrants, these new arrivals of color were entitled, as British *subjects*, to enter Britain unconditionally, and to settle wherever they could find housing and a job. Thus, these immigrants of color were vigorously recruited by public service organizations and industry to come to Britain and were strongly encouraged to do so by the British government. In the West Indies, British industry and the British government widely publicized the shortage of manpower and the opportunities for employment in Britain: "London Transport system officials once opened an office in the West Indies to recruit men to work on the city's subways and buses."[50] As a consequence recruitment in the West Indies was extensive and exhaustive. Nonetheless, except for the reception made by West Indian governments themselves, and augmented by voluntary agencies in Britain, no provisions were made by industry or government for the orientation and integration of these British *subjects* into metropolitan British life,[51] although, in 1961, the Home Secretary told the House of Commons,

It cannot be denied that immigrants who have come to this country in such large numbers have presented the country with an intensified social problem. They tend to settle in communities of their own, with their own mode of life, in big cities. The greater the numbers coming into this country the larger will these communities become and the more difficult will it be to integrate them into our national life. . . . [To the question] what had been done to help immigrants . . . I refer, in particular to the Migrants Services Division of the Office of the Commissioner for

the West Indies, the welfare officers of the Indian and Pakistan High
Commissioners, and the committees set up in many areas under the aegis of local
authorities. We welcome the work they have done, but they can deal with limited
numbers only, and, if the numbers of new entrants are excessive, their assimilation
into our society presents the gravest difficulty. . . .[52]

The first wave of immigrants of color, whom the Home Secretary
referred to as *excessive* and *arriving in large numbers* came from the
West Indies, with smaller contingents from Cyprus and West Africa,
although, "Throughout the last three hundred or four hundred years the
number of emigrants from this country has far exceeded the
immigrants."[53] Or, as Nigel Fisher, the Labor MP for Surbiton, told the
House of Commons in 1961, "Over the last decade our population has
increased by over 2 million but in the same period the emigration to the
Commonwealth has actually exceeded immigration from the
Commonwealth."[54] By 1962, immigration from the newly independent
states of India and Pakistan had accelerated and overtook the West Indian
influx. Just how many immigrants were involved?

Before the [1962 Commonwealth Immigration] Act came into force the
U.K. government had no statutory powers for the collection of such statistics
although estimates of movement between certain tropical Commonwealth countries
and the U.K. had been made since 1955. Before 1962 the only way of trying to
measure the movements of Canadians, Australians and citizens of other
"temperate" Commonwealth countries was to go to those countries and obtain
details of the migration to and from Britain from their official statistics.[55]

In 1961, members of the House of Commons complained vigorously
about the inadequate and inaccurate emigration and immigration figures
available to them. For instance, Patrick Gordon Walker, the Labor MP
for Smethwick and one of the most vehement opponents of the 1961
Commonwealth Immigration Bill, told the House of Commons,

In its six annual reports the Overseas Migration Board has deplored the absence
of decent statistics about emigration and immigration into this country. It has said
over and over again in its reports that the figures now in use are almost
meaningless and unreal.[56]

Nevertheless, the Home Secretary told the House of Commons,

A new factor in the last eight years or so is immigration from other parts of the
Commonwealth, notably the West Indies, India, Pakistan and Cyprus, and to a

lesser extent, from Africa, from Aden and from Hong Kong. Immigration from these sources first became a noticeable figure in 1953, and since 1955 we have endeavoured to keep figures of the numbers going in and out. The net intake in 1955 was about 43,000 and an inflow of approximately the same dimensions went on for the next two years. The figure dropped to 30,000 only in 1958 and to 21,000 in 1959. This striking drop was attributable in part to a slight economic recession which we had . . . but it was also due to efforts made by other Governments to restrain their emigrants . . . . Despite the action taken, a rapidly increasing number of immigrants is managing to come here from all these countries. In 1960, the figure rose to 58,000, and in the first ten months of the current year it was 113,000. Of this figure, in the first ten months about 57,000 have come from the West Indies and about 19,000 each from India and Pakistan.[57]

Charles Royle, the Labor MP for Salford, West, offered these figures: "From 1945 to 1959 there entered into this country 353,000 Irish and 330,000 from the Commonwealth."[58] Finally, John Hare, the Conservative Government's Minister of Labor, gave the House of Commons the most complete figures that were available to him:

In 1959, the net intake of immigrants—the number of people who came to this country less the number who left—from the West Indies, Pakistan, Cyprus and, to a lesser extent, from Africa, Aden and Hong Kong, was 21,000. In 1960, this net figure rose to 58,000. In the first ten months of 1961, the figure was 112,000. That shows the rate of growth. . . . It is not easy to give absolutely accurate figures for the Commonwealth as a whole, but the Overseas Migration Board do attempt to give the best answer possible. . . . If hon. members will look at the Sixth Report of the Board, in December, 1960, they will see the following figures. In 1957 there was net outward balance of 72,000. In 1958 this changed to a net inward balance of 45,000. In 1959 the inward balance was 44,000,and in 1960 it was almost doubled to 82,000. The corresponding figures for 1961 are of course not yet available, but they will be very much more than that.[59]

Fenner Brockway, the Labor MP for Eton and Slough, asked the Minister of Labor,

Is the right hon. Gentleman aware that the Home Office, on 3rd November [1961] supplied me with the following figures? Between 1952 and 1959, emigration from the Commonwealth to the United Kingdom was 481,710, while emigration from the United Kingdom to the Commonwealth was 911,897.[60]

The Minister of Labor rejoined,

I am sure that the hon. Gentleman does not want to mislead the House. In that
document it was made clear that the only figures given in it related to long sea
passages. I did not give the figures of those coming into this country by other
means.[61]

From 1955 to 1962, the Commonwealth immigration figures by
country and region were: Pakistanis 68,000, Indians 76,000, and West
Indians 260,000. The West Indian figure seems large, and it was.
However, before 1952, more West Indians migrated to the United States
than to Britain: "They are forbidden now to go to the United States."[62]
This was the consequence of the 1952 McCarran-Walter Immigration Act,
signed by President Harry Truman, which strictly limited legal West
Indian immigration into the United States. Unofficially, thousands,
perhaps millions, of West Indians simply entered and resided in the
United States illegally. Nonetheless, after 1952, many West Indians who
sought a better life for themselves and their children chose Britain, which
in imperial mythology had been enshrined as the Mother Country: the
safe haven for all of Britain's subject peoples. Again, how many
immigrants of color were the British being asked to integrate into their
society? "By the end of 1963 it is estimated that there were
approximately 750,000 coloured people of Commonwealth origin in
England and Wales—including 400,000 West Indians, 150,000 Indians,
and 90,000 Pakistanis."[63]

Britain's open door immigration policy was a long held imperial right: It was the
right of any citizen in any part of the Commonwealth—an absolute, undeniable
right—to come here and stay here at any time just as easily and readily and with
as much right as any of us who were born here.[64]

This open door policy was a legacy of two British 19th century liberal
traditions, one political and the other economic. On the political side was
the liberal tradition of the Empire and the Dominions, which had
substantial white populations, with every Empire citizen a British subject
and, therefore, assured unrestricted entry into the Mother Country. On
the economic side was the liberal tradition of free trade, which required
a free market and the free movement of labor within the Empire but
which disregarded long range planning and the social environment created
by the free movement of labor.

Before the Second World War, the small numbers of white immigrants
from the outposts of the Empire had been easy for the British people to

accept and absorb, because of cultural similarities, including language and religion, reinforced by *invisibility*. Moreover, the British people were willing to accept the small numbers of Asians, Africans, and other *visible* elites, who came to Britain for education, business, and holidays. However, after the Second World War, and especially after the partition of the subcontinent in 1947 into the independent states of India and Pakistan, most Britons viewed very differently the mass influx of non-white, non-elite, and mostly non-skilled peoples into their country. Furthermore, most of these immigrants, from newly independent Commonwealth countries, were not only *visible* by reason of their color but also by reason of their very different cultural backgrounds, including language and religion, i.e., *ethnicity*.

Despite increasing pressures from within its party for control of Commonwealth immigration in the decade before 1961, the British Conservative Party staunchly denied that Commonwealth immigration posed any special problem; this was in accord with its traditional open door policy. Nevertheless, persistent demands for controls were heard. For instance, in 1961, Sir Cyril Osborne, the Conservative MP for Louth and one of the staunchest advocates for controls, told the House of Commons,

> I have been agitating for this type of legislation for ten years. I make no bones about it and do not apologize for it. . . . I support the Bill wholeheartedly . . . but I believe that it is ten years too late and that it is still inadequate. I think that far greater controls will be necessary before long.[65]

Moreover, the rank and file of working class supporters of both the Conservative and Labor parties were vehement in their demands for controls, especially in regions such as the industrial midlands, which felt that they were most affected by increased Commonwealth immigration. As Nigel Fisher, the Labor MP for Surbiton, said,

> The public obviously wants a Bill of this type. From the Gallup Poll of last week, there is no doubt about where the public stands on this issue. I believe that the public is wrong, but I do not think that hon. Members should utterly disregard a strong expression of opinion by 90.3 per cent of our own electors. It would be rather stupid and unrealistic if we did.[66]

However, the Leader of the Labor Party, Hugh Gaitskell, pointed out,

It may be said that this is the wish of the nation, though I would beware of over-simplifying questions in Gallup Polls[67] when all the implications are not explained to those who are answering. But, even if this were the case, I do not believe it to be our duty merely to follow what we are convinced are wrong and dangerous views.[68]

Nevertheless, the rising number of immigrants from India and Pakistan, countries which between them had more than 600 million people, made most Britons feel certain that some kind of control over Commonwealth immigration was essential.

Why were these migrants of color coming to Britain? The House of Commons was told by Sir Cyril Osborne that in June 1961 the *Economist* stated:

Englishmen find themselves increasingly too fastidious to perform unsavoury or unpopular duties." Therefore, the *Economist* went on to say that we must import the semi-slave, second-class citizens to do the unsavoury jobs which we English are not prepared to do ourselves.[69]

Hugh Gaitskell, the Leader of the Labor Party, added, "The movement which we have been experiencing in the last few years is a reflection of the full employment which, in the main, since the war we in this country have enjoyed. In other words, these people have come here because they were wanted."[70] In an emotional outburst, Charles Royle, the Labor MP for Salford, West, said,

Most of the things I want to say are inspired by my love of the people of the West Indies. . . . Why do they come to this country? . . . it is because of the economic and social conditions which prevail in the West Indies. . . . I know the circumstances, economic and social, in which these people live. Therefore, I am not surprised that they desire to lift their living standards and to improve themselves. I am not surprised that they wish to learn trades . . . nearly all of them hope to return home ultimately having re-established themselves and taken the opportunity to become able to earn better wages. They believe that their stay in this country will result in their living fuller lives.[71]

During the historic 1961 debate over Commonwealth immigration, non-whites could not present the House of Commons with their points of view, as they were not then nor were they 25 years later members of the *Mother of Parliaments*,[72] although Shaurji Saklatvala, a Communist, had represented Battersea in the British House of Commons from 1924 to

1929.[73] Sir Cyril Osborne, the Conservative MP for Louth, who strongly supported the 1961 Commonwealth Immigration Bill, inadvertently, put his finger on the reason why migrants of color came to Britain:

> It is due entirely to poverty and numbers. . . . In my opinion, had they faces as white as snow, their great numbers and their great poverty would have made control of their coming into this country inevitable. . . . The dilemma facing our country is this. . . . Either we have got to bring their standards nearer to our standards or we have got to let them drag our standards down to theirs. . . . The New Zealanders, the Australians, the Canadians they are not coming here in great numbers and that has nothing to do with the colour of their skin. They are not coming here because their standard of living is so very much higher than ours, and therefore there is no temptation for them to come. This problem has nothing whatever to do with skin . . . . The real way to deal with this problem . . . of the poverty of the coloured people in the Commonwealth is not to bring what is a tiny fraction of them into this country, because a tiny fraction over there is a great flood for us and still leaves them with this basic problem. They have to face poverty and increasing population.[74]

Clement Davies, the Labor MP for Montgomery, agreed that poverty in Commonwealth countries was a major issue but added:

> To me the Bill is a confession of failure in two important respects. First, there is the failure to tackle the problem which confront these people in their country of origin, and they are people for whom we have been responsible for well over a century. Now when we are handing over self-government to them we are merely leaving them to do the best they can . . . . [Second], there has been complete failure to tackle the problem, on this side, of how these people are to be housed when they come here.[75]

Patrick Gordon Walker, the Labor MP for Smethwick, blamed the Conservative government for the housing problem:

> The Government are to blame for this situation. The Government have totally failed to relate the increase in the number of jobs to housing. They have totally failed to disperse industry. They have contributed to homelessness and overcrowding by their Rent Act and by cutting back local authority house building.[76]

Ostensibly, the problems caused by the presence of migrants of color in Britain revolved around two issues, jobs and housing. However, with full employment in 1961, jobs for these immigrants was not a problem. "Ninety-five per cent of immigrants get jobs quickly."[77] As for housing,

> The fact is that there is a great housing problem . . . there is a great shortage of housing accommodation. The immigrants are not responsible for it. The Government are responsible for it because they have failed to provide sufficient housing for the people . . . . I repeat that West Indians and other coloured immigrants are in no way responsible for the general housing situation in this country.[78]

In summing up the Labor Party"s opposition to the 1961 Commonwealth Immigration Bill, Hugh Gaitskell said,

> There is a problem here. None of us has ever denied that. There are social problems and an appalling housing problem. We concede the existence of these problems in certain areas, but we do not believe . . . that this Bill is the way to handle them.[79]

If jobs and housing were not the real issue, what was? Charles Royle, the Labor MP for Salford, West, went to the heart of the matter:

> It is generally accepted that the influx of white people from the Commonwealth is infinitesimal in comparison with the total amount of immigration. If we rule that out and rule out the Irish, who are left? We have the coloured people from the Commonwealth. The Bill becomes a colour bar Bill from that moment. Any hon. Member who votes for the Second Reading of this Bill—make no mistake—will be voting for a colour bar in this country and this legislation will be based on racial factors alone.[80]

Unlike the United States with its Jim Crow laws and South Africa with its Apartheid laws, Britain never had racial segregation or racial discrimination by statute. In and out of Britain, many people perceived the Commonwealth Immigration Act of 1962 to be an irrefutable break with that tradition:

> This is a hypocritical Bill. It is clothed and cloaked as if there was no racial discrimination involved. . . . The net effect of the Bill is that a negligible number of white people will be kept out and almost all those kept out by the Bill will be coloured people. That is why I say that this is a hypothetical [sp. hypocritical] Bill. . . . The exclusion of the Irish makes all this blatant, obvious and undeniable.[81]

Why were the Irish, especially those from the Republic of Ireland, excluded from the final Act, although they had not been when the Bill was originally drafted. R. A. Butler, the Home Secretary, presented the Conservative Government's argument, and Patrick Gordon Walker, who in an earlier Labor Government had been Secretary of State for Commonwealth Relations, refuted it.

The Bill itself was in three parts dealing with control of immigration, deportation of immigrants, and supplementary matters. Clearly, the first part was the most important, for it identified what people were or were not subject to these controls. Those excluded were people born in Britain, i.e., British citizens, and people holding passports issued by the British government, i.e., British subjects. Clearly, the Irish, of the independent Republic of Ireland, fell into neither of these two categories. So, why were they excluded? R. A. Butler explained:

> There are a great many anomalies connected with our relations with Ireland, one of which is that the citizens of the Republic, although no longer British subjects, possess under Statute all the privileges and obligations of British subjects. . . . The Government have always realised the very great difficulty there would be in operating the control against the Republic. . . . The reasons are as follows. First, the history of previous attempts has left in the minds of all concerned the determination to try to avoid such controls in the future. This was the war-time experience. Secondly, many of those who come from the Republic are seasonal workers who are coming to a job and who would, in any case, be let in under the provisions of the Bill. It is when we come to the difficulties of physical control that we realise the problem. . . . First, if we established a control we should have to operate it against a large number of British citizens who use the Irish ports. I am here supposing that we could control the Eire—that is, the Republic—and Ulster border and limit the problem simply to shiploads from the Republic to the English ports, but all experience and information indicates how very difficult it is to police the Republic-Ulster border and prevent people getting across it either by day or, especially, by night. We are, therefore, forced to the conclusion, as we were in war-time and after, that if we are to operate a control against the citizens of the Irish Republic, we should have to institute a control within the United Kingdom itself; that is, against Northern Ireland and Belfast. I repeat—against the United Kingdom itself and against United Kingdom citizens. The Government take the view that this would be an intolerable imposition upon British citizens, and would be treated as such. I feel certain that to insist on all passengers from Northern Ireland carrying passports and being subject to examination would present us with a political and practical problem as severe as that which emerges by our decision not to impose control against the citizens of the Republic. . . . Any proposals to restrict freedom of travel between Northern Ireland, which is an

integral part of the United Kingdom,[82] and the rest of the country would be unacceptable to the Northern Ireland Government.[83]

Patrick Gordon Walker replied:

[The] passage which startled me was the right hon. Gentleman's very embarrassed account of why the Government were excluding the Southern Irish from the Bill. . . . Why did the right hon. Gentleman put this in the Bill in the first place . . . ? He put it in as a sort of fig leaf to preserve his reputation for liberalism. Now he stands revealed before us in his nakedness. He is an advocate now of a Bill which contains bare-faced, open race discrimination. He advocates a Bill into which race discrimination is now written—not only in its spirit and its practice, but into its very letter. . . . In its first form, before the Irish were taken out, the Bill was very careful to cover up this racial discrimination, but this only makes it worse, because a colour bar clothed in hypocrisy provokes even deeper resentment than a straight-forward colour bar. . . . We bitterly oppose the Bill and will resist it. . . . It is a Bill, as the *Economist* said, that is a ramshackle monstrosity.[84]

Notwithstanding the Labor Party's categorical and uncompromising opposition, the Bill became law in 1962. During the lengthy debate which preceded its enactment, a subject, understood by both sides but never mentioned by either, was the greater propensity of Commonwealth immigrants to vote Labor rather than Conservative.

When the immigrants were on the register and actually in a position to vote the majority of them probably supported the Labour party. . . . Since a disproportionate number either come from a working-class background or live and work in working-class surroundings in this country, it is likely that the easiest identification for them to make was with the party of the working class.[85]

A more perceptive explanation of the West Indian electorate was made by David Pitt, a physician of West Indian origin:

Most [West Indians] feel that the politics of this country do not concern them and, to use words that were used to me "this is Red man's business, not mine." Further, they fear victimization if they find themselves identified with any political party and prefer to be strictly neutral. Also they are not helped by the attitude of many political leaders in the areas in which they live. They refuse to join the political parties because they are often invited to join when elections are in the offing, and they feel that the invitation to membership is merely a ruse to safeguard their vote and they strongly resent being used. Many immigrants do not get their names on the electoral roll because they feel that they are being spied upon and the attempts to get them on the electoral roll are merely a way of trying to be sure of their whereabouts. The landlords think that it is a means of trying to find out their incomes and do not put their tenants' names on the roll. The tenants believe they are safer if their addresses are not known.[86]

Nevertheless, for basic political reasons, both political parties cared how many immigrants were allowed in. Who were the Commonwealth immigrants subject to the new legislation? R. A. Butler explained the three categories:

The first category is defined in subsection (2,a): people coming here for the purpose of employment and holding vouchers issued by the Ministry of Labour. These vouchers will be issued to three kinds of applicant: first, those who can satisfy the Ministry of Labour that they have jobs to come to; secondly those who can satisfy the Ministry that they possess training, skill or technical qualifications, which are likely to be useful in this country, and thirdly, those who fall into neither of those categories and vouchers for this third category will be issued on a first-come first-served basis. The Government will decide from time to time how many such vouchers can be issued having gone into all the factors which bear on our capacity to absorb further immigrants without undue stress or strain. . . . The second category of immigrants who will be granted entry are those defined in subsection (2, b). That is to say, those who can satisfy the immigration officers that they are in a position to support themselves and their dependents, if any, without working. This will cover not only visitors, including business visitors, but also, for example, retired people who come to live here on pension. The third main category allowed in will be those who are granted entry by the immigration officers under administrative arrangements. . . . I have particularly in mind students, returning residents and wives and dependent children. These categories . . . will be best dealt with at the discretion of the immigration officer, in accordance with general directions which I shall issue from time to time. . . . At present, a citizen of any other self-governing Commonwealth country has the right after twelve months' ordinary residence in the United Kingdom to be registered as a citizen of the United Kingdom and Colonies. Clause 12 raises this period of twelve months to five years. . . . five years is the period laid down in the equivalent legislation of Canada and Australia.[87]

Smethwick: Ethnicity Enters the Mainstream of British Domestic Politics

For its aggressive opposition to the 1961 Commonwealth Immigration Bill, the Labor Party was subjected to charges of hypocrisy and expediency by members of the Conservative Party. These charges were made on the eve of a national election, when the 1962 Act came up for renewal in 1963 and when the Labor Party announced that it no longer categorically contested the need for Commonwealth immigration controls:

The Labour party, as it prepared for the General Election of 1964, was confronted with a particularly difficult situation. In the previous autumn, faced with the necessity of taking up a position on the renewal of the Commonwealth Immigrants Act, the leadership had substituted for its previously clear-cut hostility to the Act a compromise approach by which opposition to the Act was maintained on the grounds that restrictions had been imposed on the Commonwealth unilaterally and without consultation, but the principle of restriction was conceded. As a manoeuvre for getting the Parliamentary Labour Party out of an awkward situation this device was a success, but subsequently proved to have made little impact on the electorate, who generally continued to identify Labour with free immigration.[88]

Conservative Party accusations of hypocrisy and expediency continued after the Labor Party came to power and not only renewed the Act in 1964 but introduced additional controls of its own in 1965. The Labor Party member whose previous stance was considered most reprehensible was Patrick Gordon Walker: "Mr. Gordon Walker had betrayed the town by not voting for the renewal of the Immigration Act. From this day on Smethwick has no MP."[89]

In the 1964 National Election, Smethwick, a Midlands industrial town near Birmingham, elected its first Conservative MP since the Second World War. His name was Peter Griffiths. The Smethwick electorate rejected Patrick Gordon Walker, who had represented the town in Parliament since 1945.[90] Had he been re-elected in 1964, Patrick Gordon Walker would have been the British Foreign Secretary in the newly elected Labor Government.

The election at Smethwick marked the beginning of race as a prominent factor in British domestic politics, although not the first time that the race factor had decided an election. For instance, in 1961, Denis Howell, the Labor MP for Birmingham, Small Heath, recounted in the House of Commons how the race factor had been prominent in two recent elections in which he was a candidate:

As recently as March of this year it fell to my lot to contest the by-election at Small Heath largely on this issue . . . . [Earlier] I became the Member of Parliament for All Saints. I lost that seat by 20 votes. . . . My experience in All Saints was that a large number of immigrants were persuaded that if they voted for me in 1959 that would be an end to their prosperity, they would lose their jobs and they would all have to go home. As a result of that I lost my seat by twenty votes. In Birmingham, Small Heath, this year I had the same position again. I have never been so nauseated as I was by the campaign of the Conservative Party in the Small Heath by-election. It was shocking and disgraceful. . . . This campaign ended by an anonymous loudspeaker van and the people being told, "You do not want blacks here, do you?" There was not a single speech made in that by-election by any Conservative speaker of repute dissociating the party from this conduct. It was really disgraceful. It was despicable.[91]

What made the election at Smethwick so special was that, "The national press probably devoted more column inches to Smethwick than to any other constituency, and almost all that they printed was on the immigration issue."[92] More importantly, the 1964 election at Smethwick was a milestone in British domestic politics because, before Smethwick, the Conservative Party had not perfected an effective formula for removing a very stubborn electoral stumbling block. That stumbling block was the loyalty of the industrial working class to the Labor Party. This class loyalty was undeniable because, at every national election since 1956, some 13 million industrial workers had consistently voted for the Labor Party. Peter Griffiths and his Conservative colleagues understood that, in a shrinking economy in which unemployment was replacing full employment, working class people were more affected than any other group by the presence and competition of non-skilled, non-professional immigrant workers. These working class people made immigrants of color the scapegoats for their anomie. As a consequence, Griffiths and his Conservative colleagues used the Commonwealth immigration issue to obtain the white working class votes they needed to win. For instance, one of the slogans openly voiced during the Smethwick campaign was, "If you want a nigger neighbour, vote Labour." To this Griffiths commented,

I should think that is a manifestation of the popular feeling. I would not condemn anyone who said that. I would say that is how people see the situation in Smethwick. I fully understand the feelings of the people who say it.[93]

In 1961, Patrick Gordon Walker told the House of Commons,

There are some elements that are stirring up race hatred. We should consider legislation to punish deliberate incitement of race hatred. We must certainly have legislation to stop the practice of the colour bar in places to which the public has access.[94]

The Commonwealth Immigration Act in Action

In 1964, one of the first pronouncements made by the new Labor Government was its intention to introduce a Race Relations Bill that would prohibit discrimination on racial grounds. The Bill, which became the Race Relations Act of 1965, provided for the establishment of a Race Relations Board. In its first report, the Race Relations Board gave as the following the role legislation could play against racial discrimination:

1. A law is an unequivocal declaration of public policy.
2. A law gives support to those who do not wish to discriminate, but who feel compelled to do so by peer or social pressure.
3. A law gives protection and redress to minority groups.
4. A law thus provides for the peaceful and orderly adjustment of grievances and the release of tensions.
5. A law reduces prejudice by discouraging the behavior to which prejudice finds expression.[95]

For these reasons, the Race Relations Board recommended that the Race Relations Act be amended to include employment, housing, and financial institutions, such as insurance companies and banks, which were not covered by the existing legislation.[96] However, before the new legislation could be implemented, a new factor entered the race-immigration equation of British domestic politics. This new factor appeared in the person of Enoch Powell.

On April 20, 1968, while a member of the Conservative Party's Shadow Cabinet,[97] Enoch Powell made one of the most inflammatory speeches on race and immigration ever made by a public figure of such rank in Britain. When addressing the annual meeting of the West Midlands Area Conservative Political Center, Powell said,

The answers to the simple and rational question are equally simple and rational: by stopping, or virtually stopping, further inflow, and by promoting the maximum outflow. Both answers are part of the official policy of the Conservative Party. . . . As I look ahead, I am filled with foreboding. Like the Romans, I seem to see "the River Tiber foaming with much blood." That tragic and intractable phenomenon which we watch with horror on the other side of the Atlantic but which there is interwoven with the history and existence of the States itself, is coming upon us here by our own volition and our own neglect.[98]

In order to promote maximum outflow, Powell advocated that the British government give generous financial assistance to non-white immigrants to enable them to return permanently to their countries of origin. The leadership of the Conservative Party repudiated Powell's claim that his solution was part of the party's official policy. Subsequently, Powell was removed as a member of the shadow cabinet, and, in 1974, he left the party, ostensibly, over its decision to support Britain's entry into the Common Market. Nonetheless, Powell remained a member of the House of Commons as a representative, "from Northern Ireland, where he has identified himself with the extreme Protestant position."[99] He continued to maintain that "rivers of blood would flow," if Britain did not halt non-white immigration and institute a system of voluntary repatriation: "Today, he said the presence of two million non-whites in Britain was responsible for the wave of violence. He said, "nobody doubts that, except when talking in public.""[100]

In June 1970, the British went to the polls for a national election in which political pundits predicted an easy victory for the Labor Party. The outcome, however, was the biggest electoral surprise in the Western World, since Harry Truman upset Tom Dewey in the 1948 American presidential election. At the time few political commentators said so, but later ones speculated that the 5% swing in votes from Labor to Conservative, which enabled the latter to win, was the result of promises made by the Conservatives, during the campaign, on the matter of race and immigration.

In February 1971, the new Conservative Government introduced an immigration Bill that was intended to be the definitive legislation on the matter. In March 1971, when introducing the Bill for its Second Reading in the House of Commons, Reginald Maudling, the Home Secretary, said, "The Bill carries out the undertaking which we gave at the election in our party manifesto to introduce a new system of control over permanent immigration from overseas."[101] Immediately, many political commentators saw this as blatant duplicity, for the Home Secretary had to know that the flow of Commonwealth immigrants had been reduced to a trickle under the existing legislation. For instance, in 1965, a limit of 8,500 had been set by the Labor Government on the number of work permits to be issued each year to Commonwealth immigrants.[102]

These work permits—vouchers which were strictly controlled—were the determining factor of how many Commonwealth immigrants could enter Britain in a single year. Thus, the new Bill would have little effect on the number of Commonwealth immigrants entering Britain but would have an enormous effect on how they were treated once they arrived.

Under the new Bill, which became law, a Commonwealth immigrant needed a work permit before being allowed to enter Britain. This work permit was granted for only one year, and then had to be renewed annually. After four years' residence, the Commonwealth immigrant was eligible for permanent status. However, other restrictions existed. First, upon arrival, the Commonwealth immigrant had to register with the police and had to continue to do so periodically throughout his probationary stay in Britain. In 1961, R. A. Butler, then the Home Secretary, said: "To follow an immigrant moving from place to place in this country would be almost impossible. Also, this would be a power in excess of what we use in deciding with aliens. Therefore, we rejected it."[103]   Nevertheless, under the new law, "Commonwealth citizens would be treated exactly as aliens."[104]   More importantly, this close relationship between white police and non-white immigrants had the combustible ingredients of a time-bomb. Second, during his probationary stay in Britain, the Commonwealth immigrant had to obtain official permission for any change in job or residence. Again, this was a Home Office affair which could involve the non-white immigrant with the white police.[105]

In May 1986, Joseph Lelyveld—who had completed two tours of duty in South Africa, who was now the *New York Times* chief correspondent in London, and who had just received a Pulitzer Prize for his book *Move Your Shadow: South Africa, Black and White*—wrote of the British police, "Almost 10 years after the Metropolitan Police first tried advertising for black recruits, the 27,000-member force remains nearly 99 percent white with only 286 Indians, Pakistanis, Chinese and blacks."[106]   Lelyveld also described the experiences of

Sgt. Andrew Simons, a London police officer with nearly 10 years' experience [who] never wears his uniform when he is traveling to or from work. About 95 percent of black policemen here, he estimates, feel the same inhibition. Riding in uniform on the subway or a public bus, he would expect to be accosted by hostile questioners wanting to know what a black thought he was doing in a police uniform. "White people never approach you," he said over coffee in the canteen of the station house. . . . "You can sit here in this canteen and get a table full of policemen and one of them will say, "I stopped this nigger." Then he'll say, "Sorry, Andy." Usually, I say, "If I wasn't there, you'd call them that. Why apologize?""[107]

The new restrictions, imposed by the 1971 Bill, applied to all Commonwealth immigrants except *patrials*, who enjoyed automatic entry into Britain without any police supervision. Critics referred to the *patrial scheme* as the *grandfather clause*, because it applied to anyone who had been born or naturalized in Britain, or who had a parent or grandparent born or naturalized in Britain.

The London Times and Mark Bonham Carter, chairman of the Community Relations Commission, denounced the *patrial scheme* as transparently "racist, divisive, and unnecessary."[108] Why? Because the overwhelming majority of *patrials* were descendants of whites who once manned the outposts of the empire in Southern Rhodesia, Canada, Australia, New Zealand, and South Africa. In the House of Commons some enlightening exchanges took place of the issue of *patrials*:

Mr. Evelyn King asked the Secretary of State for the Home Department what estimate he has of the number of Anglo-Indians who can qualify as patrials. . . . Mr. Mandling: The number of people involved is no more than a few thousand.[109]

Miss Lestor asked the Secretary of State for the Home Department how many people in Southern Rhodesia are covered by the patrial clause. . . . Mr. Sharples: I estimate the number at between 150,000 and 200,000.[110]

Mr. Evelyn King asked the Secretary of State for the Home Department (1) what estimate he has of the number of Australians, New Zealanders and Canadians, respectively, now living overseas who can qualify as patrials under the provision of the Immigration Bill; (2) what estimate he has of the number of persons now living overseas, who can qualify as patrials . . . excluding Australians, New Zealanders and Canadians. . . . Mr. Maudling: It is not possible to give reliable estimates. The total would run into some millions.[111]

The 1971 Bill took a definitive step in the direction of Enoch Powell's scheme for the voluntary repatriation of immigrants by authorizing the provision of state funds for Commonwealth immigrants who might want to leave Britain permanently. *The London Times, New York Times*, and the Community Relations Commission feared that the overall effect of the Bill's provisions would be to unravel whatever progress Britain had made in the previous decade in the area of race relations and, "to erode further the already tenuous ties that link the Mother Country with non-white members of the Commonwealth."[112]

Further complicating the issue of Commonwealth immigration, in 1972, when the Asians[113] of Uganda were expelled from that country by the African dictator, General Idi Amin, many of them held British passports which identified them as British *subjects*. In 1947, under a scheme devised at a meeting of Commonwealth representatives, each Commonwealth country agreed to recognize as British *subjects* or Commonwealth *citizens* both its own nationals and nationals of other Commonwealth states. Therefore, when the Asian refugees from Uganda turned to Britain for succor, in 1972 Britain admitted about 20,000 as British *subjects*.[114] However, life was not easy for these Asian refugees in Britain, as the value of the pound sterling evaporated daily during their first three years in the country, as inflation continually ran to over 20% annually, and as unemployment became endemic in a country that once scoured the globe recruiting workers for its industries.

The total influx from Uganda of approximately 40,000 Asian refugees, as British *subjects*, caused many Britons to wonder aloud what constituted a British *subject*. During the golden age of the empire, one was a British *subject*, if one came under British rule. However, with the demise of the empire, a fierce debate arose over the concept of British *subject*. Ultimately, this debate included the question, who qualifies for British citizenship?

In the summer of 1980, after years of acrimonious debate in and out of the House of Commons, the Conservative Government of Margaret Thatcher drew up a new set of stipulations for British citizenship which would augment, and in important instances replace, the British Nationality Act of 1948 and all subsequent citizenship legislation. These new stipulations were presented on July 30, 1980, in a government White Paper and reiterated, on the same day in the House of Commons, in a special Statement by the Home Secretary, William Whitelaw. Both the White Paper and Mr. Whitelaw stated that the idea was to grant citizenship only to those people, "who have close connections with the United Kingdom."[115] Furthermore,

The main reason why it is necessary to replace the existing law is, quite simply, that the citizenship created by the British Nationality Act 1948 no longer gives any clear indication of who has the right to enter the United Kingdom. Citizenship and the right of abode, which ought to be related, have over the years parted company with each other. One can be a citizen of the United Kingdom and Colonies and not have the right of abode in the United Kingdom. Conversely, one can have the right of abode here without being one of our citizens. The Labour Government, in their Green Paper, said almost exactly the same thing.[116]

The new rules would exclude millions of people in British dependencies and former colonies whose connections with Britain were considered more tenuous. Since most of those included as British citizens were white, while most of those excluded were not, the Conservative Government's latest scheme went to the heart of Britain's growing problem of race as a dominant factor in domestic politics. Civil rights critics denounced the 1980 policy paper, which formed the basis of the new rules that became operative in January 1983, as overtly and covertly racist. Nevertheless, Whitelaw, in his special Statement on July 30, 1980, and again when the Bill had its Second Reading in the House of Commons on January 18, 1981, referred continuously to an earlier Labor Government Green Paper on British nationality law in April 1977 which stated, "The most serious drawback to the status of citizen of the United Kingdom and Colonies is that it [Nationality Act 1948] does not provide a ready definition of who has the right of entry into the United Kingdom . . . there must be a more meaningful citizenship for those who have close links with the United Kingdom."[117] In fact, many of the ideas and approaches to the question of British nationality were much the same in the Labor Green and the Conservative White papers.

To the charge of racism, the Conservative Government countered by saying that the intent of the new legislation was to avoid irregularities and to do away with complicated classifications of citizenship and national privilege which dated from the days when one fourth of the world's population came under British rule. The 1980 policy paper stated:

> The citizenship laws of the United Kingdom no longer accurately define those who have the normal attributes of citizenship. This leads to considerable uncertainty and misunderstanding, both at home and overseas, about the United Kingdom's obligations to its citizens.[118]

As one step towards clearing up the ambiguity, the Conservative Government proposed to do away altogether with the term British *subject*, which it said once seemed meaningful and relevant but was no longer. The term *subject*, which applied to more than a billion people living in Commonwealth countries, was out of date, declared the 1980 policy paper, since most of the people who are citizens of countries that used to be in the empire are in no sense subjects of Britain. However, the Irish anomaly continued, as certain citizens of the Irish Republic again came in for special consideration. In his special Statement the Home Secretary said,

> The proposal about certain citizens of Eire being British subjects is limited. It is confined to people who were British subjects before 1949. The proposal does not affect civic rights, or the right to vote. The right of citizens of Eire to vote [in British elections] was given in the Representation of the People Act 1949, and if there is to be any change, that Act will have to be amended. . . . The relationship that was enshrined in the original Acts between this country and the Republic of Ireland, . . . is somewhat different from nationality all over the world.[119]

Therefore, and ironically, the designation British *subject* did not disappear entirely from the new legislation and applied primarily to "certain citizens of Eire as British subjects."

The British Nationality Act of 1981 replaced the existing citizenship classifications with three categories: British citizenship, citizenship of the British Dependent Territories, and British Overseas citizenship. The last category was not contained in the earlier Labor Government's Green Paper of 1977: "We changed to three citizenships instead of two because it was the wish of some of the dependencies concerned."[120]

The first category, *British Citizenship*, is granted to people closely connected with the United Kingdom, the Channel Islands, and the Isle of Man. Generally, these are people who were born or naturalized in Britain or were born overseas of British parents. The second category, *Citizenship of the British Dependent Territories*, is granted to people connected with dependencies, most of whom are in Hong Kong and Gibraltar. They number about three million persons. The third category, *British Overseas Citizenship*, which caused a great deal of discussion in the House of Commons, is granted to those citizens of the United Kingdom and Colonies who do not acquire either a British citizenship or a British Dependent Territories citizenship. The number of people who qualify for British Overseas Citizenship, most of whom were born in one part of the Commonwealth but now live in another part, such as missionaries and their children, is difficult to estimate. They may run in the hundreds of thousands but, as the Home Secretary said,

> This is a residual category. Many of its holders indeed already possess another citizenship. . . . I want to stress, however, the continuance of the special arrangements for certain United Kingdom passport holders who are mainly in or originate from East Africa. The Government intend to continue the special

voucher scheme for them. Clause 27 [of the British Nationality Bill][121] would ensure the continuation of the current provisions regarding British subjects without citizenship by virtue of sections 13 and 16 of the 1948 Act. Those are the people who in 1948 were regarded as potentially citizens of other Commonwealth countries. Those countries, however, did not in the event cover them in their citizenship laws. The category diminishing since it relates to people born before 1949.[122]

The Conservative Government claimed that the Nationality Act of 1981 was color-blind, but critics rejoined that parts of it seemed designed to let whites in and keep non-whites out. For example, critics deplored the change under which citizenship would no longer be automatic for all children born in Britain. The Home Secretary responded,

A child of parents neither of whom is a British citizen and neither of whom is settled here should not acquire British citizenship solely by his birth in the United Kingdom. . . . All adults, whether Commonwealth citizens or foreigners, who wish to obtain British citizenship will do so by naturalisation. The present automatic entitlement of wives to obtain our citizenship by registration will be ended. Instead, both husbands and wives will be able to apply for naturalisation on the same terms as others, though after three years' residence instead of five.[123]

Nevertheless, citizenship will be withheld for at least 10 years, if the foreign mother giving birth was in Britain temporarily or illegally, as for example, a student, tourist, or illegal alien. Timothy Raison, the Minister of State for the Home Office, rejoined,

The present arrangements mean that citizenship is acquired by many children whose parents are here only temporarily, as students or visitors, for example, or who are working here for short periods or are here illegally. Any child who obtains our citizenship in this way and then leaves with his parents will at present transmit that citizenship in due course to his own children from abroad. With air travel and much greater mobility, the situation today is very different from that which existed when concepts like *jus soli* grew up. The arguments for continuing to confer citizenship in the present indiscriminate manner are clearly weak.[124]

The debate over British citizenship went to the heart of the British people's perceptions of themselves. Furthermore, it reflected some of the social tensions that had arisen in the previous generation, as Britain ceased to be virtually an all-white society: a textbook example, as Furnivall would call it, of a homogeneous society. The debate also prompted a new evaluation of the golden age of the British Empire, for the empire and its aftermath[125] produced the situation of millions of people, all over the world, who considered themselves British *subjects*. However, as Timothy Raison, the Minister of State for Home Office, said,

> We have got finally to dispose of the lingering notion that Britain is somehow a haven for all those countries we once ruled. . . . Our present pattern of citizenship is clearly out of date. It reflects an imperial idea, which no longer exists. . . . Our new citizenship law will reflect the reality of today's world rather than our imperial past.[126]

The British Nationality Act of 1981 states that the expression *British subject*, as a common description of all Commonwealth citizens, would cease to be used and that instead the expression *Commonwealth citizen* would be applied. What this would mean, in practice, worried some Britons. For instance, the Roman Catholic Bishops of Britain expressed this opinion:

> Britain has become irreversibly a multiracial, multicultural society. Any new nationality law should state, as a matter of principle, that our national identity is multiracial, thereby avoiding any potentially racialist conception of national identity.[127]

Many other Britons were not prepared to accept that theirs was a multi-racial society, despite a non-white population of 4% nationwide with much higher percentages in urban areas.[128] This view was reflected by a number of speakers during the debates in the House of Commons, but none so bluntly as John Stokes, the Conservative MP for Halesowen and Stourbridge:

> The ordinary Englishman still clings obstinately to his Englishness and to the old, known ways. He knows only too well that if immigration continues at the present rate the indigenous population will in time be supplanted by aliens and British people will gradually disappear from these islands. It has already started to happen in certain areas.[129]

In 1983, Britain had an estimated population of 56 million people. Of these, approximately one and a half million were of Asian ancestry, mainly Indian and Pakistani, while an estimated half million were of African and West Indian descent. Altogether, non-whites made up about 4% of the total British population. During the 1970s, the only group of non-white immigrants to arrive in significantly large numbers were

Asians, mainly from India, Pakistan, Hong Kong, and East Africa. During the same period, among West Indians, who preceded Asians to Britain in significantly large numbers, the number of immigrants dropped so sharply that more West Indians were leaving the country than entering it. In fact, in 1961, "The Economist Intelligence Unit study on migration from the Commonwealth suggests that the outflow is very much larger than is generally thought. For instance, it is estimated that between 1955 and 1960 no less than 20 per cent of the West Indians went back."[130] In 1972, the *New York Times* reported, "More people have left Britain in recent years than have arrived as immigrants."[131] In 1978, in the first report of the British government's Select Committee on Race Relations and Immigration, the situation was summarized this way: "More people leave the United Kingdom each year than enter. [Last year] 190,000 came to live in Britain and 230,000 left."[132] In other words, the United Kingdom was consistently losing more people to the West Indies, rather than gaining them, as was the case until 1969.

Summary

At the end of the 1960s, about 25% of the non-white population in Britain had been born there. By the early 1980s, "nearly half the non-whites living in Britain were born here,"[133] and among those under the age of 21, an estimated 5 out of every 6 were born in Britain. Still, these figures could be deceptive: "There are no reliable figures about immigrants now resident in the United Kingdom; no reliable statistics which can be described as indicators of immigration; and no details have been kept from which such statistics might have been compiled."[134] Nevertheless, these young men and women born in Britain refuse to see themselves as immigrants or to find consolation in comparing their circumstances in Britain with the often wretched conditions in their parents' homeland. Britain is their homeland; therefore, these young people measure their status not with others overseas but with fellow citizens in Britain. While their parents may have accepted second class citizenship in Britain, these young people expect more from British society and are increasingly frustrated and exasperated by that society's persistent xenophobia and racial discrimination. For instance, in Britain, unlike in America, non-whites have had little success in penetrating the middle and upper echelons of power in the professional, economic, or political worlds. Their attitude of despair was expressed by Lord David Pitt, Britain's only black peer and an unsuccessful candidate for a seat in the House of Commons: "People are no longer ashamed of being bigots. Ten years ago, they would say, "Sorry, no coloureds." Today, they don't bother to say . . . sorry.""[135]

Race as a dominant factor in domestic politics has turned out to be a painful, embarrassing, and ugly experience for Britain. Britain is not alone in this experience. For years, Europeans chastised white Americans for their discrimination and segregation of black Americans. Now, Europeans from the icy Baltic to the balmy Mediterranean find themselves guilty of similar abuses. Especially European powers, such as Holland and France, whose colonial empires once stretched round the globe, have not fared well, when they have met their colonial progeny face to face in the Mother Country.[136] In Britain, however, the issue of non-whites has resulted in violent confrontations between whites and non-whites at regular intervals. In fact, over the past two decades, racial violence in Britain has become so commonplace as to resemble an epidemic. For instance, in August of 1977, more than 250 people were injured during a West Indian carnival that turned into a race riot in London's Notting Hill district, a riot reminiscent of racial violence in the same district in 1958. In January of 1978, 200 West Indian youths battled with the police and other white youths in the industrial city of Wolverhampton, while in the spring and summer of 1981, almost continuous racial violence raged over a dozen cities and towns with fighting, burning, and looting the likes of which [Britons] had not seen in their century. Nevertheless, not all of Britain's racial disharmony has been as visible as these episodes:

> Racial discrimination has become a continuing, if rather low-keyed, scandal. Only last week, the Guardian newspaper reported a confidential Government survey that found systematic discrimination in the Department of Health and Social Security. Similar studies have found widespread bias in industry.[137]

Race as a factor in British domestic politics did not begin with Mrs. Thatcher's government in 1980, nor with Smethwick in 1964, but rather, it is a bitter legacy of Britain's imperial past. The first seed of that imperialism was planted in 1562, when John Hawkins laid anchor in the Caribbean after having taken a cargo of Africans from Africa and deposited them in the New World as slaves. Ironically, Liverpool, which was once the greatest port in Europe, is today a deeply depressed economic area. At its height, Liverpool was at the vortex of a system referred to as the *golden triangle*: from Africa, where the cargo was Africans, from the West Indies, where the cargo was sugar, coffee, cotton, and other primary produce, and finally from Liverpool, where the cargo was manufactured goods from Birmingham and the industrial midlands that were sent round the world. The second seed of British imperialism was planted throughout the 17th century: under James I, Ulster was forfeited to the British Crown in 1611, after the Irish rebellion led by Hugh O'Neill was crushed and the Ulster Plantation was established. By mid-century, 1649, Oliver Cromwell had rewarded his victorious Protestant soldiers, many of them Scotsmen, with land belonging to the Irish Catholics, much of it in Northern Ireland. The third seed of British imperialism was planted in the 18th century when Britain's supremacy in India was assured: by her defeat of her commercial rival, the Dutch, in 1759, and her defeat of her fellow-imperialists, the French, guaranteed by the Treaty of Paris in 1763, which also brought Canada into the imperial fold. Sadly and ironically, the fruits of these imperial adventures—Africa, Ireland, and India—all ripened at the same time to produce a bitter fruit for the British lion to savor.

The theory that Britain aimlessly, carelessly, and with no foresight accumulated a vast empire that eventually contained one fourth of the earth's inhabitants, with imperialism following trade and commerce, is flawed. The error and inadequacy of this explanation of British imperialism are visible in Ireland, for in Ireland the theory, practice, and moral justification for British imperialism was established.

Ireland was one of the first of the English imperial colonies, for it was Irish trees that produced the wood that gave England the finest naval ships in the world. But, by the end of the 17th century, Ireland had been denuded of most of her indigenous trees for this imperial project.

Prior to the First World War, Irish freedom seemed imminent, under a political expediency termed Home Rule, but also imminent was a sectarian civil war in Northern Ireland—fostered by Protestants in the North and nurtured by Unionists in the South of England—if Prime Minister Herbert Asquith's government proceeded with its Home Rule project. Consequently, the Irish Issue was left unsettled until after the First World War. Now, after trying for more than a hundred years, it is from Northern Ireland—the last of the imperial colonies—that the British find it impossible to disentangle themselves.

Notes

1. Theodore Rabb, *Enterprise and Empire: Merchant and Gentry Investment in the Expansion of England, 1575-1630* (Cambridge: Harvard University Press, 1967), 1.

2. Margaret Hodgen, *Early Anthropology in the Sixteenth and Seventeenth Centuries* (Philadelphia: University of Pennsylvania Press, 1964), 34-35.

3. "When Christopher Columbus [returned] he brought with him seven kidnapped Indians. . . . During the years which followed, Indians captured by other explorers were exhibited in other capitals of Europe. In 1494, six hundred were sent home as slaves; in 1496, thirty; in 1499, two hundred and thirty-two; while Vespucci's first voyage netted two hundred and twenty-two. In England, Sebastian Cabot appears to have been the pioneer showman." Ibid., pp. 111-112.

4. Ibid., 19-20.

5. Thomas Hobbes, *Leviathan* (Penguin Books, 1968), 186.

6. Ibid., 187.

7. John Locke, *Two Treatises of Government* (New York: Cambridge University Press, Mentor Books, 1965), 348.

8. Ibid., 369.

9. John Stuart Mill, *On Liberty* (New York: Norton and Company, 1975), 11.

10. Nicholas Canny, "The Ideology of English Colonization: From Ireland to America," *William and Mary Quarterly*, 30, no. 4 (1973), 583.

11. In 1589 Spenser became secretary to Lord Grey de Wilton,

Lord Deputy of Ireland, whom he accompanied on his ruthless expeditions against the Irish. After service with Lord Grey, Spenser stayed on in Ireland to serve in several minor governmental posts. He lived on a government-confiscated Irish estate near Crok at Kilcolman Castle. When his finances were low, Spenser often returned from England to Kilcolman Castle until December 1598, when the castle was sacked and burned by Irish rebels. Thereupon, Spenser returned to England in January 1599, where he died in poverty.

12. "The influence of Spenser's life in Ireland on *The Faerie Queene* has usually been under-estimated. The opinion most commonly held is that the influence was not important, that it was external and did not affect the inner stream of poetry, that none of the greater passages in *The Faerie Queene* owe anything either in feeling or picture to that life. This is an inadequate estimate, for it is possible to trace the influence of his Irish experiences not only in the background and incident, but in the emotional and imaginative life of the poet as these are reflected in the poem." M. M. Gray, "The Influences of Spenser's Irish Experiences on *The Faerie Queene, Review of English Studies*, 6:24 (October 1930), 413.

13. Hodgen, 365.

14. Edmund Spenser, *A View of the Present State of Ireland*, edited by William Lindsay Renwick (London: Eric Partridge, 1934), 109. (Note: The Spenser citations have been transposed from archaic 16th century usage to modern 20th century usage, by the editor, for ease of understanding by the reader.)

15. Ibid., 109-110.

16. Ibid., 111.

17. William Shakespeare, *The Tempest*, edited by Frank Kermode

(Cambridge: Harvard University Press, 1954), act 1, sc. 2, p. 29.

18. Ibid., 31.

19. Ibid., 32-33.

20. Canny, 583.

21. Herodotus is called the Father of History. "It was his hand ... which set down in an organized and vivid form a description of a series of human cultures, later to be deformed and disfigured to suit the twisted imaginations of his successors. It was his mind, brooding restlessly over strange cultural contrasts in Mediterranean lands, which first formulated some of the persisting problems of anthropological inquiry." Hodgen, 20-21.

22. "On the question, then, of the view to be taken of savagery—a question which ultimately raised the issue of human homogeneity, or the common humanity of the civil and savage peoples—the accounts of Renaissance voyagers were almost unanimous. For upwards of two hundred years an unfavorable, or *anti-primitivistic* verdict was rendered. The Church, with its distaste for the unconventional in marriage and funeral not to mention the non-Christian in religion, may in this have exercised an overwhelming influence upon the explorers." Ibid., 361-362.

23. Canny, 586.

24. Ibid., 588.

25. Ibid.

26. Ibid., 598.

27. Ibid., 596-597.

28. Hodgen, 214.

29. In 1735, Carl Linné (1707-1778), also known as Carolus Linnaeus, published *A General System of Nature, through the Three Grand Kingdoms of Animals, Vegetables, and Minerals: Systematically Divided into Their Several Classes, Orders, General, Species and Variations.* The ostensible purpose for Linné's producing this work was to codify the thousands of plants he and other scientists had in their possession. Thus, he invented his system of classification called Taxonomic Classification. "Thus, though Linnaeus may be generally regarded as one of the chief founders of the botanical and zoological studies, his place in the history of ethnology is less eminent. He not only believed in the existence of human varieties of race, but he failed as a proponent of the hierarchical arrangement of things to preserve any discernible order in their listing. He subscribed to the reality of fabulous, monstrous men. He was subservient to unexamined medieval ideas." Ibid., 426.

30. Clifford Hill, *West Indian Migrants and the London Churches* (London: Oxford University Press, 1963), 1.

31. The "British" Commonwealth does not exist, although there is a Commonwealth of independent states, whose headquarters are in London, composed of former dependencies within the British Empire with the British monarch as its titular head. "As defined by the politicians attending the Imperial Conferences in the 1920s and as enacted by the Statute of Westminster in 1931, the Commonwealth members were to be "autonomous communities within the British Empire equal in status, in no way subordinate one to another in any aspect of their domestic or foreign affairs, though united by a common allegiance to the Crown." That was a cosy white man's club consisting of Britain, Canada, Australia, South Africa, Newfoundland, and New Zealand. But starting with the

independence of India in August 1947, the Commonwealth began to widen and change. Now its member states embrace about a billion people, living around the world from the tiny atolls of the Pacific to the northern expanses of Canada." Thomas Butson, "For All Britain's Loss of Empire, the Commonwealth Still Matters," *New York Times*, 12 June 1977.

32. John Furnivall, *Colonial Policy and Practice* (London: Cambridge University Press, 1948), 305 and 311.

33. The terms migrant, immigrant, and emigrant refer to people, who sometimes are different and sometimes are the same. For instance, a migrant is one who moves from one place to another in search of temporary employment. An emigrant is one who *leaves* his home country for another to establish permanent residence. An immigrant is one who *enters* another country with the intention of settling there permanently. There are a number of personal reasons for these moves: psychological, economic, social, and better living standard, and a more compassionate system of justice in the host country.

34. Bernard Weinraub, "Broad British Laws Proposed to Curb Racial Discrimination," *New York Times*, 12 September 1975.

35. *British Parliamentary Debates [Hansard] House of Commons Official Report*, Fifth Series, London, Her Majesty's Stationery Office [HMSO], Volume 649, No. 13.

36. "Lord Butler, known popularly as "Rab" from the initials for Richard Austen Butler, was twice expected to become Prime Minister. Dubbed by many in the Conservative Party as the greatest Prime Minister they never had, he lost his chances to run the country to Harold Macmillan in 1957 and to Sir Alex Douglas-Home in 1963. Equipped with a sharp mind and a fierce loyalty, he became one of the chief architects of the

modern Conservative Party, serving seven of its governments in a range of positions. . . . He [made] a name for himself in the Foreign Office defending Prime Minister Neville Chamberlain's policy of appeasement." *New York Times*, Obituary, 10 March 1982.

37. Hansard, Volume 649, No. 13, 687 and 693.

38. Ibid., 750.

39. Ibid.

40. Ibid., 781.

41. Ibid.

42. Ibid.

43. Ibid., 795.

44. Irish nationalism will be discussed in the next chapter.

45. Hansard, Volume 649, No. 13, 734.

46. Ibid., 808: John Hare the Conservative Government's Minister of Labor.

47. Ibid., 688.

48. Ibid., 800.

49. Ibid., 733.

50. Tom Lambert, "British Race Relations Worsen . . . ," *Los Angeles Times*, 23 June 1976.

51. "Race in Britain," *The Economist*, 27 April 1974.

52. Hansard, Volume 649, No. 13, 694.

53. Ibid., 732.

54. Ibid., 779.

55. R. B. Davison, *Commonwealth Immigrants* (London: Oxford University Press, 1964), 1.

56. Hansard, Volume 649, No. 13, 707.

57. Ibid., 689.

58. Ibid., 747.

59. Ibid., 804.

60. Ibid.

61. Ibid.

62. Ibid., 734: Clement Davies, the Labor MP for Montgomery.

63. Nicholas Deakin, ed., *Colour and the British Electorate 1964: Six Case Studies* (New York: Praeger, 1965), 6.

64. Hansard, Volume 649, No. 13, 729.

65. Ibid., 716-717.

66. Ibid., 782.

67. "A Gallup Poll taken in June 1961 found that only 21 per cent of the sample were in favour of maintaining freedom of entry, as opposed to 67 per cent in favour of restrictions and 6 percent who advocated a complete stop on entry." Deakin, 5.

68. Hansard, Volume 649, No. 13, 801-802.

69. Ibid., 725

70. Ibid., 793.

71. Ibid., 743 and 746.

72. "Only three nonwhites have ever sat in the House of Commons. . . . "The reason why there are no nonwhites in the House of Commons is that the Tories and Labor have not adopted ethnic candidates in any of their safe seats," said Maurice Nadeen, a London lawyer born in India 52 years ago." Jon Nordheimer, "British Nonwhites Seek Bigger Voice," *New York Times*, 8 June 1983.

73. "There are no blacks in the House of Commons, although the Labor Party, under pressure from its Black Sections Committee, has six black nominees for the next election." Jo Thomas, "In Riot's Wake, Black Leader's Words Roil Britain," *New York Times*, 28 October 1985. However, since 1985, several blacks have been elected to the House of Commons.

74. Hansard, Volume 649, No. 13, 721 and 727.

75. Ibid., 728-729.

76. Ibid., 715.

77. Ibid., 710.

78. Ibid., 748-749: Charles Royle the Labor MP for Salford, West.

79. Ibid., 796

80. Ibid., 748.

81. Ibid., 709: Patrick Gordon Walker the Labour MP for Smethwick.

82. The term United Kingdom refers to England, Scotland, Wales, and Northern Ireland.

83. Hansard, Volume 649, No. 13, 700 and 701.

84. Ibid., 706, 708, and 716.

85. Deakin, 7.

86. Ibid., 6-7.

87. Hansard, Volume 649, No. 13, 696, 697, and 704.

88. Deakin, 8.

89. Michael Hartley-Brewer, "Smethwick," in *Colour and the British Electorate 1964*, ed. Nicholas Deakin, 82.

90. From 1926 to 1931, Smethwick had been represented by Oswald Mosley, who was renowned during the inter-war period for his sympathies for fascism and Adolf Hitler.

91. Hansard, Volume 649, No.13, 757-761.

92. Hartley-Brewer, 90.

93. Deakin, 8-9, as reported in *The London Times*, 9 April 1964.

94. Hansard, Volume 649, No. 13, 716.

95. *Report of the Race Relations Board 1966/1967* (London: HMSO, 1968).

96. In 1976, a government body called the Race Relations Commission replaced, "two bodies, the Race Relations Board and the Community Relations Commission. The Board, set up under the 1964 Race Relations Act, was empowered to investigate complaints and seek to conciliate. But it proved virtually impotent because it had no power to end discriminatory practices, and relied upon the voluntary cooperation of those against whom complaints had been made. The Community Relations Commission was largely

designed to provide advice and information to Asians and West Indians." Bernard Weinraub, "Broad British Laws Proposed to Curb Racial Discrimination," *New York Times*, 12 September 1975.

97. In the British system of Parliamentary government, the Shadow Cabinet is composed of members from the opposition party, who are prepared to take office immediately at the fall of the political party in power.

98. "Enoch Powell's Speech of 20 April 1968, Roy Jenkins' of 4 May 1968, et al.," *Race*, July 1968, 95 and 99.

99. *New York Times*, 26 January 1977.

100. R. W. Apple, "Labour Is Scornful of Mrs. Thatcher in Debate on Riots," *New York Times*, 10 July 1981.

101. Hansard, Volume 813, No. 99, 42.

102. "At present, the Home Secretary can issue in a year as few as 8,500 work permits—the document which must be held by any arriving head of a family on entry. . . . Only 4,000 heads of families came here to settle in 1970." *New York Times*, 1 March 1971 and 28 February 1971.

103. Hansard, Volume 649, No.13, 695.

104. *New York Times*, 28 February 1971.

105. An angry poem—written by Janet Morris, an 18-year-old West Indian student who was born in Britain, and entitled *Babylon*, a slang term used by West Indians for a white policeman, caused an uproar in Britain, especially among the metropolitan police. The poem reads as follows:

> Babylon patrolling the streets,
> Always spitting at a nigger's

feet.
You try to fight back
    But you're outnumbered
'Cause they bring the fleet.
    The day will come when
we'll be strong
    To fight the Babylon back.
Rise up you niggers and face
    the facts, You'll always be
harrassed [sic] because you're black.
    Meat wagons heavily rum-
bling down the street,
    You hear the patter of a
nigger's feet.
    A scream rings out, a shout
is muffled.
    Another nigger just been
gutted.
    When will it end?
It will be soon.
    They said man could never
reach the moon.
    But brothers and sisters, all
you niggers,
    Our time will come soon.

Bernard Weinraub, "Poem by Black Annoys London Police,"
New York Times, 8 July 1975.

106. Joseph Lelyveld, "Being a Black Bobby Means Hearing "I'm
     Sorry,"" *New York Times*, 14 May 1986.

107. Ibid.

108. Editorial, *New York Times*, 1 March 1971.

109. Hansard, Volume 813, No. 104, 243.

110. Ibid., Volume 812, No. 98, 544.

111. Ibid., Volume 814, No. 110, 101-102.

112. Editorial, *New York Times*, 1 March 1971.

113. Before the division of the Indian subcontinent into independent states of India and Pakistan, these Asians were generally referred to as Indians.

114. "London is Seeking to Ease Immigration for Whites," *New York Times*, 26 January 1973.

115. Hansard, Volume 989, No. 224, 1516.

116. Ibid., Volume 997, No. 35, 931.

117. Ibid.

118. *British Nationality Law*, White Paper, Cmnd. 7987, London, HMSO, July 30, 1980.

119. Hansard, Volume 989, No. 224, 1521-1522, and 1526.

120. Ibid., 1521.

121. British Nationality Bill, London, HMSO, June 8, 1981.

122. Hansard, Volume 997, No. 35, 939-940. "British overseas citizenship represents, in essence, the relationship with the United Kingdom held by people connected with countries that were once part of the British Empire, or whose ancestral connections with the United Kingdom or its present dependencies are not sufficiently close to qualify them for British citizenship or citizenship of the British dependent territories. Children born after the Act comes into force to parents who have become British overseas citizens will not themselves hold that citizenship." Ibid., Volume 989, No. 224, 1517.

123. Ibid., Volume 989, No. 224, 1516 and 1517.

124. Ibid., Volume 997, No. 36, 1035.

125. Roy Reed, "The Trouble Began When the Colonies Came Home," *New York Times*, 21 August 21 1977.

126. Hansard, Volume 997, No. 36, 1033.

127. William Borders, "Britain Debates Immigration and Race," *New York Times*, 8 February 1981.

128. On November 16, 1961, Patrick Gordon Walker told the House of Commons, "The latest figures which I have been able to obtain show that 40 per cent of the coloured immigrants in this country live in London, 30 per cent in the West Midlands and 3 per cent in Scotland. The position is worse than the figures show, because the immigrants are concentrated in small areas within larger conurbations like London and the West Midlands." Hansard, Volume 649, No. 13, 714.

129. Ibid., Volume 997, No. 35, 984.

130. Ibid., Volume 649, No. 13, 706. The statement is by Patrick Gordon Walker.

131. Garry Wills, "Mrs. Thatcher's Racist Appeal," *Hartford Courant*, 26 April 1978.

132. Select Committee on Race Relations and Immigration, First Report, Session 1977-1978, "Evidence and Appendices," Volume 2, 13 March 1978, 16.

133. William Borders, "British Weigh Racial Factors in Disorders," *New York Times*, 22 July 1981.

134. Select Committee on Race Relations and Immigration, First

Report, Session 1977-1978, 16.

135. *New York Times*, 22 February 1978.

136. James Markham, "Minorities in Western Europe: Hearing 'Not Welcome' in Several Languages," *New York Times*, 5 August 1986.

137. Roy Reed, "The Trouble Began When the Colonies Came Home," *New York Times*, 21 August 1977.

Chapter Three
Northern Ireland: A Question or a Problem?

An erroneous belief, propagated by the British, is that each time they come close to solving what they call *The Irish Question*, the Irish change the question. That is not so. For what the British term *The Irish Question*, the Irish call *The British Problem*, and for the Irish, *The Problem* has always been the same: How to get the British out of Ireland.

For almost 500 years, the British, for political, economic, social, and ethnic reasons, have refused to accept their withdrawal from Ireland as *the* basic problem. The continued rejection of this fundamental Irish demand, by successive British governments, led to a gradual change in what the Irish considered an acceptable response to their demand. As a consequence, by the beginning of the 20th Century, the various Irish nationalist groups—discouraged by the intransigence of the British against their efforts to obtain some measure of internal self-government—turned away from *Home Rule* as a goal, until, in 1918, the majority of Irish nationalists supported the goal of a free and independent Irish State.

This, however, still left a significant part of *The Irish Question* and *The British Problem* unanswered and unresolved, which was: What to do about Ulster? In these six northeastern counties of Northern Ireland, in 1920, the Protestant minority opted out of political union with the Catholic majority in the new Irish State in order to retain political alliance with Britain. Today, *The Question* and *The Problem* remain, as the answer and the solution continue to elude Britain's political leaders.

During the 16th century and the reign of Henry VIII the basic pattern of Irish-British relations was established. First, Irish Catholics' resentment of Anglicanism, the new English religion, produced strong resistance to the English presence. Second, English persecution followed the Irish Catholics' refusal to be subjugated and converted to Protestantism. Third, Irish resistance to the English presence and persecution stiffened, while the English presence and persecution persis-

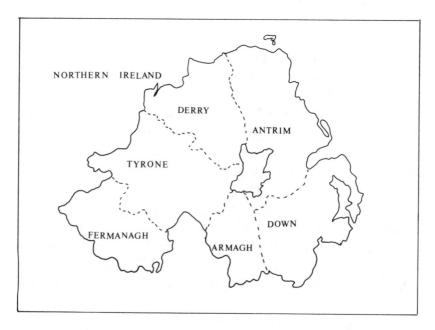

ted. This pattern of Irish-British relations grew out of two diametrically opposed objectives: the Irish determination to get the British out of Ireland, and the British determination to stay.

The English presence was made more oppressive by the English policy of populating Ireland, especially Northern Ireland, with Protestant immigrants. For example, in the early 17th century, during the reign of James I of England who was also James VI of Scotland, England invited 150,000 Presbyterians from the Scottish lowlands to settle in Ireland, especially in the Ulster region. They were lowlanders rather than highlanders because the highlanders were Catholic, spoke Gaelic, and could not be trusted not to be sympathetic to the objectives of their co-religions, the Irish Catholics. Later, in the mid-17th century, Oliver Cromwell, England's military, political, and religious leader as well as Lord Protector and dictator of the Commonwealth, rewarded his victorious Protestant soldiers with Irish lands, especially in Northern Ireland.

Thus, the English made overt public policy decisions to colonize Northern Ireland with Presbyterian Scots who would be loyal to England and to her interests. Today, the descendants of these Scottish immigrants constitute the nucleus of the Protestant majority in Northern Ireland. This adds another dimension to the Irish-British equation, the Scottish factor, for many of these descendants have relations in Scotland who would be loath to have their kinsmen evicted or in any way displaced, by Irish Catholics, from their advantageous position of dominance in Northern Ireland. This realization has not eluded the consciousness of decision-makers in London.

This onerous calamity was exacerbated by the Irish hatred of the English system of absentee landlords: English landowners collecting rents from impoverished, Irish peasants, who subsisted on lands that once was theirs, while English lords languished in London. Does this dilemma have a *solution*?

After much rancor, negotiations, and compromises, Britain and the Irish Republic introduced the Ulster Peace Plan on February 22, 1995. The *solution* presented seems to comprise a patch-work of other unsuccessful proposals, some reaching as far back as the 1973 Sunningdale Agreement. For instance, the Northern Ireland Assembly of elected officials has been proposed numerous times in the past, and consistently evolved into a forum for virulent Unionists. Furthermore, with the exception of Ireland's renounced constitutional claim to Northern Ireland and Britain's legal changes to allow Ulster to determine its own political future, the rest of the document remains relatively unprogressive. What does this proposal entail that past proposals have lacked? What makes John Major and John Bruton think that this *solution* will street around the unchartered territories of compromise in Northern Ireland. The answer has two parts: 1) the timing is right, and 2) the balance is right.

Since the IRA declared cease-fire in September 1994, Northern Ireland in the following months has made some phenomenal progress in the peace process. Not only has Britain begun to substantially withdraw its troops; the IRA consented to begin disarming. To predict these events in the escalating violence in 1992 would have been considered at best naive and at worst ludicrous. Now, Ulster is being tempted with this new-found peace, and to revert back to a civil war would be self-defeating. Furthermore, Northern Ireland's economy begs for attention. Economic development has taken a blow in the last twenty-five years since the commencement of violence. Unemployment sky-rocketed and investment plummeted. A stable society in Ulster would allow for the much needed increase in economic productivity. John Hume, also asserts that economic advancement would alleviate ethnic tension and aggression.

The balance of concessions within the proposal between Catholic and Protestant interests also contributes to its possible success. While the proposal in general may lean towards the Catholics, the Protestant concerns, such as insuring that the majority in Ulster will determine its political future and confirming that the Republic of Ireland has to withdraw its constitutional claim on Northern Ireland remains somewhat satisfying. Protestant leaders still refute the role of the Republic of Ireland in the new structure of government, however, their contention has remained mild in comparison to past response.

Ulster is exhausted, politically, economically, socially, and physically. The Ulster Peace Plan almost solely relies on this point. Whether it succeeds will depend on how much Protestants and Catholics will be willing to compromise, a concept almost completely alien to both groups. However, the incentives for finding a compromise are high. Peace and stability will assuredly bring productivity and prosperity. With the IRA willing to put down arms and join the political process, perhaps the Ulster Peace Proposal will finally find a common ground for Protestant and Catholics and end a conflict that has lasted too long.

Ireland Must be Free

In the late 19th century, in all of Ireland, Irish nationalists were faced with their own dilemma: they had the option of accommodating the claims of Ulster Protestants. If they did so, they would have to recognize a minority with a separate identity and different loyalties in their midst, and encourage an increase in that minority's claims. Irish nationalists adroitly avoided that option: "From Parnell to Redmond, to Pearse and de Valera no Irish leader consistently pursued a policy of conciliation."[1] However, the extent of the Catholic majority's ability to consciously decide what policy to pursue was not distinctly and sharply defined.

> There is an element of political determinism in the working out of majority-minority relations in dependent societies as the time for a transfer, or possible transfer, of power approaches and the pattern in Ireland had so much in common with events as they later unfolded in India, in Cyprus, and in parts of Africa, as to suggest that the freedom of choice before majority and minority community leadership was more limited than may retrospectively be supposed.[2]

The policy which the Irish nationalists ultimately pursued depended largely upon Prime Minister Gladstone, who publicly announced his support of Irish Home Rule in 1885. However, Gladstone's first Home Rule Bill in Parliament contained no provisions for the Ulster minority. He said,

> I cannot conceal the conviction that the voice of Ireland, as a whole, is at this moment clearly and constitutionally spoken. I cannot say otherwise when five-sixths of its lawfully chosen Representatives are of one mind in this matter. . . . I cannot allow it to be said that a Protestant minority in Ulster, or elsewhere, is to rule the question at large for Ireland.[3]

In Parliament, Gladstone's support of Irish Home Rule was not only challenged by the Conservative Party's opposition; it split his own Liberal Party.

> Ireland kept the Tories in power almost continuously for twenty years after 1886 because of the Liberal split over Home Rule. Ireland brought the greatest political figure of the age, Joseph Chamberlain, into the Tory camp and kept him there, in a subordinate role. Ireland distracted the attention and diverted the passion of Englishmen from their own social problems and gave Conservatives the excuse they needed for not tackling them. Ireland seemed to be the cockpit of the struggle for property, aristocracy, Protestantism, empire and civilization. . . . Yet Ireland's troubled state . . . was symptomatic of a widespread desire for radical change at the turn of the century. In particular, the condition-of-England question remained unanswered. Never had there been such hideous poverty amid such ostentatious plenty. Malnutrition was more rife in the Edwardian era than it had been since the great famines of Tudor times.[4]

The most vocal Conservative, Lord Randolph Churchill, coined the phrase, "Ulster will fight; and Ulster will be right."[5] Churchill reiterated the Conservative Party's sentiment that Britain could not leave Ulster Protestants in the lurch. Joseph Chamberlain, a Liberal Unionist, "was the first middle-class politician to reach the highest rank [and] in a sense the first *professional* politician [in Britain],"[6] he defended the Protestant minority by saying, "One of the great difficulties of this problem [is] that Ireland is not a homogeneous community—that it consists of two nations—that it is a nation which comprises two races and two religions."[7]

Gladstone's first Home Rule Bill was defeated in July of 1886. It would have established a separate Irish Parliament, but legislation relating to such matters as the army, navy, trade, and navigation would still be dealt with by the British Parliament, in which Irish members *would no longer sit*. The defeat of Gladstone's first Home Rule Bill was due to the absence of any safeguards for the interests of Ulster Protestants and to the reaction of the British public, especially its reaction to the murder, in broad daylight, in Phoenix Park, Dublin, in May of 1882, of Lord Frederick Cavendish, the Chief Secretary for Ireland, and Thomas Burke, the Permanent Undersecretary.

In 1893, Gladstone's second Home Rule Bill passed the House of Commons but was overwhelmingly defeated in the House of Lords. Its principal difference from the first Bill was that it *did* allow Irish representatives to sit in the British Parliament. However, this safeguard was not considered sufficient to Ulster Protestants. Moreover, Victorian England was again outraged—this time not by murder, but by adultery.

By the early 1880s, politically important Irishmen and Englishmen had become committed to a form of Irish self-government called *Home Rule*. The most prominent of these was Charles Stewart Parnell, the dominant figure and spokesman for the Parliamentary Home Rule Party. Parnell was also an Irish member of the British Parliament, an Irish Protestant landowner, and a man consumed with hatred for England.

In December of 1889, Captain William Henry O'Shea filed suit for divorce and named Charles Stewart Parnell as co-respondent. O'Shea was one of Parnell's followers. From 1880 to 1886, Parnell had been living with Kitty O'Shea. Parnell maintained that Captain O'Shea had, at least, known of his wife's relationship with him. Nevertheless, "After a two day hearing, the divorce court delivered its verdict against Mrs. O'Shea and Parnell, the suit being undefended."[8] In his hour of dread, Parnell's constituency did not desert him: he was re-elected leader of the Irish Parliamentary Party. The Conservative Party opposition, however, saw its opportunity to defeat Home Rule by refusing to negotiate with the Liberal Party unless Parnell resigned.

The tragedy of Parnell and Home Rule was that, as a consequence of his involvement with Kitty O'Shea and being named as co-respondent in a divorce suit brought by her husband, the Liberal Party Government of Gladstone was constrained to support Home Rule, as long as Parnell led the fight, however, he refused to step down. Under pressure, Gladstone requested Parnell's resignation. Leaders of his own Party publicly supported Parnell, while privately they urged him to resign, but he refused. His refusal caused a split within his own Party.

The tragic effects of the behavior of Ireland's greatest parliamentarian are still felt today, more than 100 years after the facts. At the time, Parnell's determination to retain power destroyed the Home Rule Bill, until the eve of the First World War. More importantly, it destroyed any hope for achieving some semblance of unity among Ireland's sectarian groups. Finally, the schism within the Irish Parliamentary Party was permanent. Justin McCarthy became leader of the majority wing, while John Redmond became leader of the minority faction, but the Party's credibility was devastated, as it came to be viewed merely as the handmaiden of the British Liberal Party. Ironically, Parnell created and destroyed the most potent Irish political party ever to sit in a British Parliament.

> The most tragic spectacle, in 1891, was not that of the doomed hero, but that of a great work laid in ruins: the work of reconciliation which Gladstone and Parnell with their parties seemed, by 1890, to have established on solid foundations.[9]

In October of 1891, Charles Stewart Parnell died at the young age of 45, but, by then, the momentum for House Rule had waned. Thus, as with Henry VIII, Parnell's licentiousness had grave and unexpected repercussions: it caused a split in both the Irish and British bases for the Home Rule movement and a golden opportunity for a nonviolent, constitutional resolution of the Irish Question was lost, perhaps forever. Home Rule was, eventually, agreed to by the British Parliament in 1914, but, by then, Irish nationalists wanted not only complete independence but the total withdrawal of the British presence from Ireland. Ultimately, the study of politics involves the study of individual, human behavior.

The repercussions of Parnell's lasciviousness were not all calamitous. In 1893, the Gaelic League was founded with the intent of restoring Irish self-respect by emphasizing Ireland's cultural heritage. In fact, the twenty years before the First World War ushered in a cultural renaissance for all things Gaelic, especially the language. At the beginning of the 19th century, probably two million Irish spoke Gaelic, but by the end of the century, Gaelic-speaking Irishmen were a vanishing species. The aim of the Gaelic League was to reverse this trend. Furthermore, linguistic nationalism was another reaction to English dominance on the Gaelic Isle. These years also marked the rise of such Irish literary greats as the dramatist John Millington Synge (1871-1909) and the brilliant poet and playwright William Butler Yeats (1865-1939) who, like the flamboyant Oscar Fingell O'Flahertie Wills Wilde, created their art in English but who, unlike *that* precious Irish wit, were profoundly influenced by Irish traditions and customs rather than by English upper class manners. In 1906, the Sinn Fein (Gaelic for *Ourselves Alone*) Party, with roots in the Fenian movement, came into existence.[10] The Sinn Fein Party was not so much a fallout of Parnell's ruin as a continuation of militant Irish nationalism. The Sinn Fein demanded total withdrawal of all Irish members from the British Parliament. Paradoxically, members of the Party—especially after the Easter Rebellion of 1916—won election after election to that august body but, as a strategy, always refused to occupy their seats.

British Problems and the Irish Question

In 1894, William Ewart Gladstone (1809-1898) retired from politics, after four times serving as Britain's Prime Minister between 1868 and 1894. Having lost his fight for Home Rule the year before, Gladstone resigned the premiership and was succeeded by the Liberal Imperialist Lord Rosebery (1894-1895). At the turn of the century, Arthur James Balfour succeeded his uncle, Lord Salisbury (1895-1902) as Prime Minister (1902-1905). Balfour, alluded to by some as "the first gentleman of Europe" and by others as "the laziest man in town," launched a program of "killing Home Rule with kindness,"[11] and, for several years, this seemed successful, as the 1890s and early 1900s saw continued improvements in the life of the Irish farmer. Moreover, in the political arena, renewed Irish factionalism prevented any united parliamentary effort for 10 years following Parnell's fall. Not until 1900 was John Redmond able to string together the discordant strands of the Irish Parliamentary Party, but, by then, many Irishmen felt that reconciliation had come too late: their faith in constitutional methods of change had died with Parnell's reputation.[12]

Between 1905 and 1914, the Liberal Party—first under Henry Campbell-Bannerman (1905-1908) and then under Herbert Asquith (1908-1916)—was again in power and again pledged to the attainment of Home Rule for Ireland. The great parliamentary road block was the British House of Lords. Irish Home Rule was but one of numerous reforms that the Liberals were pledged to institute, but they were thwarted at every turn by the veto of the Conservative-controlled House of Lords: "Mr. Balfour's poodle—this was Lloyd George's famous description of the House of Lords as, obedient to his master's voice, the huge Tory majority therein mangled bill after Liberal bill."[13] Eventually, the Liberals' budget proposals rather than Irish Home Rule spelled the death knell for the House of Lords not only as an instrument of political obstruction but as a political force of any kind, although the two issues were intricately locked in the Liberal Party's strategy.

In 1909, David Lloyd George, as Chancellor of the Exchequer and as the leading force behind Liberal reforms in the Asquith government, faced an enormous budget deficit, which was due mainly to "guns and butter" expenditures: defense (meaning naval expenditures) and the cost of the much-needed Liberal Party's social reform program. To offset this deficit, Lloyd George proposed a budget which would shift the tax burden from the working and middle classes to the affluent upper class in the form of an income tax, a tax on unearned income, an inheritance tax, and a tax on unearned increments of land. The upper class, especially the land-endowed members of the House of Lords, was outraged by this Welshman's presumptuousness. To the British hereditary lord *his* land was sacrosanct—in fact, nothing was more sacred—which made all of Lloyd George's budget proposals an abomination. The budget passed in the House of Commons but was defeated in the House of Lords. Prime Minister Asquith denounced the Lords' actions as obstructionist and a breach of the Constitution. Although talk of King Edward VII (1901-1910) creating enough Liberal peers to the House of Lords to overcome the Conservative majority was rampant, the Liberals had a shrewder plan than this mere expediency.

In 1910, the British general election was fought over three issues: the budget, the veto power of the House of Lords, and Irish Home Rule. The Liberals lost considerable support among the electorate but won the election. Moreover, they had the support of the remnants of Parnell's Party, but only if the power of the Lords was so crippled that they could not prevent an Irish Home Rule Bill from becoming law.

In 1910, the Liberal-controlled House of Commons passed two resolutions: (1) that the House of Lords should have no right to veto a money bill passed by the House of Commons and (2) that any other bill should become law after being passed in three successive sessions of the House of Commons, even if vetoed by the House of Lords. In 1911, these resolutions, which had become part of the Liberals' larger Parliament Bill, were passed—after much rancor—by both Houses. Thus, with the House of Lords' veto power abolished, the way was opened to introduce an Irish Home Rule Bill, which the Liberals did in 1912. This Bill provided Ireland with a bicameral legislature as well as continued representation in the British Parliament. However, for the Unionists and Conservatives, the Bill was viewed as unjust to Ulster Protestants who, they claimed, would be swamped in a united Catholic Ireland. In 1913, the Irish Home Rule Bill was twice passed in the Commons and twice defeated in the Lords. Meanwhile, Ulster Protestants took heart from the machinations at Westminster, and, under Edward Carson's orchestration,[14] its opposition to Home Rule grew steadily more virulent. In 1913, Ireland was on the brink of a bloody sectarian war. Only a greater tragedy prevented it: the First World War.

In 1914, the British Parliament passed the Irish Home Rule Bill for the third time, and, under the stipulations of the 1911 Parliament Act, no further action by the House of Lords was either necessary or meaningful. Ireland obtained a unitary parliamentary system with no separate safeguards for Ulster Protestants, such as a second chamber. However, before the Bill's final passage, Prime Minister Asquith offered a concession to Unionists and Conservatives: the electorate in each of the nine counties in Ulster could have the right to determine whether their individual county would become an immediate part of the new polity or be excluded for six years in order to think. This concession represented "the nose of the camel" entering "the tent of partition" and did not bode well for the future of a united Ireland. However, during the course of the First World War, this issue was moot because, when George V (1910-1936) gave his royal assent to the Home Rule Bill, making it law, by a simultaneous Act, Irish Home Rule was not to be implemented until after the First World War was over. Ominously, the Liberals pledged that, before Irish Home Rule became effective, an amendment would be introduced in the Commons dealing with the issue of safeguards for Ulster Protestants. The Irish Catholics had reasons, based on past experiences, for not trusting British parliamentarians. As for the Ulster Protestants, what they feared was what white South African reactionaries feared: that when they were no longer the dominant minority, they would face retribution from the dominant majority.

The institution of martial law as a result of the 1916 Easter Rebellion and the threat of Irish conscription to help Britain fight its war against Germany aroused intense bitterness and fear in Ireland. Consequently, several by-elections in 1917 resulted in the defeat of Irish Parliamentary Party members by Sinn Fein candidates. Furthermore, actions by the British government to halt the growing influence of Sinn Fein only increased that organization's prestige while damaging the prestige of the Irish Parliamentary Party and its leader, John Redmond.

Although he was widely respected, Redmond's commitment to constitutional methods for attaining a united Ireland's independence became increasingly detrimental to his popularity. His Party remained influential, ironically, until 1914, the year it achieved its greatest goal, Home Rule. However, by 1914, Home Rule was no longer acceptable to a great many Irishmen, and Redmond's inability to influence a resolution of the Ulster dilemma soured his victory. Moreover, Redmond's enthusiasm for Irish volunteers, not conscripts, to fight with the British in the First World War showed how *out of touch* Irish parliamentarians at Westminster were with sentiments back home. Irish nationalists were thoroughly disgusted with the British Liberal Party, which they believed had compromised a *just* settlement of the Home Rule issue by giving in to reactionary forces in Ulster and in Britain, and these nationalists were fast becoming dissatisfied with Redmond, the man who continued to deal with the British in their Parliament.

After the First World War, the Sinn Fein Party emerged as the most potent of the various nationalist forces in Ireland. In October of 1917, the Sinn Fein held a convention in Dublin, adopted a constitution for the Republic of Ireland, and elected Eamon de Valera its president.[15] In March of 1918, John Redmond died. The next month, the British government of Lloyd George proposed the extension of conscription to Irishmen, and the members of the Irish Parliamentary Party walked out of the British Parliament. They returned to Ireland where they joined with the Sinn Fein in a pledge to resist the conscription move. The Catholic Church also announced its opposition to Irish conscription. This was a *rare* display of solidarity among Irish nationalist forces. The British responded to their defiance with massive arrests of almost the entire Sinn Fein leadership, including de Valera, under the pretext that they were a part of a *German plot*.

In December of 1918, Britain held its first general election since 1910. The result was an overwhelming victory for the Sinn Fein, even though most of the Party leaders were in jail. In accordance with a campaign promise, those Party members who were not in jail refused to take their seats at Westminster. Instead, they met in Dublin, again declared Ireland's independence, and organized a parliament of their own, the Dail Eireann. The British reacted with their usual practice of harassment: the Dail Eireann was denounced, and the headquarters of the Sinn Fein were raided. This attempt to suppress the Sinn Fein led to a bitter war between Sinn Fein and British forces.

The Black and Tan War, or the *Troubles*, as the Irish euphemistically refer to this period, was fought mainly between Irish guerillas and the Black and Tan, a British auxiliary police force which became infamous for its use of terror tactics. Eventually, these tactics led to the alienation of the British public. Irish manpower never approached that of the British, nor were the Irish ever adequately armed, in fact, a large part of their endeavors were attempts to secure arms from the enemy. The Irish did, however, have the support of most of their countrymen, which proved to be an essential asset. Moreover, strict discipline existed within the Irish forces, largely as a result of the influence of Michael Collins, the Head of Intelligence for the Volunteers and Minster for Finance in the rebel government. At the age of 31, Collins wielded tremendous power throughout the Black and Tan War: he succeeded in completely incapacitating British intelligence efforts, while daily riding his bicycle through the streets of Dublin back and forth to work.

Infamous atrocities were committed on both sides during this war, but the policy of the British government, called *official reprisals*, was particularly reprehensible. The British perpetrated a policy of killing one Sinn Fein for every British soldier killed. If a Sinn Fein member could not be found, then two sympathizers were to be executed, and if sympathizers were not available, then three Irish houses were to be burned down. The horror of these actions caused revulsion among the British public:

> In every part of Ireland that we visited we were impressed by the atmosphere of terrorism that prevailed. . . . We have no desire to overstate the facts; but the atmosphere of terrorism which has been created and the provocative behaviour of the armed servants of the Crown, quite apart from specific *reprisals* are sufficient in themselves to arouse in our hearts feelings of the deepest horror and shame. (Report of the British Labour Commission to Ireland)[16]

> We saw such a scene of wanton destruction of houses and shops that made me and members of the Commission ashamed of being Englishmen. (Arthur Greenwood, British Labour leader)

> Deeds have unquestionably been done by them [the Forces of the Crown] in Ireland which have lastingly disgraced the name of Britain in that country. British processes of justice which for centuries have commanded the admiration of the world have been supplanted by those of lynch law. (Editorial from the *London Times*)

> The British Government committed worse crimes in Ireland than Germany had ever committed in France. (General Sir Hubert Gough)

Constitutional Government in Ireland has been suspended and a state of affairs
prevails which is a disgrace to the British race. (The Right Honorable A. Henderson
[later Foreign Secretary])

I say deliberately that never in the lifetime of the oldest among us has Britain sunk
so low in the moral scale of nations. . . . Things are being done in Ireland which
would disgrace the blackest annals of the lowest despotism in Europe. (Lord Oxford
and Asquith)

King George V implored Prime Minister Lloyd George to quit killing
his people. The Black and Tan War epitomized Britain's grotesque
relationship with Ireland, for in that war Britain acted contrary to its
values and beliefs in attempting to come to terms with a people whom it
was not interested in assimilating and found impossible to destroy.
Despite the claim that the British could have won the war, the situation
seems analogous to the American presence in Vietnam. The United
States took ten years to realize its mistake; the British have taken
centuries to realize theirs. In any case, the cost of a military victory, in
terms of money, military morale, and public opinion was too high for
Britain to pay.

What Happens after Partition?

By the spring of 1921, British leaders realized that they were not
dealing with a small band of extremists but were fighting a united
nation. By then, however, Lloyd George's government had passed the
Act of Ireland in 1920. An amending act to the Home Rule Bill which
Prime Minister Asquith had threatened, in 1914, was to safeguard the
interests of Ulster Protestants. Lloyd George's Act partitioned Ireland.
The most important element of the Act of Ireland was the way in which
the boundaries of partition were decided. In 1910, Sir Edward Carson
was made head of the Ulster Unionist Council. As leader of the Ulster
Protestants, Carson and the Council were allowed to draw up the
boundaries of Northern Ireland. In making this concession to the Ulster
Protestants, the British government seemingly failed to envision the
consequences of allowing the Unionists to design a part of Ireland for
themselves in such a way as to create a permanent Catholic minority.
Carson and the Council decided that the largest land area the Ulster
Protestants could reasonably control would contain only six of the nine

original counties of Ulster. Therefore, they excluded Donegal County, which occupied all of northwestern Ulster, and the counties of Monaghan and Cavan, which were located at the southern extremity of Ulster Province. Fermanagh and Tyrone counties contained large Catholic majorities, but those people were never asked to vote on whether they wanted to be included in Northern or Southern Ireland, and once included in the North they would be neutralized through the process of gerrymandering. The boundaries were expressly fixed to insure the Protestants' supremacy. They were never redrawn, although supposedly the issue was to be redecided by a boundary commission. The Act of Ireland of 1920 not only partitioned a country but divided a province within that country.

What were the actual terms of the 1920 Act of Ireland? The first section stated:

> For the purposes of this Act, Northern Ireland shall consist of the parliamentary counties of Antrim, Armagh, Down, Fermanagh, Londonderry and Tyrone, and the parliamentary boroughs of Belfast and Londonderry, and Southern Ireland shall consist of so much of Ireland as is not comprised within the said parliamentary counties and boroughs.[17]

This section created Northern Ireland with an area of 5,242 square miles and a population of approximately one million Protestants and a half million Catholics.

The governmental structure of Northern Ireland was set up in the following manner. The Parliament, called the Stormont, was to sit in Belfast and contain two Houses: the Senate and the House of Commons. The Senate was to consist of 26 members who were elected by the 52 members of the House of Commons who were elected by the people. The Stormont was to meet at least once a year, and its members to the House of Commons were to be elected by universal adult suffrage. The Cabinet was to consist of a Prime Minister and six other ministers, all members of the Stormont. Parliament was given the power to make laws concerning peace, order, and good government. The Act specifically restricted its other powers. The powers delegated to the Stormont were granted by a method known as *devolution* and could be amended or withdrawn by the British Parliament at Westminster to which Northern Ireland was to send 13 representatives. Definite limitations were fixed by the Act of Ireland on the powers held by the Stormont, both in the internal and external realms of policy making. For example, the

Stormont could not change its constitutional structure. The armed forces and foreign affairs were assigned to the British Crown, while land purchase and taxation were assigned to the Parliament at Westminster. The Crown's representative in the governmental structure of Northern Ireland was the Governor-General, who could summon or dissolve Parliament. He had the function of giving or withholding the Royal Assent on the bills passed by the Stormont. In other words, Northern Ireland was not created as a sovereign state but rather as a subordinate territory within a kind of *federalized* system.

The Act of Ireland established a third set of powers which were originally under the jurisdiction of the Council of Ireland. These included railway and fishery administration and dealing with contagious animal diseases. The Council of Ireland was to be composed equally of members from the Parliaments of Northern and Southern Ireland. Its primary function was to facilitate the reunion of the two parts of Ireland. However, it was never properly constituted and, in reality, never operated.

Further provisions of the Act of Ireland imposed restrictions which were designed to safeguard the rights of minorities and would, theoretically, prohibit all legislation which would interfere with religious equality or which would allow discrimination. The Superior Courts of Northern Ireland remained under the jurisdiction of the Parliament at Westminster, and judges to those courts were appointed by the Crown. The Inferior Courts remained under the jurisdiction of Northern Ireland. Finally, Northern Ireland could not regulate matters relating to the franchise, the system of election, or the size of constituencies for three years.[18]

At the time the Stormont was established, three major political parties existed in Northern Ireland: the Unionists, the Nationalists, and the Republicans or Sinn Fein Party. At the first session of the Stormont, the Unionists stated that their goal was "to return a Parliament of our own and not to come under a Dublin Parliament."[19] Prime Minister James Craig put it more succinctly when he described Stormont as "a Protestant government for a Protestant people."[20] The two opposition parties, the Nationalists and the Republicans, both favored an end to the Stormont and the reuniting of Northern Ireland with the rest of Ireland. The Nationalists tended to hope that these goals would be achieved through constitutional means, while the Republicans had little faith in constitutional channels and refused to recognize the fact of partition.

These three divergent orientations have influenced the political history of Northern Ireland from 1920 to the present.

The first elections to the Stormont were held in May of 1921. During the election campaign, a reign of terror and violence was waged against the Catholic minority. Their candidates, organizers, and tally clerks were arrested, election literature was confiscated and destroyed, and voters were harassed and actually barred from entering the voting booths.[21] The results of the elections were 12 seats between the Nationalists and Republicans and 40 seats for the Unionists. The Nationalists and Republicans refused to take their seats in the House of Commons, thereupon, the 40 Unionists elected an entirely Unionist Senate. James Craig, the first Prime Minister, created his Cabinet; Stormont announced its policy; and every indication was given that the Unionists were determined to maintain their supremacy and control in Northern Ireland.

The Unionists have employed numerous tactics to insure their supremacy, tactics which, despite the restrictions of the Act of 1920, were within their power. For example, the Act of 1920 stated that the Stormont could not regulate matters relating to voting and elections for three years. So, the government waited until late in 1922 to abolish the system of proportional representation in local elections, which gave the Catholic minority a fairer representation, then altered the electoral divisions within several constituencies. The results of these machinations were demonstrated in the elections of 1923, when fifteen public bodies and nine rural counties, which had previously had Catholic majorities, were either abolished or became controlled by the Unionists. In 1927, Prime Minister Craig, speaking at the annual Orange celebration, announced an end to proportional representation in parliamentary elections, which eliminated all but one opposition party in Northern Ireland, the Nationalist Party. The rationale behind this action was obvious: proportional representation encouraged the development of several parties; the existence of several parties might erode the politico-religious division in the province, and Protestant supremacy depended upon the existing politico-religious division. Thus, instead of wanting to end hostilities between Catholics and Protestants, the government encouraged it. The words of the Minister of Agriculture, spoken in 1933, are typical of the government's attitude:

> Many in the audience employ Catholics, but I have not one about my place. Catholics are out to destroy Ulster with all their might and power. They want to

nullify the Protestant vote, take all they can out of Ulster, and then see it go to Hell.[22]

Not only government officials but also the police worked at enlarging the cleavage between Catholics and Protestants. In the early 1920s, a Special Constabulary was formed which was revived from the days of Sir Edward Carson's activities during the battle over Home Rule. Ostensibly, this Special Constabulary was created to protect the rights of all citizens in Northern Ireland, but, in practice, it only protected the interests of Ulster Protestants. Placed at Prime Minister Craig's disposal, this police force was anti-Nationalist, and the majority of the men were fanatically anti-Catholic. Together with members of other Protestant extremist groups, the Special Constabulary attacked Catholics on their jobs, on the streets, and in their homes.

The anti-Catholic attitudes displayed by government officials and members of the police force were dramatized in the politically and socially discriminatory tactics they employed against their fellow citizens. These tactics served to strangle the Catholic population both politically and economically and resulted in the level of hatred and violence which exist in Northern Ireland today.

The first of these tactics was the use of gerrymandering, which is the redrawing of electoral districts to the disadvantage of the victims. For example, the Wards in Derry City (Londonderry, as it is called by the British) were set up in such a way that more Catholics lived in the South Ward of the city than there were Protestants in the entire city. Consequently, with a Catholic population of 63%, not one of Derry City's elected officials was a Catholic. In some national elections, up to 70% of the seats in Parliament were Protestant-controlled and went uncontested year after year, all because of gerrymandering.[23]

Closely related to gerrymandering was the system of housing discrimination: concern for electoral consequences determined the location of new housing and who got the new units. Again, in Derry, all new Catholic housing was restricted to the South Ward ghetto known as the Bogside, which was becoming a dense and rapidly deteriorating slum. While in Belfast, 100,000 Catholics were stacked into an overcrowded area called Falls Road. If new housing were built in an area where Protestants were the majority, Protestant applicants would always be considered before Catholics. Furthermore, a Protestant family with only one child would be *imported* from outside a district before a

Catholic family, two blocks away with six children, would be considered for new housing.

The general rule was that Catholics were placed where their votes would be wasted. When they did vote, Catholics found that they were again the victims of discrimination: polling booths were located to discourage them from voting. For example, in Down County, some Catholics had to cross a mountain and walk five miles in order to vote. Others had to pass ten election centers before they reached their own. In 1948, this practice, of locating voting booths to discourage Catholics from voting, was brought up in discussions at Westminster. Westminster said the matter was for Stormont, Stormont said the county councils (which, of course, were controlled by Unionists), were responsible, and nothing was done to change the practice.

Finally, the Unionists maintained a very successful system of job discrimination against Catholics. Their hope was to drive Catholic workers to emigrate in order to find work, either to the Republic of Ireland[24] or to Britain. A typical example of the effectiveness of this system was the case of Bernadette Devlin's father, a carpenter, who had to go to Britain because he could not find work in Northern Ireland. Business was in the hands of Protestants, men like John Barnhill, a Unionist Senator and grain merchant, who proudly boasted about how few Catholics, if any, they hired.[25] The Harland and Wolff shipyards, Belfast's most important company, employed 10,000 men but only 500 of them were Catholics.[26] Those Catholics who did not emigrate might never find work. For example, when Derry's unemployment rate for men was 18%, the Bogside's rate was 36%.[27] Often a graduation certificate from a Catholic school was enough to disqualify a job applicant. Furthermore, many employers set up elaborate qualifications rules, such as residence or military service requirements, which applied only to Catholics.

In addition to these tactics, the government of Northern Ireland passed and enforced laws which aided in the oppression and harassment of Catholics. Specifically, the Special Powers Act of 1922 allowed search without warrant, arrest without charge, and imprisonment without trial or counsel. By the time it was amended in 1951, this Act also banned flag flying and demonstrations:

> These Special Powers Acts are not designed, as such Acts are in other nations, solely to meet some great emergency. They have become part of the ordinary law and

were added to in the second half of 1951 when an Act called the Public Order Act was passed.[28]

Throughout the years, the Special Powers Act was applied almost exclusively to Catholics and was effectively enforced by the *B-Specials*, a partisan wing of the Constabulary force.

These policies and practices—discriminatory, harassing, and oppressive—illustrate the extent to which the Unionist Party, for fifty years, acted in its own interests, though it did so within what were called legal limits. The Stormont encouraged unfair religious differentiations, which had enormous political and economic repercussions, in areas where it was constitutionally allowed to legislate. The Catholics, severed from their political and religious compatriots in the South and forced into the role of a permanent minority in the North, were trapped in frustration and hopelessness without political channels through which to work. True, their local councils were democratically elected, in the sense that everyone could vote, and the manipulations, which resulted in Unionist majorities, were engineered within the law. The law, however, also operated to perpetuate their oppression. For example, no Catholic was issued a gun permit for years before the events of 1969, furthermore, it would have been futile to have brought this matter up before a Unionist-controlled court, for the court system too was unfair. All these factors contributed to an emphasis on the divisive nature of Northern Ireland's society: the supremacy of one group over the other, and the increased separation, hatred, and distrust between the two religious segments of the population. The bitter frustration felt by the Catholics had been building up for at least fifty years, as was the narrow-minded bigotry of the Protestants. Inevitably these dichotomous emotions would explode into relentless violence, which happened in 1969.

Derry County has traditionally been the Catholic stronghold with Protestants outnumbered by a ratio of 2 to 1. Derry was also the site of the most reprehensible gerrymandering and the location of the most abominable slums in Northern Ireland. If hell were to break loose, the rupture inevitably would be in Derry.

In October 1968, the Civil Rights Association, an avowed non-sectarian group, was formed. Defying a ban imposed under the Special Powers Act, the group marched in the town of Derry in a demonstration against the government. The police stopped the demonstration and wounded 77 of the marchers. This episode marked the beginning of a non-violent resistance movement on the part of civil rights workers. At about the same time, a new political party was being formed by Bernadette Devlin and other students at Queen's University. This organization with its socialist orientation was called the People's Democracy Party and stood for the civil rights of all the people in Northern Ireland. Together, these two groups became the nucleus of the Civil Rights Movement.[29] The most important characteristic of the CRM was that, taken as a whole, it contained people from almost all sectors of Northern Ireland's society, expressing widely disparate political and religious views. This kind of unity was unique in Northern Ireland and took its lead from the civil rights movement in the American South and from the student demonstrations which were becoming quite common in Europe and other parts of the United States. The CRM sought to secure for the Catholic community the same political and economic rights that were enjoyed by the other citizens of the United Kingdom by staging marches and protests. If Stormont held firm, then the British government hoped to intervene in the same way that the Federal government had intervened in Little Rock, Arkansas, and other places in the United States where local authorities persisted in carrying on discriminatory practices.

Meanwhile, in Belfast—the Protestant stronghold, the capital of Northern Ireland, and the county seat of Antrim—the Reverend Ian Paisley was drawing a large following while preaching the piety of bigotry. Making a virtue of hating Catholics, Paisley said that he had "hated God's enemies with a perfect hate."[30] His sermons on the "wantonly reproductive" Catholics, who threatened the jobs of good Protestants, appealed to the bigotries of his congregations: the poor, the farmers, and the small businessmen. The Protestant poor were not as poor as the Catholic poor, but any advancement by Catholics represented a threat to them. The Protestant disadvantaged classes had been persuaded that they were a part of the Ascendancy, so long as their status was superior to that of the Catholics. Paisley, however, appealed as well to their sense of alienation from the affluent class power structure of Stormont. Finally, Paisley succeeded in having many Protestants identify all civil rights workers with Catholics, as he played upon their fears of possible Catholic economic competition.

Confrontation between members of the CRM and Paisley's followers was inevitable and took place in January of 1969, when the Civil Rights Association and the People's Democracy Party held their first joint demonstration for the purpose of pressuring Prime Minister O'Neill into carrying out the reforms he had been promising. They planned to march between Derry and Belfast but were set upon by a large group of Protestants, armed with bottles, stones, and nail-studded cudgels, at Burntollet Bridge on the outskirts of Derry.

This violent episode set a precedent which has plagued the leaders of Northern Ireland ever since. Inevitably, if a leader, especially the Prime Minister, even hinted at making necessary reforms to satisfy the basic and rightful needs of the Catholics or simply tried to *quiet things down*, as Westminster continued to implore, an angry and violent Protestant backlash was unleashed. After fifty years, the Unionist leaders had created a beast that could not be calmed.[31] Thus, Terence O'Neill, who came into the Prime Minister's seat in 1963, was forced to resign from office in April of 1969, shortly after the confrontation at the Burntollet Bridge.

In March of 1972, Stormont was prorogued, and Britain assumed direct rule of Northern Ireland in response to an ever-worsening situation. Britain's direct administration of Northern Ireland was only supposed to last for one year, but Britain has been there ever since. It is locked in, and it cannot get out. It has produced a stream of White Papers and made numerous efforts to extricate itself and to establish some form of power-sharing, but the intransigence of the doctrinaire Unionists has made British failure inevitable. The Unionists will not compromise; they insist upon *their* majority rule. For a country to disengage itself from a reprehensible situation by repudiating almost 500 years of its political history is no easy matter.

Summary

The outbreak of sectarian violence in Northern Ireland in 1968-1969 originated, "because a young generation of college-educated Catholics decided to emulate the nonviolent movement of American blacks led by Martin Luther King, Jr., and to challenge the inequities in Northern Ireland's society by passive resistance."[32] The Catholics' nonviolent, civil rights movement evoked brutal suppression by the Northern, Protestant police and inflamed the smoldering hostility of the Protestant majority. Reluctantly, on March 24, 1972, the British government imposed *Direct Rule* on the province.

Throughout the 1970s, 1980s, and early 1990s, the British government put forward several proposals and mechanisms in Northern Ireland for accommodating the Protestant majority and ameliorating the Catholic minority. All failed because of the use or threat of violence by either the Catholic IRA or Protestant extremists. For instance, in 1973, the British established a power-sharing assembly based on proportional representation, which was Britain's first attempt to assuage the Catholic Nationalists' demands for greater participation in the province's governance and greater equity in its social services. "The politicians worked well together but the Protestant gangs, whipped up [Reverend] Paisley and other hard-line politicians, organized a general strike in May 1974 that paralyzed the province."[33] The British experiment with multi-party coalition lasted from January 1974 to May 1974.

The Sunningdale Agreement of 1974 was a second attempt at power-sharing. It was a collaborative attempt of the British and Irish Republic governments and three principal parties in Northern Ireland—the Unionist Party, the Alliance Party, and the SDLP, the Social Democratic Labor Party—to form a power-sharing executive for the province. It collapsed in a matter of months: "The success of the first Ulster Workers' strike, which brought down the Sunningdale Agreement, remains a significant folk symbol for [Protestant] loyalists."[34] The Unionist point of view has remained unchanged since the Partition:

Protestants had been loyal to the British Crown; therefore, only Protestants were deemed worthy of participation in government. As long as Catholics resided in Northern Ireland, they would be expected to comply with the regime's laws; their support was neither sought nor obtained.[35]

In May 1984, "Constitutional Nationalists, North and South . . . [produced] . . . the Forum Report which proposed three solutions to the Northern Ireland problem: a unitary state, a federal/confederal arrangement, and joint authority by both governments [British and Irish Republic] over the North."[36] The Forum Report stated calmly, cogently, but forcefully:

The immediate outlook for the north is extremely dangerous unless an acceptable political solution is achieved. The long-term damage to society worsens each day that passes without political progress. . . . There are at present no political institutions to which the majority of the people of the nationalist and unionist traditions can give their common allegiance or even acquiesce in. The fundamental social bonds which hold people together in a normal community, already tenuous in the abnormal conditions of Northern Ireland, have been very largely sundered by the events and experiences of the past fifteen terrible years. . . . The immense challenge facing the political leaders in Britain and Ireland is to create the conditions for a new Ireland and a new society acceptable to all its people.[37]

The Anglo-Irish Agreement of November 15, 1985, was a first step in creating a new Ireland and a new environment for the whole island. The essential clause states:

There is hereby established . . . an Intergovernmental Conference . . . concerned with Northern Ireland and with relations between the two parts of ireland, to deal, as set out in this Agreement, on a regular basis with (1) political matters; (2) security and related matters; (3) legal matters including the administration of justice; (4) the promotion of cross-border cooperation.[38]

By the Anglo-Irish Agreement of 1985, Britain acknowledged that the Republic of Ireland had a formal and vital role to play in resolving the Northern Ireland Crisis, albeit a consultative role, as all final decisions remained in the hands of the British government. Nevertheless, the Unionists were incensed, accusing the British government of "betrayal," and set about immediately to wreck the Agreement, as it had the 1973 and 1974 agreements, with strikes, boycotts, and violence.

In October 1993, the Prime Ministers of Britain and Ireland issued a joint statement from Brussels, "promising *that new doors could open* for peace talks on [Northern Ireland] if the Irish Republican Army ended its campaign of violence."[39] This new initiative would allow the Sinn Fein, the political wing of the IRA, to sit at the negotiating table. The Unionists were outraged and during the week that the new initiative was made sixteen people in Northern Ireland were killed.

Northern Ireland is a difficult problem for the outside world to understand because it arises from religious antagonisms within the Christian community. In an age when the agnostic spirit prevails elsewhere, a conflict between Presbyterians and Anglicans on the one side and Roman Catholics on the other seems an incomprehensible throwback to the seventeenth century. It is made all the more incomprehensible when leading Irish church leaders and politicians periodically insist that the dispute is not religious in nature. In reality, although the problem has significant political and economic dimensions, it would dwindle away if it were not for the religious antagonisms.[40]

"The result is today's bitter sectarian stalemate from which no easy exit is evident."[41] *Plus ça change, plus c'est la même chose.*[42]

Notes

1. Nicholas Mansergh, *The Irish Question: 1840-1921*, rev. ed. (London: George Allen and Unwin, 1965), 189.

2. Ibid., 188.

3. Ibid., 192.

4. Piers Brendon, *Eminent Edwardians* (Boston: Houghton Mifflin, 1980), 94-95.

5. Mansergh, 165.

6. Peter Fraser, *Joseph Chamberlain* (London: Cassell, 1966), xii.

7. Mansergh, 194.

8. Conor Cruise O'Brien, *Parnell and His Party* (Oxford: Clarendon Press, 1957), 28.

9. Ibid., 352.

10. "Arthur Griffith (1871-1922), editor since 1899 of *The United Irishman* . . . had launched in 1905 the slogan Sinn Fein." Hugh Seton-Watson, *Nations and States: An Enquiry into the Origins of Nations and the Politics of Nationalism* (Boulder, CO:Westview Press, 1977), 38. Sinn Fein, however, was not founded as a political organization until 1906.

11. "Balfour would never insult the Irish as Lord Salisbury did—his uncle did not conceal his view that they were a race of bog-trotting Hottentots, quite incapable of self-government." Brendon, 88.

12. "Griffith urged complete abstention from parliamentary politics and an uncompromising priority for Irish national interest in all fields, especially in the economic." Seton-Watson, 38.

13. Brandon, 106.

14. Edward Carson (1854-1935) was the man who led Ulster against Home Rule and the man who defended the Marquess of Queensbury in the first trial of Oscar Wilde: "A vain, hatchet-faced, hypochondriacal but talented lawyer with a penchant for histrionics, Carson was a fervent Unionist from Dublin." Patrick Buckland, *A History of Northern Ireland* (New York: Holmes and Meier, 1981), 11.

15. Eamon de Valera, American-born in 1882 of a Spanish father and an Irish mother, was thrice Prime Minister of Ireland (1937-1948, 1951-1954, 1957-1959). He served as President of Ireland from 1959 to 1973, retiring after serving the maximum 14-year period allowed under the Constitution. He died in 1975.

16. This and the following quotations are from Frank Gallagher, *The Indivisible Island: The History of the Partition of Ireland* (London: Victor Gollancz, 1957), 146-147.

17. Mansergh, 209.

18. Nicholas Mansergh, *The Government of Northern Ireland: A Study in Devolution* (London: George Allen and Unwin, 1936), 104-122.

19. Ibid., 113.

20. Max Hastings, *Barricades in Belfast* (New York: Taplinger Publishing, 1970), 26.

21. Gallagher, 148.

22. Mansergh, *The Government of Northern Ireland: A Study in Devolution*, 240.

23. Gallagher, Chapter 15, *Gerrymandering*.

24. In 1949, Southern Ireland, which had since the Anglo-Irish Treaty of 1921 been known as the Irish Free State, declared itself a Republic and withdrew from the Commonwealth.

25. In December of 1971, John Barnhill was killed by the IRA.

26. Miriam Reik, "Ireland: Religious War or Class Struggle," *Saturday Review*, 18 March 1972, p. 28.

27. Bernard Weinraub, "Free Derry, Run by IRA, is a State Within a State," *New York Times*, 27 April 1972.

28. Frank Gallagher, 194.

29. London Sunday Times Insight Team, *Northern Ireland: A Report on the Conflict* (London: Penguin, 1972). This book arose out of articles that appeared in the *London Sunday Times* in 1971.

30. Reik, 26.

31. For forty years after partition, Northern Ireland had only two Prime Ministers—James Craig and Sir Basil Brooke (later Viscount Brookeborough)—both served terms of twenty years and both were ardent anti-Catholics. Lord Brookeborough was the founder of the *B-Specials* and, in 1933, was the Minister of Agriculture who exclaimed vehemently against Catholics. Both men sowed well their seed of hate.

32. William Shannon, "The Anglo-Irish Agreement," *Foreign Affairs*, Spring 1986: 852.

33. Ibid., 854.

34. Michael Connolly and John Loughlin, "Reflections on the
     Anglo-Irish Agreement," *Government and Opposition* 21, no.
     2 (Spring 1986): 158.

35. Richard Rose, *Governing without Consensus: An Irish
     Perspective* (Boston: Beacon Press, 1979), 97.

36. Connolly and Loughlin, 151.

37. Shannon, 858.

38. Ibid., 849-850.

39. *New York Times*, 30 October 1993.

40. Shannon, 851.

41. Ibid., 853.

42. The more things change, the more they remain the same.

Chapter Four
Canada: Political Integration Or Territorial Disintegration?

The most obvious obstacle to Canada's pursuit of political integration has been the demand of French Canadians in Quebec Province for a sovereign, independent state separate from the rest of Canada in all but matters of common economic interest.[1]   However, other obstacles to political integration face Canada that could portend the nation's territorial disintegration: the country's size, the heterogeneity of its population, its federation, its constitution, and the formerly dormant issue of what to do about the *First Nations*.

Canada is enormous. Until the dismemberment of the Union of Soviet Socialist Republics, Canada was the world's second largest land mass.[2] This enormous size, coupled with a population approximately the same as the state of California, estimated at 30 million people in 1990, has always been a threat to Canada's territorial integration. For instance, despite trans-continental railways and national airlines, Canadians of the Atlantic maritime provinces have more contact with New Englanders than with their own countrymen west of Toronto. Thus, when Quebec separatists threatened to take their province out of the federal union, distance, both geographic and psychological, contributed to the western Canadian's attitude of *Let them go!* Furthermore, when the French language was placed on an equal status with English, in all branches of the federal government, non-French-speaking western Canadians grumbled that a language spoken mainly in Quebec Province should not be made an official language for the whole country. Geography, therefore, added to the contentiousness between Quebec separatists and Canadians living west of Ontario.

As 90% of all Canadians live within 200 miles of the United States border, geography has separated Canadians from one another more than it has separated them from Americans. Even more amazing, 80% of all Canadians live within 50 miles of the United States border.

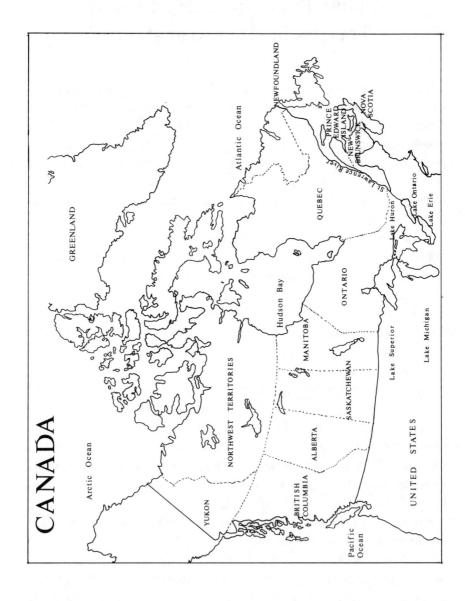

Over the years hundreds of thousands of Yankees have moved to Canada, while an even larger number of Canadians have sought improved opportunities to the south. This constant shift back and forth has been so widely accepted that it is largely ignored. Yet the migration between Canada and the United States has totaled more than six million people, one of the greatest population movements in history. And it has created one of the world's most unusual borders, a porous line which saw barely monitored crossings by 70 million people.[3]

Pierre Eliott Trudeau, when Prime Minister of the Canadian Federation, once remarked about Canada's relationship with the United States that "living next to you is like sleeping with an elephant: no matter how friendly and even-tempered is the beast, one is affected by every twitch and grunt."[4] In 1975, a report by the Canadian Senate's Standing Committee on Foreign Affairs was more explicit about that relationship:

This report deals mainly with government-to-government contacts. It is important to recognize, however, that this is not the whole picture but only the tip of an iceberg. In the private sector, financial, business, and private transactions are not statistically visible but number millions per month by telephone and mail alone, not to mention the enormously high number of daily border crossings. This interchange goes on largely independent of and beyond the control of governments. It is one of the basic strengths of the relationship. . . . [However], it is not a relationship of equals. The United States has 10 times the population and over 10 times the gross national product of Canada. In military terms it is a super-power, in economic terms a giant. *Because of this disparity, Canada is more dependent, more sensitive, and more vulnerable to the state of the relationship than is the United States.* For Canada, it is by far the most important of all its external relationships.[5]

Karl Deutsch has referred to Canada's *external* political integration, concerning the United States, as a *Pluralistic Security Relationship*, where few if any political institutions have been merged and which has existed between the two nations for almost 200 years, along the longest undefended border in the world.[6]

Deutsch emphasizes that mutual trust and understanding are achieved between the two nations through an expansion in channels and processes of communication both private and governmental, which is reiterated in the report of the Canadian Senate's Standing Committee on Foreign

Affairs. And yet, it is what Deutsch refers to as a country's *internal* political integration, its *Amalgamated Security Relationship* in which the major political institution have been merged, that has most vexed the Canadian Federation, especially as related to the heterogeneity, the multi-ethnicity, of its population.[7]

While French and English are both official languages for federal purposes, until recently only 13% of the population were bilingual. Sixty-seven percent spoke only English; 18% spoke only French; and 2% spoke in their mother tongue such languages as German, Dutch, Italian, and Ukrainian. In fact, one-fifth of the Canadian population was neither of French nor of British ancestry. Most came from Europe seeking refuge from war, tyranny, prejudice, and poverty. One Canadian in twenty was of German descent, and one in fifty was of Italian or Dutch descent. These and other European immigrants brought with them their cultural heritage as well as their brains, muscles, and ingenuity. Moreover, just as English- and French-speaking Canadians had retained some of their most cherished ethnic traditions, so too had these European immigrants preserved some of their old values and ways of life. While they had learned English, though not so often French, many have retained their mother tongue and other cultural attachments. More important, because of their color, they had not appeared dissimilar from the majority of other white Canadians. But this has not been the case for those of a darker skin, whom white Canadians refer to as *visible minorities*, many of whom now call Canada their home and many of whom are viewed as a threat by many white Canadians.

Canadians have always believed themselves to be more tolerant and less racist than their southern neighbors. However, events of recent years have caused shadows of doubt in many Canadian minds. For instance, in the spring of 1992, following the riots in Los Angeles, California, that accompanied the Rodney King verdict, Toronto experienced severe but less violent race-related events. As a consequence, Stephen Lewis, a former Canadian ambassador to the United Nations, was assigned the task of reporting on race relations in Ontario, Canada's largest province. Ambassador Lewis produced a scathing report in which he said that, "It is blacks who are being shot [by police]; it is black youth that is unemployed in excessive numbers; it is black students who are being inappropriately assigned to lower tracks in school."[8]

The original, non-indigenous, non-white people of Canada were the runaway slaves, who escaped the ravages of American slavery via the underground railway to Canada. Their descendants, until recently, have been relatively invisible to most white Canadians. However, in the past few decades, especially since the end of the Second World War and the demise of the British empire, they have been joined by growing numbers of non-whites from Asia, East Africa, the West Indies, and the Middle East, and suddenly Canada has a visible racial minority and a concomitant racial problem:

> In Vancouver, Indian school-children are now sometimes called *ragheads*, an allusion to the turbans that some of their fathers wear. . . . One Indian man moved his family twice during the last two years, once after *nigger* was painted on his front steps, and again after a series of rock attacks on his teen-age daughter.[9]

A large percentage of these non-white immigrants have few skills and little education, which has consigned them to the lowest rung of the economic ladder. Moreover, most of them are concentrated in Canada's major urban areas, such as Vancouver, Montreal, and Toronto, where they are often blamed for many urban ills. For example, in Toronto, armed robberies were about 20% higher in 1974 than they had been in 1973, and many policemen insinuated that the non-white immigrants, especially those from the West Indies, were responsible for the increase. Whether or not their insinuations were justified; they could not be verified because Canadian crime statistics were not kept by race, and that they were made at all troubled many Canadians, white and non-white.[10]

Until the end of the 1960s, white immigrants made up more than 70% of all new immigrants to Canada. In recent years, white immigrants make up less than 35%, and the percentage is steadily falling. For instance, in 1992, "Canada grants entry to far more blacks and other so-called *visible minorities* than to white," and this steady influx of non-whites was unnerving to many of Canada's traditional, white population.[11]

By the early 1970s, approximately 62,000 blacks and many fewer Asians were living in Canada: the majority were citizens or legal residents living in urban areas such as Toronto, but many were illegal aliens. For instance, in 1974, 800 Haitians had entered Canada legally as tourists, but Canadian immigration officials wanted them to depart as illegal aliens. The Haitians claimed that they were political refugees who faced certain imprisonment, if they were sent home, because if they left Haiti for social or economic reasons, their political loyalty to the Haitian government was suspect. A spokesman for the Canadian Department of Manpower and Immigration was quoted as saying, "If we gave the kind of special treatment that they want to everyone who came here because he was displeased with the economic or political situation of his own country, we would have them coming by the millions."[12] In 1966, there were 84 legal Haitian immigrants in Canada, but, by 1974, their numbers had increased to over 3,000, not including the disputed 800.

From 1969 to 1974, the influx of immigrants from Asia, the West Indies, East Africa, and the Middle East had risen from 19,000 to 71,000. In the two years from 1972 to 1974, the number of immigrants from the West Indies had nearly tripled from 4,000 to 11,000. The influx from Africa was increasing at an annual rate of 230%, and from Asia, mainly from India and Pakistan, at an annual rate of 177%. In terms of actual numbers. Asians represented the largest influx and not just Asians from the subcontinent but from East Africa as well. The 104,000 immigrants of all races admitted to Canada during the first six months of 1974 represented an increase of 46% over the number admitted during the first six months of 1973 and an increase of 92% over the number admitted during the first six months of 1972.[13] In the twenty years since 1972, in addition to the continued influx of Asians from the subcontinent, immigrants from Hong Kong, predominantly Chinese, have added to Canada rapidly becoming a multi-ethnic society. Thus, in 1992, "A recent poll showed that more than half of Canadians *fear* their country has taken in more multiracial immigrants than it can comfortably absorb."[14]

Canada has never wished to emulate the American pattern of amalgamating diverse ethnic groups into a melting pot. Instead, the Canadian goal has been to create a mosaic of ethnic groups, each retaining its separate identity with pride in its heritage. No European immigrants have taken this idea of separate identity and ethnic pride further than have the French-speaking Canadians, who represent one fourth of the country's total population and who have remained virtually self-segregated in Quebec Province for very specific survivalist reasons.[15]

The most conspicuous disintegrative factor in the Canadian mosaic of ethnic harmony has been the consequence of the ethnic enmity between the English-speaking, Protestant majority, and the French-speaking, Catholic minority. Today, outside of Europe, only in South Africa does a similar communal clash between descendants of European ethnic groups exist. In South Africa, this clash has been between those of English-speaking and Dutch-speaking descent.

In Canada the problem is this: how can a self-conscious ethnic minority preserve its distinctiveness in a country governed by the democratic principle of majority rule, which Henry Mayo says is one of the four, "tightly knit principles characteristic of democracy as a political system."[16] In such a society, if an issue arises which divides the country along ethnic lines, then the French-speaking, Catholic minority inevitably finds itself subjected to the tyranny of the English-speaking, Protestant majority.

For example, in each of the major wars in which Canada has been involved this century (the Boer War 1899-1901, the First World War 1914-1918, and the Second World War 1939-1945), French Canadians were adamantly against Canadian troops being conscripted to serve under the British flag. Nevertheless, the English-speaking majority got its way and conscription was instituted. During the Boer War, riots between French- and English-speaking students at McGill University broke out in the streets of Montreal over this issue of conscription. During the two World Wars, violence again broke out in the streets of Montreal, although thousands of French Canadians fought and died in both wars. They did so, not because they loved the British sovereign or hated the Kaiser and Hitler, but for the adventure. Nevertheless, many French Canadians resisted conscription by seeking refuge with relatives in the backwoods of the massive Quebec Province. In fact, their numbers were so large that the federal government ended the whole business by proclaiming a general amnesty, after the Second World War, rather than trying to bring all these deserters to court.

In 1980, 44.6% of the Canadian population was of British ancestry; 28.7% was of French ancestry; 23% was of other European ancestry; and 3.7% was of non-European descent. With regards to sectarian affiliation, 41.2% were Protestant; 47.3% were Catholic; 1.5% were Eastern Orthodox; 1.2% were Jewish; 1.3% were of other religious persuasion, such as Muslim; and 7.4% were of no religious affiliation.

The foundation of today's English-speaking, Protestant dominance was laid in the eighteenth century by British loyalists who fled the thirteen colonies, after the British lost the American revolutionary war for independence. However, and in spite of this dominance, French-speaking Catholic Canadians still maintained their identity as a separate ethnic entity, but not by increasing their numbers through immigration but by segregating themselves in Quebec Province. There the majority of French Canadians reside today, although pockets of French-speaking Catholic Canadians are found throughout the federation with substantial numbers in New Brunswick, Manitoba, and Ontario. The survival of French-speaking Catholics as a distinctive ethnic group, despite English-speaking Protestant dominance, may be described as a cultural miracle.

Twenty years after the Treaty of Paris of 1763, which ceded Canada to Britain, the 70,000 French-speaking Catholic settlers were a crushed people. Their misfortune, however, was not due solely to the victorious British, for, after the British conquest of Canada, the French civilian elite who had governed them abandoned them and returned to France or went elsewhere in the French empire. Within a generation, the entire French-speaking Catholic population of Canada became identified with subsistence farming, while the new English-speaking Protestant settlers concentrated on trade and commerce. This focus on agriculture was deliberate and was helped by two factors: the education that French Canadians received and the Catholic Church which disseminated that education.

The rudimentary educational system under French rule was completely disrupted by the British conquest. For several decades, practically no organized education was given to French-speaking Catholic children. In fact, by 1800, the vast majority of these children were unable to read and write, in any language. They had no choice but to turn to subsistence farming in order to survive. The only organized education offered to French-speaking Catholic children was given in cities such as Quebec and Montreal to young men and women preparing to enter Catholic Church service as priests and nuns.

After the British conquest, the role and power of the Catholic Church, among French-speaking peasants, was awesome. As an elite, only the Catholic clergy stayed behind. Under French rule, French civilians had served as a counterbalance to the clergy's power. With the departure of these bureaucrats and administrators, the clergy assumed their vacated roles, thereby enhancing the Catholic Church's position as the only institution to which the French-speaking Catholic peasants felt they could turn with any confidence, trust, and sense of identity. The British regime relied upon the Catholic clergy to act as an intermediary by using its influence to ensure the loyalty of French-speaking Catholic peasants to British rule. For its part, the Catholic Church had been a consistent advocate of a rural, agricultural, Catholic life—one divorced from the influences of the eighteenth century's enlightenment and the nineteenth century's progress. Furthermore, the Roman Catholic Church dreamed of establishing in North America a model colony founded on agriculture and its own authoritarian dogma, as was the case in Latin America but had not been possible in the thirteen American colonies. After the British conquest, the Catholic Church in Quebec was in an optimum position for achieving such goals.

After the British conquest, French-speaking Catholic peasants instilled in their children two slogans that became their credo: *la survivance*, survival, and *Je me souviens*, I remember. In 1977, *Je me souviens* replaced *La Belle Province* as the motto on the license plates of motor vehicles in Quebec Province. By 1977, the province was being governed by those whose avowed aim was to separate Quebec Province from the rest of Canada and to establish an independent state.

Ironically, the main battlefield between the French-speaking Catholics and the English-speaking Protestants has not extended to the rest of Canada but has remained in Quebec Province itself, where more than 80% of the approximately 6,770,800 inhabitants are of French ancestry. In the nineteenth century, rural French-speaking Catholic peasants were able to compete with their English-speaking Protestant countrymen in an economy based primarily upon agriculture. However, by concentrating on trade and commerce, the English-speaking Protestant Canadians were able to accumulate the capital necessary for industrial development and investment. On the other hand, rural French-speaking Catholic peasants, tied to the soil, were in no position to compete with their fellow-countrymen when, in the early twentieth century, industry and not agriculture became the basis of the country's economy.[17]   Moreover, Quebec Province—blessed with rich forest and mineral resources, waterways which could produce an opulent supply of hydroelectric power, excellent harbors at Quebec City and Montreal, and a reservoir of abundant cheap labor—was in an optimum position to participate in Canada's rapid industrial development. However, while the impoverished French-speaking Catholic peasants represented a cornucopia of cheap labor, the affluent English-speaking Protestant entrepreneurs constituted the home-spawned capitalist class. Along with British and American capitalists, these English-speaking Protestant entrepreneurs became the owners and managers of the new industries, while the French-Canadian peasants became *the hewers of wood and drawers of water*. No longer were they masters even in their own house, but they became chattel in a province dominated by the English-speaking Protestant capitalist class. This impoverished, powerless situation was self-inflicted not by the French Canadian peasants but by their French Canadian leaders who encouraged the English-speaking Protestant capitalist class to make the financial outlays in the growing industrial economy which the survivalist peasants had not been able to accumulate. Later, these leaders would be condemned for selling Quebec Province to outside interests:

> Is there another people whose elite betrayed it so lightedheartedly, almost without exception? For is it not betrayal to constantly preach patience, resignation, and fear of change in order to keep the herd well under control? . . . Quebec is . . . a nation one has tried to smother forever in the depressing cotton wool of a paternalistic social and political climate. . .[18]

Political leaders were not the only ones censured for this sell-out. The Catholic Church also earned condemnation, for the Catholic Church had supervised an educational system that had not prepared French Canadian men and women to be technicians and specialists in the science and techniques of modern business, industry, and organization.

Until 1982, the British North America Act of 1867 was Canada's written constitution. It guaranteed the cultural and civil rights of the English-speaking Protestant minority in Quebec Province as well as to the French-speaking Catholic minority living outside Quebec. However, the French-speaking Catholic minority soon learned that a piece of paper was no guarantee of their actual rights. For instance, in 1870, the province of Manitoba was organized with a population of less than twenty-five thousand,[19] and the organizers promised to respect the cultural and civil rights of the French-speaking Catholic minority. But, in 1890, Manitoba abolished French-language schools and ended the right of members to use French in the provincial legislature.[20] In other words, outside Quebec Province, French Canadians were like Indians living off the reservation; only in Quebec Province could they live out their cultural heritage. However, even in Quebec Province, English increasingly became the language of prominence and dominance.

Today, in Quebec Province, one refers to a French-speaking Canadian as a francophone and an English-speaking Canadian as an anglophone. "Until just a few years ago a francophone entering one of Montreal's fashionable department stores and addressing a salesclerk in French would be answered in English with: "Speak white.""[21] Canada might possess two dominant languages and two cultures, but evidently only French Canadians had to be bilingual and bicultural, even in Quebec Province.

By the end of the Second World War, all sectors of the French Canadian community were unhappy with the situation in Quebec, but nothing changed. Their greatest discontentment was with their provincial government and especially with the leader of that government, Maurice Duplessis.

Maurice Duplessis, a French Canadian, was the Premier of Quebec Province from 1936 to 1940 and again from 1944 until his death in 1959. He skillfully manipulated French Canadian nationalist emotions as a shield behind which to protect his paternalistic, retrogressive policies in the mock battles he staged with the federal government. Consistently, Duplessis fought progressive federal welfare programs as being infringements upon the authority of the provincial government, the French Canadian culture, and their civil rights. Rarely, however, did Duplessis produce any progressive alternatives of his own. Furthermore, in labor battles, the Duplessis regime often sided with management against French Canadian labor interests. Duplessis was able to get away with such shenanigans due to the under-representation of urban areas in the provincial legislature. His National Union Party had little to fear from trade unions whose members were predominantly urban and French-speaking. Despite his retrogressive policies, Duplessis was regularly re-elected through a combination of electoral corruption, political patronage, charlatanism disguised as charisma, and an ear finely tuned to the nationalistic frustrations and the inferiority complex of French Canadians.

While Duplessis was in power, a quiet revolution was in progress, as a new, ambitious, and aggressive French Canadian middle-class was being spawned. This middle-class was composed of men and women who turned away from the traditional French Canadian vocations of the Church, the law, and medicine towards science, business, and technology. This transformation, however, was slow to develop because of the continued dominance of Catholic Church-directed classical education, which emphasized language, literature, and culture. Throughout the 1950s French Canadian discontent mounted, the quiet revolution progressed, and so too did ominous ethnic tension. Finally, in 1961, the anachronistic politicians of the National Union Party were swept from office by the provincial legislative victory of the Liberal Party, which came to power on promises of radical social, economic, and political changes. Once in office, it sponsored legislation for changes in education, which weakened the stranglehold of the Catholic Church. It instituted social and economic programs which helped to alleviate the everyday misery of peasant and working class Quebec Province residents, and it gave greater representation to urban trade unions which increased their clout in the provincial legislature.

Out of fear that more disruptive and possibly revolutionary changes might spill out of Quebec Province into the rest of Canada, the federal government, business organizations, and English-speaking Canadians encouraged the Liberal Party government in its pursuit of this progressive agenda. For its part, the Liberal Party government, to assuage those fears, contended that the demands of French-speaking Quebecers could be fulfilled within the framework of the administration's forward-looking but gradual changes. The majority of French Canadians seemed convinced by the Liberal Party government's arguments and programs. However, a strident minority was not convinced. By the beginning of the 1970s, alarming signs indicated that not only was the pace of change too slow for these strident nationalists but that the changes themselves were irrelevant. Exploding bombs planted in mail boxes in Quebec Province became a regular occurrence, culminating in more virulent acts of terrorism involving two officials of the British and Quebec governments. In October 1970, James Cross, the British Trade Commissioner in Canada, was kidnapped. However, before the Cross kidnapping, Pierre Laporte, the Minister of Labor for Quebec Province, was abducted, slain, and his body found during the Cross captivity. This extreme act of violence prompted Canadian authorities to fly Cross's kidnapper to Cuba in exchange for his release. Not even this concession seemed to assuage such extremists, as the left-wing secessionist Front for the Liberation of Quebec would be satisfied only with a sovereign and independent Quebec NOW!

In 1968, the year after Canada commemorated the British North America Act of 1867 and celebrated the formation of the federal union with *Expo 67*, disparate groups of moderate and militant nationalists, left-wing socialist activists, and radical separatists in Quebec Province came together to form a mass political party. This coalition was led by René Lévesque, a journalist, who had left the Liberal Party because of its gradualist approach to change. The coalition called itself the Parti Québécois and promised that, once elected to provincial power, it would extricate Quebec Province from the Canadian federation.

As in the case of Jurassian separatism in Switzerland, by the beginning of the 1970s, Canada was at a crucial crossroad in its political development. The axiom applied in the Jura situation aptly fits here: when those who believe that, in the past, they have been oppressed or denied their rights begin to achieve some of their goals, their demands become more strident, as they develop a thirst for even greater concessions. The corollaries to this axiom also apply: if these demands are not granted, social unrest in the form of communal violence may ensue; if they are granted, regional autonomy may become more appealing and perhaps result in the creation of a new political entity, an independent state.

In November 1976, the Parti Québécois defeated the Liberal Party, and René Lévesque became Premier of Quebec Province, only four months after he had published his blueprint for extrication, the so-called *sovereignty-association* plan, which would render Quebec Province politically independent, although retaining its economic ties with the rest of Canada.[22]   Once in power, the separatist-minded Parti Québécois made known its intentions to seek the views on separation from the electorate of the province by means of a referendum. However, the years 1977 and 1978 came and went without any signs of an imminent referendum, although the threat of Quebec's secession persisted.

During this time, Lévesque and the Parti Québécois expended much energy in trying to convince the world of the inevitability of Quebec's independence.   However, the major objection to the *sovereignty-association* scheme came from the leaders of the other nine provinces, who showed no interest in an economic association with an independent Quebec. Within the province itself, the Liberal Party, which was the chief opponent of the Parti Québécois' quest for independence, said that the province could obtain all the changes and power it sought without dismembering the Canadian federation. Furthermore, public opinion polls failed to substantiate that independence for Quebec Province was inevitable, despite Lévesque's confident and unequivocal assertions that it was.

Finally, after weeks of bitter, emotional, and often recriminating debate, Quebec's provincial legislature, the National Assembly, approved by a vote of 68 to 37 a question, the language of which had been drafted by the Parti Québécois, to be put to the province's electorate in the form of a referendum. On April 15, 1980, Lévesque, appearing more confident than ever, announced to the provincial legislature that the date of the referendum would be May 30, 1980.

The English text of the referendum question, which asked for a provincial government mandate to negotiate with the rest of Canada a new partnership of economic association and, eventually, the province's independence, stated:

> The Government of Quebec has made public its proposal to negotiate a new agreement with the rest of Canada, based on the equality of nations;
>
> This agreement would enable Quebec to acquire the exclusive power to make its laws, levy its taxes, and establish relations abroad—in other words, sovereignty—and, at the same time, to maintain with Canada an economic association, including a common currency;
>
> No change in political status resulting from these negotiations will be effected without approval by the people through another referendum;
>
> On these terms, do you give the Government of Quebec the mandate to negotiate the proposed agreement between Quebec and the rest of Canada?[23]

Prime Minister Trudeau, although a French Canadian and a native of Montreal, was staunchly anti-separatist and vehemently opposed to any special economic relationship between Quebec and the rest of Canada. To the members of the House of Commons in Ottawa he explained that if the Lévesque government could not receive a mandate to negotiate for economic association with the rest of Canada neither could it negotiate for Quebec's political separation from the rest of Canada because the two issues were indissolubly united. Therefore, Trudeau implored the Quebec electorate to reject the Quebec government's tentative plan to negotiate a vaguely defined Quebec sovereignty.

The result of the May 1980 referendum was a resounding defeat for Lévesque and the Parti Québécois, with 87% of the electorate voting, 2,717,913 voted *NO*, and 1,478,200 voted *YES*. Frenzied jubilation on the part of the anti-separatists was uncalled for because, although Quebec had said NO to the dismemberment of the Canadian federation, it had not said YES to the current federation. Political observers viewed the outcome of the referendum as having been as much determined by French-speaking Quebecers' fear of the unknown as by their affection for federal Canada as it existed.[24] Furthermore, because the 20% English-speaking Quebecers voted overwhelmingly against separation, the result of the referendum meant that the province's French-speaking majority was divided roughly 50:50 on the issue. This indicated formidable separatist support. For the future, it represented a serious challenge to Trudeau as he sought to placate not only Quebec's leaders but leaders of governments in other provinces who demanded greater autonomy and power, especially economic power over the allocation of revenues in their provinces. Nevertheless, the results of the referendum gave credence to the proposition that economic interests held as much sway with the French-speaking electorate as did ethnicity, for no greater unknown existed than how Quebec would manage economically on its own. In April 1981, the Parti Québécois won 80 of 122 seats in the National Assembly and the right to govern the province for another five years. During the interim, Premier Lévesque persistently urged his party to step up its separatist campaign and, at a special convention of the Parti Québécois in February 1982, delegates reaffirmed their goal of eventual independence. Nevertheless, after the 1980 referendum, the Parti Québécois was deeply divided over the pace and tactic necessary to achieve that goal. For instance, in November 1984, five provincial ministers, two of whom were among the most powerful in the Cabinet, resigned over their perception that Lévesque had demoted the separation issue as a priority on the government's agenda.[25] Lévesque had not abandoned Quebec's independence as a goal, although he had de-emphasized it for the immediate future and for a very practical political reason. By April 1986, Quebec had to hold new provincial elections, and Lévesque correctly perceived that his constituents were less enamored with separation than they had been in 1976.

A sense of security has developed among Quebec's French-speakers that did not exist a decade ago. Confident that their language and traditions are no longer endangered, they are now concerned above all with economic problems. According to a recent survey, only a fifth of Quebecers still favor some form of sovereignty, while more than half want their province to be like any of the other nine.

Quebec has felt the recession of recent years more than most other provinces. The unemployment rate at the end of 1984 was 11.9 percent compared with 8.7 percent in neighboring Ontario. Independence has become a moot issue for many people anxious about their jobs, particularly when the best chances for recovery seem to lie in strong economic ties with the other provinces.[26]

Were economic interests or ethnic pride more important to French Canadians? At a December 1981 convention of the Parti Québécois, militant separatists, who were angry and impatient with Lévesque's gradualist program towards Quebec's independence, rewrote the Party's program and removed almost all references to *association*. What they wanted was *sovereignty* NOW! In a referendum, by mail, of the Party's 300,000 members this hardline approach was rejected by 95% of the 290,000 members who voted. The vote was regarded as an endorsement of Lévesque, for he threatened to resign, if the referendum had opposed his policies. Not only the province's electorate but also the Party's members had shifted their priorities over the previous decade and had accepted economic interests over ethnic pride; self-interest defeated fear of the unknown. The Party's members feared loss of political power, if they could not appeal to the majority of the Quebec electorate. All the major polls indicated a Liberal Party resurgence and a possible victory at the next provincial election. If the Parti Québécois were to place the independence issue at the top of its agenda, that tactic could cost them more votes than such a strategy might gain.

The vision of an independent Quebec had become blurred, perhaps even obsolete.[27] Clearly, the Quebec electorate believed that both their economic and ethnic goals could be more readily accomplished within a Canadian federation rather than outside it. In fact, in December 1985, that electorate said so definitively, for, in the provincial elections for the National Assembly, the Liberal Party won 99 of the 122 seats contested. During the election campaign, the incumbent Parti Québécois never once made Quebec's independence an election issue.

Throughout the referendum campaign for Quebec independence, Prime Minister Trudeau, a passionate federalist, vowed to fight the dismemberment of the Canadian federation. Following the defeat of the 1980 referendum, Trudeau said, "Now that we have reaffirmed our will to live together, we must apply ourselves without delay to the task of rebuilding our home to conform to the needs of the Canadian family."[28] Later, Trudeau told the Canadian House of Commons, "We Canadians are now agreed on a common destination. What we must now do is chart a new course and a common itinerary toward that common destination."[29] However, Trudeau gave no precise indication of what changes he was prepared to implement in order to satisfy Quebec and the other provinces in their desire for more power. Then, in an interview in February of 1982, Trudeau said that instead of trying to please the provinces, the federal government would now try to please itself and "hopefully those Canadians who think there must be a Government of Canada that will have some powers and some tax room left." He ended by saying, "And that is the New Federalism, if you want to call it that."[30]

What Prime Minister Trudeau wanted to do was increase the federal government's role in almost all fields, and to put a stop to what he called centrifugal tendencies of parochial interests and the insatiable appetite of the provincial governments for more money and more power. Unlike the United States, Canada has not had to suffer the ravages of a civil war to determine whether the regional or the central government possessed the ultimate power. In Canada, the pendulum of power has swung back and forth between Ottawa and the provinces. In recent years, however, the provinces had been demanding more power—so much so that Trudeau had said that the ability of the federal government to govern was threatened.

One particularly sensitive issue had been the struggle between the provinces and the federal government for control over natural resources. The provinces, especially those rich in natural resources, wanted the power to determine the production and allocation of natural resources, as well as the distribution of revenues derived from them.[31] On the other hand, Trudeau wanted those powers to rest mainly in the hands of the federal government. The recent revision of the British North America Act of 1867 makes some concessions to the provinces on this issue. Nevertheless, richer regions of a country rarely wished to support the poorer regions through general revenues. These more richly endowed regions felt that money gained from their own natural resources were primarily for their own benefit. For instance, in 1975, Alberta Province produced 83% of Canada's oil, but the provincial government felt that it was not being paid enough for the oil it produced by the other Canadian provinces, because of the federal government's regulations and interference. Putting this point quite bluntly the Premier of Alberta, Peter Longheed, said "that oil belongs to Albertans—to you and me and our grandchildren. . . . But we're asked to sell this depleting resource far below its value."[32]

Until 1982, the Canadian constitution was the British North America Act of 1867. In other words, an act of the British Parliament and not of the Canadian federal or provincial legislatures brought the provinces together to form the Canadian federation. Trudeau and almost everyone else including the British government wanted to *repatriate*[33] this basic document in order to end the British Parliament's control, however tenuous, over the Canadian federation. But problems existed.

The BNA of 1867 granted Canada the right to internal self-government within the British empire and later within the British-organized Commonwealth of Nations. The intent of that document, in the Age of Pax Britannica, was to pacify the two dominant ethnic groups, the French-speaking Catholics and the English-speaking Protestants. The hope was that the two would live in harmony, if their ethnic interests were not infringed upon by either of the other or by the central government. As Ottawa was the citadel of the English-speaking Protestants and Quebec the heartland of the French-speaking Catholics, this solution seemed reasonable and appropriate. Therefore, the BNA gave to each province control over the matters which were special to its ethnic majority, such as education, with certain guarantees for the minority living in the other's province. However, unlike the American constitution, the BNA had no Bill of Rights which could ensure, nationwide, the protection of minority rights. The central government was entrusted with the responsibility for those matters which were common to both ethnic groups, such as trade, foreign policy, the military, and the common currency. However, the BNA was promulgated before Canada *imitated* America and pursued its own *manifest destiny* from ocean to ocean rather than from the Atlantic to the Great Lakes. This sweep across the continent not only meant adding new ethnic groups to the Canadian family but adding those groups' special interests as well.

Since 1927, Canada tried, without success, to repatriate its constitution from Britain in order to ameliorate its continental concerns and not just the concerns of the original European immigrants. But, because tradition required the unanimous consent of the provincial governments to any constitutional changes, this unanimity was almost impossible to achieve. The one instance of unanimity was the Citizenship Act of 1977, which finally ended Canadians' legal status as British subjects. But despite such revisions, all constitutional changes had to be approved by the British Parliament, after the customary unanimous consent of the federal and provincial governments. The British Parliament was willing, even eager, to hand over to Canada its basic laws, but, until 1981, the Canadians could not agree among themselves how to amend the BNA and bring it home. Even, in 1981, that decision was not unanimous.

One major reason for the lack of unanimity was that the four western provinces felt abused by the eastern provinces:

> British Columbia, Alberta, Saskatchewan and Manitoba always have felt remote from, neglected by and vaguely hostile to the distant center of federal power in Ottawa, which is not much closer to Calgary than Mexico City. This feeling of alienation, born of geographical isolation and neglect, festered during the Depression of the 1930s when the federal government imposed tariffs that protected the industrialized eastern provinces at the expense of western farmers and ranchers.[34]

Therefore, the western provinces were extremely reticent about agreeing to constitutional changes, or even making the constitution a Canadian rather than a British act of law. They rightly feared domination by the two ethnic and more populous provinces in the east, Ontario and Quebec.[35] In other words, westerners perceived the interest of the federal government in them and their region was power grabbing by Ottawa and the eastern majority. As a consequence, a major tenet of their consensus politics was to curb rather than expand federal jurisdiction and power, which was the reverse of the avowed intention of Prime Minister Trudeau's New Federalism. Therefore, when, in the 1970s, Trudeau began suggesting amending and repatriating the BNA, westerners became extremely suspicious.

Since the early 1970s, serious attempts at a Canadian accord had been sought for revising the constitution. However, attempts to delineate the scope of federal authority while protecting provincial prerogatives were hampered by a lack of agreement over just what powers should be consigned to the provinces. In 1971, at a meeting in Victoria, British Columbia, Prime Minister Trudeau and the ten provincial premiers reached an apparent accord on a new Canadian constitution. The proposal, known as the Victoria Charter, would have entrenched[36] certain fundamental rights, such as French and English language rights. It would have entrenched a constitutional commitment to end regional social and economic disparities, and it would have provided a method for amending the Constitution without any involvement of the British Parliament. The Victoria Charter was to have been approved by each province, but, although accepted by the majority, its enactment became impossible when Quebec rejected it because it did not provide assurance of provincial control over all social policies.

In 1976, Prime Minister Trudeau clearly indicated that his government was determined to revise the constitution, and, in a letter to the provincial premiers, he made proposals based on the Victoria Charter. In this letter, Trudeau maintained that the federal government was determined to achieve revision, even if revision required a unilateral action by the federal government. Following the angry responses of the provincial premiers in October 1976, Trudeau dropped this threat of unilateral action.

In 1978, Prime Minister Trudeau presented to the federal parliament a twenty-five page document entitled *A Time for Action: The Renewal of the Canadian Federation.* In it he proposed a two-phase program for constitutional changes. Phase One would deal with matters which the federal government could change unilaterally; Phase Two would deal with matters which required provincial consent. The proposed changes included incorporating a Charter of Human Rights, giving the provinces a say in the appointment of Justices to the Supreme Court, and establishing a new upper House to replace the existing Senate which was appointed and not elected. Trudeau made little headway with his *Time for Action* project.

In 1961, a Canadian Bill of Rights was passed by the federal parliament which declared that there existed, and had always existed in Canada, certain basic rights. Nevertheless, the Act permitted the federal parliament to pass legislation in violation of these basic rights. For instance, the Act was subject to repeal by an ordinary act of the federal parliament. Moreover, the Bill of Rights was applicable only to the legislation enacted by the federal parliament, and did not affect legislation which was within the jurisdiction of the provincial legislatures.

Finally, in November of 1981, the historic constitutional stalemate was broken. After months of hard bargaining, Prime Minister Trudeau and nine of the ten provincial premiers agreed to a package of constitutional revisions that the Canadian Supreme Court ruled was legal. These revisions paved the way for the federal parliament to request the repatriation of the Canadian constitution from Britain. Quebec was the only dissenter.

Premier Lévesque disagreed so strongly with the terms of the proposed new constitution that he ordered flags in Quebec lowered to half-staff as a symbol of protest. Once again he threatened to pursue Quebec's independence from the rest of Canada. However, by now, the Parti Québécois had lost the referendum vote in May 1980; therefore, Quebec's threat to block repatriation with its customary veto was considerably weakened. Furthermore, the Canadian Supreme Court, in September 1981, handed down the decision that *as a matter of law* the federal government did not require the approval of all ten provincial governments for constitutional amendments, but "as a matter of constitutional convention and tradition" an unspecified number of those governments should agree to any constitutional changes.[37]

Based upon this Supreme Court decision, which eliminated the need for unanimity, the Canadian Parliament requested the British Parliament to transfer the British North America Act of 1867 to Canada.

> Britain will be asked to include a bill of rights guaranteeing basic freedoms and parliamentary government as well as an amending procedure that requires the assent of the federal Parliament and the legislatures of seven provinces.[38]

Nonetheless, the Lévesque government was opposed to a proposal in the new constitution which would allow all Canadians the right to live and work anywhere they wished in Canada. The Lévesque government argued that such a proposal would handicap job preference programs any province might have for its own people. However, the main bone of contention between the Lévesque government and the federal government was language rights. The Lévesque government objected to provisions in the proposed Bill of Rights which would guarantee to the English-speaking minority in Quebec and to the French-speaking minority in other provinces the right to educate their children in their own language. The Lévesque government argued that jurisdiction over this right belonged to the provincial governments. Furthermore, Lévesque insisted that only in New Brunswick, where French Canadians made up about one-third of the population, did a substantial French-speaking population exist outside Quebec.[39] Therefore, the Lévesque government argued that the rate of assimilation of French speakers outside Quebec was so high that the proposed Bill of Rights would, in fact, be protecting a vanishing breed of French Canadians, while weakening the defenses of Canada's only province which was home to most French Canadians.

In 1978, the Lévesque government had placed on the statute books *Public Law 101*, which barred English speakers, including Canadians from outside Quebec Province, from sending their children to English language schools in Quebec Province at public expense, except under special circumstances. At the time, the ethnic composition of Quebec Province was 79% French-speaking, 11% English-speaking, 87% Catholic, and 6% Protestant. The English-speaking population was concentrated in the Montreal area, and it had a large network of publicly supported primary, secondary, and post-secondary schools. Quebec's *Public Law 101*, while generally asserting the primacy of the French language, did provide for continuance of publicly supported English language schools. However, *Public Law 101* restricted entry into those schools to children whose parents had been educated in English *in* Quebec Province. The provision in the proposed Bill of Rights would impose on Quebec Province the obligation to admit into the English schools the children of all citizens educated in English anywhere in Canada, and not just in Quebec Province. The practical effect might be to increase to an unforeseen degree the English language school population in Quebec Province, but the main point of dispute was one of principle. The law would breach Quebec's previously exclusive right to legislate on educational and cultural matters. In fact, however, that exclusive right had already been struck a grievous blow on December 21,

1979, when the Canadian Supreme Court declared Quebec's *Public Law 101* unconstitutional.

The new constitution does concede that Quebec must only admit children to English language schools, if their parents were educated in English in primary schools in Canada. Parents whose mother tongue is English, but whose primary school education was received in another country, say Britain or the United States, would have to send their children to French language schools.

Another stipulation of Quebec's *Public Law 101*, whose official name was Charter of the French Language, mandated the use of French as the everyday language of business in the province. For instance, *Public Law 101* outlawed the posting of signs *outside* business establishments in any language other than French. The only concession the statute made, which pleased no one, permitted *inside* signs to appear in both French and another language, provided that French was given the place of prominence.

Ten years after the Canadian Supreme Court found Quebec's *Public Law 101* unconstitutional, that Court, in a unanimous decision, also struck down the sign law saying that it violated the guarantees of freedom of expression and nondiscrimination, found in the Canadian Bill of Rights. Nevertheless, within days of the Court's unanimous decision, the provincial government of Quebec outraged civil rights advocates by reimposing the sign law. It did so by invoking, as its mandate, a clause in the federal Charter of Rights and Freedom that allowed a province, under special circumstances, to supersede the federal Bill of Rights guarantees.

This kind of chicanery non-French-speaking Canadians fear, if Quebec Province is allowed an entrenched special status in the country's constitution as a *distinct society* owing to its status as the Federation's only predominantly French-speaking province and its system of civil laws. In and out of Quebec Province, civil rights advocates fear abuse of this special status to the detriment of non-French-speaking Canadians. For example, Noel Alexander, President of the Jamaican Association of Montreal, which represents 20,000 Jamaicans, was quoted in an interview as saying that in Quebec Province the right of new immigrants to earn a living was limited by the requirement that "even for menial jobs, people have to know the French language."[40] Nevertheless, in 1991, Ludmila de Fougerolles, a refugee from Czechoslovakia who has lived in Canada for decades, had for four years been President of the Commission for the Protection of the French Language, the province's top cop for enforcing the sign law. Ironically Mrs. de Fougerolles had two sons who were pursuing graduate university degrees, one in international relations and the other in immunology, both in English-speaking America.

Of the sign law, Julius Grey, an immigrant from Poland and a civil rights lawyer in Montreal, was quoted as saying, "The sign law is really just an illustration of the pettiness of nationalism."[41]

On April 17, 1982, Queen Elizabeth II of Britain proclaimed a new Canadian constitution, the Canada Act, which had been drafted in Ottawa, approved by the British Parliament and by nine of the ten provincial governments, and signed by the Queen. However, on that historic day, René Lévesque again condemned the new constitution and led 12,000 demonstrators through the streets of Montreal as a sign of protest.

Canada adopted federalism as a solution to its ethnic pluralism, but resistance to the expansion of the federal government's powers remains in Quebec and the western provinces. French Canadians have agitated for years for greater autonomy, indeed, for independence, but additional objections to increased centralization of power have been made by other provincial governments, which jealously guard their extensive constitutional and customary authority due to regional, not ethnic, concerns. For instance, one saying in British Columbia is that Ottawa is 3,000 miles away on the map, but 30,000 miles away in people's minds.

In many discussions of Canadian federalism, regionalism does not get its just due. While Quebec governments have been sensitive to French-speaking communalism, other provincial administrations have been sensitive to economic regionalism. For instance, in 1971, during the talks surrounding the Victoria Charter, a marked similarity existed between the position of the ethnically minded Premier of Quebec and that of his economically minded western colleagues over the expansion of federal powers. Most premiers, however, dismissed the language issue as of secondary importance to the issues of resources and revenues. As one premier put it: *What are we doing discussing the Constitution? That's not the issue. Economic problems are the issue.*

Canada's problems of internal political integration cannot be laid solely at the door of ethnicity. Indeed, the regional preoccupation of most premiers has heightened their disenchantment with both French and English ethnic problems. Canadians in the west, many of whom are descendants of immigrants who came neither from France nor Britain, simply do not care about the French-English communal controversy. Their reaction to the French Canadians' threat to secede is to say, *Let them go.* Nonetheless, regional preoccupations have combined with Quebec separatism to hinder the concentration and the efficiency of a federal government struggling with inflation, unemployment, and a deflated currency, while at the same time burdened with persistent planning and service obligations.

In December 1985, by the time of provincial elections, which resulted in the defeat of the Parti Québécois, Prime Minister Trudeau and Premier Lévesque, the protagonist and antagonist of the political drama that had consumed the attention of Canadians for three decades, had both departed the political arena. On February 29, 1984, Trudeau, in a surprisingly simple, hand-written letter to the President of the Liberal Party, announced that after fifteen years he was resigning as leader of the Party and head of the government. It was, he said, "the appropriate time for someone else to assume this challenge."[42] Then, on June 20, 1985, in an equally stunning *coup de théatre*, Lévesque announced his resignation as leader of the Parti Québécois and Premier of Quebec. These two Canadians of French ancestry had been the major combatants in one of the most thrilling and enthralling demonstrations of participatory democracy in action in the twentieth century. As a consequence, at their departure from the political arena, Canada possessed a greater sense of political integration than at any time in its political history, and to those two consummate actors and dynamic politicians went much of the credit for this phenomenal accomplishment.

However, in the drama that is Canadian ethnic politics, the French Canadian issue, that had seemed resolved in the 1980s, resurfaced in the 1990s. Moreover, an issue, that had lain dormant if not ignored for most of the twentieth century, burst like a meteorite in the late 1960s and exploded with violence in the 1990s in, of all places, Quebec Province.[43]

At issue was, "What to do about the First Nations": the indigenous Indians and Eskimos of Canada.[44]

To a society that had seemed to be all white, at the beginning of the Second World War, the new immigrants of color, who were added to the ethnic equation in the decades following the Second World War, brought with them unaccustomed ethnic diversity and, concomitantly, racial tension. While Canada becomes a multi-ethnic society at a staggering pace, there is no guarantee that Canadians will handle the situation any better than their American neighbors, as "a growing number of Canadians have had it with foreigners [i.e., immigrants] and their problems."[45] Many Canadians are discovering a kind of racism, among themselves, that they believed only existed among their white neighbors south of their immediate border. Some Canadians are of the opinion that the reason for this absence of racism, in previous years, was the white Canadians' lack of contact with non-white peoples. Actually, Canada has always had a racial secret: one which involved its indigenous Indians and Eskimos, both of whom had been excluded from the mainstream of Canada's political, economic, and social life as well as being geographically segregated and isolated and were, therefore, virtually *invisible*.

Before contact with European settlers, the Indians pursued a life of hunting, fishing, and basic agriculture for their sustenance and livelihood. However, European immigration destroyed Indian self-sufficiency and consigned most of them to reservations, where the government referred to them as *bands*, where they became *invisible* and where they became dependent for their survival on handouts from government agencies and private charities. Nevertheless, before the taming of the Canadian wilderness, Indian guides and trappers played an indispensable role in the transformation of Canada's open lands into settler closed lands suitable for European habitation:

> The Hudson's Bay Company was not interested in encouraging colonization . . . because of the resultant displacement of the fur-bearing animals so necessary to the economy of the Company. For their part, the Indians resented the establishment of a colony for they feared the loss of their territories. Nevertheless, settlers did arrive.[46]

In 1980, the Canadian Ministry of Indian and Northern Affairs reported wide disparities between Indian and white societies, despite improvements in social, economic, and political conditions over the previous 20 years for the country's approximate 300,000 Indians.[47] The Ministry's Survey noted that Indian housing and community services were better in 1980 than they had been in 1960, but that their life expectancy, a reflection of health standards, was still 10 years less than that of the national population. According to the Survey, violent deaths among Indians were three times the national level, and suicides, particularly in the 15- to 24-year-old age group, were more than six times the national rate.

The Survey noted that the strength and stability of the Indian family seemed to be eroding with higher divorce rates, more births outside marriage, and more children turned over to outside care. In 1964, the Survey reported that 36% of the Indian population received social assistance, but, by 1978, the figure was between 50% and 70%. The Survey said that levels of education, job accessibility, cash in Indian hands, and Indian acceptance into the mainstream of the country's economic life were higher in 1980 than 20 years earlier, but the proportion of Indians of high school age in school was 12% below the national level, and only 32% of the working-age Indian population had jobs.

The Survey stated that the proportion of Indians living off reservations increased from 16% in 1966 to 30% in 1979, with job-seeking young adults making up the majority of those leaving the reservation, while women, the old, and the infirm were left on the reservations to rear children. Moreover, Indians living off the reservations experienced rates of unemployment and welfare dependence of between 25% and 30%. The Survey noted that the greatest concentration of young Indian adults trying to live in white societies were found in the poor sections of Winnipeg, Manitoba, but they could also be seen wandering through the skid row sections of Vancouver, British Columbia.

The Canadian government's 1980 survey stated that the relations between the Indians and the federal government had improved and that Indians had assumed greater responsibility for their own affairs. While acknowledging that some improvements had been made, the *National Indian Brotherhood* insisted that Indian rights, including the right to an autonomous Indian state, should be included in the federal constitution then under discussion for revision. Much of that constitutional debate centered on the question of equity between the two so-called founding people, the French- and English-speaking Canadians. Indians complained that such a debate ignored their rights as people living in Canada long before the arrival of French- and English-speaking settlers.

The 1980 Report pointed out that federal expenditures for Indians increased by 14% per capita during the 1970s. However, other social programs for the entire country during the same period increased by 128%. In 1980, the budget of the Federal Ministry of Indian Affairs amounted to slightly more than $700 million, but the National Indian Brotherhood, complaining that too much went for administration and too little went directly to the Indians, said, "Give the Indians the money and see what they can do with it."[48]

Government propaganda in the past had been that Indian exclusion from the mainstream of Canadian life was mainly the result of indigenous people choosing to segregate themselves either in isolated areas or on reservations where they received certain tax and welfare benefits. What this propaganda failed to explain was why Indians became increasingly dependent upon the largesse of European settlers, their missionaries, and their governments as European colonization spread from the Atlantic to the Pacific.

Then, in the 1970s, these indigenous peoples began making land claims involving huge, rich regions in Canada's northern wilderness. For instance, in October of 1976,

Leaders of the 7,000 Indians of the Northwest Territories filed a formal demand with the Government today for ownership rights and separate jurisdiction over 450,000 square miles of the federally administered area. . . . The Indians asked that the area of their claim be placed under the jurisdiction of a new political entity, equivalent to a province, to be known as the Dene nation. *Dene, an Indian word meaning the people*, was adopted as the name of the proposed province by the Indian Brotherhood of the Northwest Territories.[49]

Earlier, in December of 1975, two Indian groups, totaling 10,500 people, spread over vast regions of Northern Quebec, won hunting, trapping, and fishing rights as well as a financial settlement of $225 million.[50]

Two decades later, in the summer of 1990, Indian legal claims and petitions turned to Indian aggressive demands—backed by assault rifles, handguns, and gas masks—for lands their ancestors occupied before they and their descendants were consigned to 2,230 reserves in the backwaters of Canada.

On June 23, 1990, a federal government plan, that would have constitutionally entrenched a special status for Quebec Province, was rejected by two of the ten provincial governments, when a unanimous acceptance by all ten provincial governments was required, if the plan was to be accepted.[51] Within a few weeks of that devastating decision, two events occurred which shocked white Canadians, especially Quebecers, who had been preoccupied with the French-English controversy, and which brought the issue of "What to do about the First Nations' to the forefront of the Canadian political agenda. First, in early July of 1990, armed Mohawk Indians confronted the provincial Quebec police and the federal Royal Mounted police in a showdown at Oka in Quebec Province over the Mohawks insistence that the extension of nine-hole golf course be stopped and that the title to the 55 acres of land, which they claimed covered a sacred Mohawk burial ground, be turned over to the Mohawks.[52] The standoff lasted for 77 days, and, in the course of the violent confrontation, on July 11, 1990, a policeman was killed. Then, within days of the Oka showdown, Mohawk Indians, armed as if for war in camouflaged uniforms, bandannas covering their faces, and assault rifles in their arms, blocked one of Canada's most crucial transport arteries, the Mercier Bridge across the St. Lawrence River with Montreal, the heart of Quebec Province. The Mohawk showdown at the Mercier Bridge brought out more federal and provincial police, as well as the national army, and put the Canadian people on notice that Indians would no longer wait patiently, with claims and petitions, for federal and provincial governments to deal speedily and judiciously with their grievances.

The enormous significance is that these two showdowns took place *in* Quebec Province, where French Canadians had been clamoring for decades for recognition of their special status but had consistently ignored the rights of the *First Nations*, the indigenous Indians. Now, on their own front door step, the indigenous peoples of Canada were putting the French Canadians' feet to the fire for the recognition of their special status. The irony of events was lost on no one.

The first provincial government to react to the events of July 1990 was the government in Ontario, the country's most populous province and the seat of the federal government in Ottawa. On August 6, 1991, the Ontario provincial government formally recognized the inherent right of Indians in that province to self-government, a recognition that had long been sought by Indian leaders. Governments in Quebec and the Western provinces were not so quick to follow Ontario's lead, for they were deeply concerned about making such a broad political statement as to their Indians right to self-government. The impetus for this concern centered around the resources, above and below the ground, that lay in their provinces, and the development of those resources, in other words the economic consequences of such an admission. Finally, the federal government, in a package that, among other objectives, was intended to assuage the ethnic aspirations of both the French Canadians and the indigenous Indians, in September 1991, proposed a plan that would recognize Quebec's special status and would grant self-government, within ten years, to Canada's indigenous peoples, Eskimos as well as Indians.[53] The issue now, however, was what did self-government mean, in fact, and who would pay for the experiment, if and when it came to fruition.[54]

Other questions continue to vex the Canadian federal and provincial governments as well as the Canadian people themselves. For instance, in response to the Ontario government's pronouncement that Indians in that province had an inherent right to self-government, Gordon Peters, the Ontario regional chief of the Assembly of First Nations stated that Indians had to be given full control and complete ownership of their own lands and the resources above and below those lands in order for them to become self-sufficient. Another vexing issue revolves around the status of two categories of Indians: the 512,000 so-called *status* Indians who live on reservations and, therefore, have land rights, and the 500,000 Indians of mixed blood, who are referred to as Métis and live off the reservations most of them in the slum regions of urban areas in dire poverty and who have no land rights and are, therefore, referred to as *non-status* Indians. The question is: how are these two categories of Indians to be accommodated in a self-government scheme?

Unlike the Indians in the 1970s, Canada's Eskimos rejected any outright financial settlement but rather claimed ownership of 250,000 square miles of northern Canada, special rights in 500,000 square miles of additional land, as well as 800,000 square miles of the ocean. The Inuit claimed that the entire land area, comprising more than one-fifth of Canada's land mass, should be separated from the federally administered Yukon and Northwest Territories. The eventual aim of the Inuit was to establish an autonomous province called Nunavut, meaning *our land*. This, however, raised another dilemma, how to accommodate two categories of Eskimos: the Inuit, the 17,500 majority, who live in the East, and the Inuvialuit, a much smaller minority of about 1,500 who live in the Western Arctic of Canada's vast northern wilderness.[55] In December of 1991, the federal government took steps to resolve this dilemma by granting to the Inuit "political domain over 770,000 square miles [and] a cash settlement from the Canadian Government that will be paid over 14 years and amount with interest to more than $1 billion."[56] At the time, no decision, however, was made with regards to the Inuvialuit in the western Arctic.

Thus, as the Indians and Inuit became more visible and aggressive in the Canadian political arena, and their demands accommodated, the issue of Quebec's *sovereignty* refused to disappear. The problem Canada faced was this: if ethnic groups within the federation expressed their ethnic pride by demanding self-determination, i.e., greater autonomy, then the state's political sovereignty was not only compromised, but its political integration jeopardized.

In 1985, with the departure of Prime Minister Trudeau and Premier Lévesque from the political scene, most Canadians believed that they had received a respite from the toils of French Canadian controversy. In 1987, and adding to this optimism, the federal government believed that it had arrived at a final solution with something called the Meech Lake Accord.[57] By this agreement,

The *preamble* to the Accord reflects the intention of the Meech Lake agreement: that is, to bring about Quebec's full and active participation in Canada's constitutional evolution, to foster greater harmony among governments through new arrangements, and to hold annual constitutional conferences, the first of which must be held before the end of 1988.[58]

The primary purpose of the meeting at Meech Lake was for the federal and provincial governments to come to some kind of agreement that would bring Quebec Province back into the political fold, for the Quebec government, under Premier Lévesque, had neither agreed to the repatriation of the BNA of 1867 nor signed the constitutional accord of November 5, 1981, which had sanctioned the repatriation and established the Canada Act of 1982. The solution of the Meech Lake Accord was, "The recognition that Quebec constitutes within Canada a distinct society."[59] To this the federal Prime Minister and the provincial premier unanimously agreed. At the eleventh hour, however, two provincial legislatures reneged on the agreement: "Manitoba and Newfoundland torpedoed a constitutional accord that would have made Quebec a *distinct society* within the Canadian union."[60] Predictably, the Quebec separatists shouted angrily of once again being humiliated by the English Canadians. The separatists' solution was to have the Quebec provincial legislature pass a law, in the summer of 1991, that called for a provincial referendum no later than October 26, 1992, on whether Quebec would remain part of the federation or would become a sovereign, independent state—"if the rest of Canada fails to come up with satisfactory proposals to keep Quebec within the federation."[61]

The federal Prime Minister, Brian Mulroney, in an attempt to preempt Quebec's October 1992 deadline, sought to mobilize support for "new constitutional provisions aimed at appeasing Quebec while addressing a list of demands from other provinces and special groups."[62]

Specifically, Mr. Mulroney offered Quebec more power in such areas as immigration and the financing for cultural institutions as well as recognition of its special status as a distinct society within the Canadian Federation because of its French language and its civil code of laws.[63]

Moreover, "For balance, he offered western Canada greater influence in Parliament, including an elected senate: members of Canada's upper house are now appointed to serve until they reach the age of 75, and have little power."[64]

The conditions surrounding Quebec's proposed October 1992 referendum were similar, in one very important respect, with the conditions that existed at the time of the 1980 referendum, when, by a ratio of 3 to 2, the Quebec electorate rejected that proposal: the province's economic uncertainty. In 1980, Quebecers were unsure of their economic future outside the Canadian union, while, in 1992, "Quebec is experiencing its worst economic downturn since the 1930s."[65] In 1992, the prolonged economic recession in Canada had affected Quebec Province more severely than any of the other provinces, "with more than a million Quebecers now on welfare rolls," out of the province's population of 7 million people.[66] Thus, "Support for a break with Canada has shown signs of slipping from the levels it attracted in the last year and a half. A poll in December by Angus Reid Associates in Winnipeg showed that Quebecers were evenly split, with 46 percent for accepting a new deal with Canada and 45 percent for independence."[67]

One significant difference existed, however, between the conditions in 1980 and those in 1992: leadership. In 1980, the Premier of Quebec was René Lévesque, who was also the head of the Parti Québécois, which held the majority of seats in the provincial legislature. In 1992, however, the Premier of Quebec was Robert Bourassa, whose Liberal Party held the majority of seats in the provincial legislature. In 1980, however, while Lévesque was the leader of the Parté Québécois, in 1992, the leader of the Parté Québécois was Jacques Parizeau.

> While Mr. Lévesque, once a journalist, remained comfortable in the blue-collar taverns of Montreal and Quebec City after he became Premier in 1976, Mr. Parizeau, son of a Montrealer who founded Quebec's largest independent insurance brokerage has held himself aloof. . . . Many who follow Quebec politics say he is a less than ideal advocate for independence when Quebec is [worried] about jobs. "René Lévesque was a populist, he was a kind of sponge, who understood all the moods of the people," said Alain Dubuc, editorial page editor of *La Presse*, Montreal's largest newspaper. "But Parizeau doesn't understand Quebecers. I know lots of Péquistes"—Quebec shorthand for members of the Parté Québécois—"who think independence is doomed because of Parizeau."[68]

What awaits the Canadian Federation political integration or political disintegration? What could be more neutral and anonymous, as a symbol of its union, than the Canadian flag with its single maple leaf?

Notes

1. In 1994, the provinces of Canada were Newfoundland, Nova Scotia, New Brunswick, Prince Edward Island, Quebec, Manitoba, Saskatchewan, Alberta, British Columbia, and Ontario, where Ottawa, the federal capital, was located. Two territories, the Yukon and the Northwest Territories, were under the direct federal administration.

2. Although there are similarities between the disintegration of the British global Empire and the Soviet Union regional Empire and its client states in Eastern Europe, the dissimilarities are so numerous and diverse as to require a separate analysis i.e., a separate book. It would be totally out of character and somewhat disingenuous to join an addendum on the dispersion of the Soviet Union to this present study, where emphasis is on the fragmentation of the British Empire and its legacies.

3. Andrew Malcolm, "Canada Is a Melting Pot for America and the World," *New York Times*, 11 March 1979.

4. Marc Leepson, "Canada, the U.S., and the Third Option," *Daily Hampshire Gazette*, Northampton, Massachusetts, 8 November 1976.

5. The Report of the Canadian Senate's Standing Committee on Foreign Affairs, *Canada-United States Relations: The Institutional Framework for the Relationship* (Ottawa, December 1975), 2, 7.

6. Karl Deutsch, "The Growth of Nations: Some Recurrent Patterns of Political and Social Integration," *World Politics*, January 1953; and *Politics and Government: How People Decide Their Fate* (Boston: Houghton Mifflin, 1970).

7. Karl Deutsch and William Foltz, editors, *Nation-Building* (New York: Atherton Press, 1966).

8. Mary Walsh, "Charges of Prejudice Rattle Canadians," *Los Angeles Times*, 13 June 1992.

9. William Borders, "A Vein of Bias Exposed in Vancouver by Immigration from India," *New York Times*, 12 April 1975.

10. William Borders, "Racial Trend in Immigration Troubling Canadians," *New York Times*, 25 November 1974.

11. Walsh, *Los Angeles Times*, 13 June 1992.

12. William Borders, "Deportation Plan Rouses Canadians," *New York Times*, 29 October 1974.

13. Robert Trumbull, "Canada Tightens Rules Covering Immigrant Flow," *New York Times*, 23 October 1974.

14. Walsh, *Los Angeles Times*, 13 June 1992. Italicized by the author for emphasis.

15. Quebec is the Algonquin Indian word meaning "where the rivers narrow."

16. The other three characteristics of a participatory democracy, according to Mayo, are "the popular control of policy makers by means of periodic elections; the political equality of adult voting; and effective choice exercised through the procedural political freedoms." Henry Mayo, *An Introduction to Democratic Theory* (New York: Oxford University Press, 1960), 166.

17. A similar phenomenon occurred in Northern Ireland and South Africa with those attached to industrialization and the British economic system in a more advantageous position to profit from the capitalist economic system than those who were attached to the land and subsistence agriculture, i.e., Irish Catholics and Dutch-speaking South Africans, the Boers.

18. René Lévesque as quoted by Gustav Morf, "The Case of Quebec," in *Ethnicity in an International Context*, eds. Abdul

Said and Luis Simmons (New Brunswick, N.J.: Transaction Book, 1979), 88.

19. The 19th-century history of Manitoba is saturated with the memory of Louis Riel, a métis—part Indian and part French—who led a rebellion in 1869 and another in 1885 for a self-governing province which would guarantee the cultural and civil rights of the métis. He was hanged in 1885 but remains one of the romantic heroes in French Canadian folklore.

20. In June 1985, the Canadian Supreme Court, by unanimous decision, declared, "all laws established by the province of Manitoba in English since 1890 were invalid because they had not been enacted in French as well. To avoid chaos in the province's offices and courts, the Supreme Court ruled that the laws would be *temporarily valid* for the minimum time needed to translate and enact them into French. But it warned that new laws would have no force if they were not bilingual." Christopher Wren, "Canada Supreme Court Rules Solely English Laws Invalid," *New York Times*, 14 June 1985.

21. William Stockton, "René Lévesque and the Divided House of Canada," *New York Times*, 20 May 1979.

22. René Lévesque, "For an Independent Quebec," *Foreign Affairs*, 54:4 (July 1976), 734-744.

23. *New York Times*, 21 May 1980.

24. Editorial, "Quebec Votes for Canada," *New York Times*, 22 May 1980.

25. By the end of 1984, seven provincial cabinet ministers had resigned over the demotion of the separation issue. The two most important ones were Jacques Parizeau and Camille Laurin. Jacques Parizeau "was responsible for much of the Parti Québécois' economic thinking and planning and is praised for giving the Lévesque government a reputation for efficiency, competence and honesty." Camille Laurin "was the

architect of the province's famous Bill #101, which entrenched French as the official language of business and education. . . . Both men were known for being firmly for independence . . . so their resignations were shocking . . . and dramatized the split." Kenneth Freed, "Dream of Independence Fades for Quebec Residents, Leader," *Los Angeles Times*, 21 December 1984.

26. Christopher Wren, "Quebecers Seem Interested in Success, Not Secession," *New York Times*, 27 January 1985.

27. Robert Bourassa, leader of the provincial Liberal Party, said, "Independence is an obsolete concept, an idea of the 1950's." Douglas Martin, "Quebec Independence: The Vision Has Faded," *New York Times*, 26 January 1984.

28. *Daily Hampshire Gazette*, 21 May 1980.

29. Andrew Malcolm, "Trudeau Calls for National Healing and Prompt Effort on New Charter," *New York Times*, 22 May 1980.

30. Henry Giniger, "Trudeau Preaches His Own New Federalism," *New York Times*, 1 March 1982.

31. In the case of Nigeria, one of the primary causes of the Biafran Civil War (1967-1970) was a similar struggle between the central government and a regional authority over the control of an indigenous natural resource, i.e., off-shore oil in Eastern Nigeria.

32. William Borders, "Oil, the Big Issue in Alberta Voting," *New York Times*, 14 March 1975.

33. Many sources refer to the process as *patriate* or *patriation*, as the BNA had never been a Canadian document.

34. Smith Hempstone, "Canadian West Gaining Attention—At Last," *Daily Hampshire Gazette*, 30 September 1977.

35. In 1981, Quebec had a population of approximately 6,438,000 and Ontario 8,625,000 for a combined total of over 15 million. At the time, Canada's total population was just under 24½ million. In a participatory democracy, numbers are the key to power, for they determine who gets what portion of the political and economic pie.

36. Entrenchment here means that something is fixed firmly in place and can only be changed or removed under very specific and extraordinary circumstances. The term becomes of major significance in the chapter on South Africa and non-white voting rights in the Cape Province.

37. Andrew Malcolm, "Pleasing Both Sides, Court Just Sharpens Canada Crisis," *New York Times*, 4 October 1981.

38. Henry Giniger, "Canadian Leaders Agree on Charter; Quebec Is Opposed," *New York Times*, 6 November 1981.

39. Other than Quebec, New Brunswick was the only province where French was an official language, although it was an official language, along with English, for federal government organizations and institutions.

40. Clyde Farnsworth, "Ottawa Plan Gets Wary Responses," *New York Times*, 29 September 1991.

41. Clyde Farnsworth, "In a Language Minefield, Enforcer Treads Softly," *New York Times*, 9 October 1991.

42. *New York Times*, 1 March 1984.

43. Andrew Malcolm, "Language Again Threatening to Split Canadian Federation," *New York Times*, 24 March 1990.

44. "Drumbeats of Rage: Native Canadians Prepare for a Showdown on Self-Government," *Maclean's Newsmagazine*, 16 March 1992.

45. Mary Walsh, "A Lamp to the Nations Flickers," *Los Angeles Times*, 18 June 1992.

46. Canadian Department of Indian Affairs and Northern Development, *Indians of British Columbia: An Historical Review* (Ottawa: Queen's Printer, March 1967), 4.

47. Canadian Ministry of Indian and Northern Affairs, *A Survey of Indian Conditions* (Ottawa: Queen's Printer, June 1980). The statistics which follow are taken from this survey.

48. Henry Giniger, "Canada Says Gap Persists Between Indians and Whites," *New York Times*, 29 June 1980.

49. "Indians Ask Canada for a Province," *New York Times*, 26 October 1976. Italicized by the author for emphasis.

50. David Vidal, "Canadian Tribes Drop Land Claims," *New York Times*, 7 December 1975.

51. Both Manitoba and Newfoundland rejected the Meech Lake Accord, and both had definite reasons for doing so. In the case of Manitoba, Elijah Harper, a 41-year-old Cree Indian, blocked the introduction of the resolution that would have approved the Meech Lake Accord. Elijah Harper was outraged that federal and provincial governments had consistently ignored Indian demands for formal recognition of their distinctiveness as the original inhabitants of Canada but were now prepared to accept the distinctiveness of the descendants of French Canadian settlers. Eventually, the Manitoba legislature rejected the accord. In Newfoundland, which by the smallest of margins had only joined the Canadian union in 1949, the Premier, Clyde Wells, the legislature, and the people recited a litany of abuses to which the province and its people had been subjected by Ottawa and by Quebec. Newfoundland was only too happy to scuttle the Meech Lake Accord. John Burns, "With Canada's Future in Question, Newfoundland Ponders a Vital Vote," *New York Times*, 18 June 1990.

52. John Burns, "Fury Rising in Quebec over Mohawk Standoff," *New York Times*, 22 July 1990.

53. Clyde Farnsworth, "Mulroney Proposes New Canadian Framework to Stall Separation," *New York Times*, 25 September 1991.

54. Mary Walsh, "Proposals for Canadian Unity Prove Divisive," *Los Angeles Times*, 27 June 1992.

55. The term Eskimo is an Indian word meaning *eater of raw flesh*.

56. John Burns, "Accord to Give the Eskimos Control of a Fifth of Canada," *New York Times*, 17 December 1991.

57. The Accord was signed by the First Ministers of all ten provinces, including Quebec, as well as Brian Mulroney, the federal Prime Minister. Office of the Canadian Prime Minster, "Meeting of First Ministers on the Constitution: 1987 Constitution Accord," 3 June 1987.

58. Ibid., "A Guide to the Constitutional Accord," 3 June 1987, 3.

59. Ibid., "The 1987 Constitutional Accord," Schedule Section 26, 1.

60. John Burns, "Quebec Isn't Feeling Especially Canadian," *New York Times*, 8 December 1991.

61. Clyde Farnsworth, "Mulroney Proposes New Canadian Framework to Stall Separatism," *New York Times*, 25 September 1991.

62. John Burns, "Quebec Isn't Feeling Especially Canadian," *New York Times*, 8 December 1991.

63. Only Quebec Province has a Civil Code system of laws. The other nine provinces have a common law system of laws. A civil code has its origins in Roman law, as distinguished from

Common law, which originated and was developed in England. Common law is based on Court decisions, on the doctrines implicit in those decisions, and on customs and usage rather than on codified written laws.

64. "A Canada Now Beyond Secessionism?" *New York Times*, 24 February 1992.

65. John Burns, "A Sovereign Quebec, He Says, Needn't Be Séparé," *New York Times*, 21 February 1992.

66. John Burns, "Quebec Isn't Feeling Especially Canadian," *New York Times*, 8 December 1991.

67. John Burns, "A Sovereign Quebec, He Says, Needn't Be Séparé," *New York Times*, 21 February 1992.

68. Ibid.

Malaysia
in Southeast Asia

CHINA

TAIWAN

HONG KONG

BURMA

NORTH
VIETNAM

LAOS

PHILIPPINES

THAILAND

CAMBODIA

SOUTH
VIETNAM

MALAYSIA

SABAH

MALAYA

BRUNEI

•Kuala Lumpur

SARAWAK

SINGAPORE

SUMATRA

BORNEO

CELEBES

JAVA

Chapter Five
Malaysia: The Consociational Experience

The races never get along. In America, blacks and whites at least speak the same language, wear the same clothes, eat the same food, and often go to the same church. The Chinese and Malays haven't any such common ground. To the Chinese, the Malays are indolent and incompetent. To the Malays, the Chinese are ruthless and unprincipled. Racial remarks roll off the tongue in Kuala Lumpur as readily as they did in America's Deep South in the 1950s.[1]

Thus far, ethnic minorities in developed nations such as Switzerland, Britain, Northern Ireland, and Canada have used tradition, tolerance, and the constitution as guides to ensure their rights and protection in pursuit of what Karl Deutsch has called *Amalgamated Security Communities*. For Deutsch, political integration is a condition or relationship achieved by political communities in which violence is excluded and in which reasonable expectations for reconciliation exist with or without a merger of their political institutions. Deutsch refers to communities that have attained this condition or relationship as *Security Communities*, which he subdivides into two types: *Pluralistic* or *Amalgamated*. Pluralistic Security Communities are those in which few, if any, political institutions have been merged. For example, according to Deutsch, Canada and the United States have been a Pluralistic Security Community since 1819. Amalgamated Security Communities are those in which political institutions have been merged. For example, according to Deutsch, the Swiss Federation has been an Amalgamated Security Community since 1848. For Deutsch, the key factor in these relationships is *mutual trust*, that is, mutual perceptions and expectations, which induce groups to reject violence as a means for reconciling their social and political differences. According to Deutsch, mutual trust and understanding are achieved through a gradual expansion of channels and processes of social communications such as economic transactions, transportation systems, mass media communications, tourism, and even the flow of mail between separate political communities such as between Canada and the United States. Karl Deutsch places great emphasis on the importance of informal social groups and informal citizens' support and activities in the achievement of political integration.[2]

In the Swiss case, the formula of tradition, tolerance, and the constitution was successful.[3] First, because the Swiss Constitution of 1848, and its revisions and amendments in 1874, entrusted to the cantonal governments, rather than to the federal government, the duties, power, and responsibilities for resolving ethnic conflicts and assuaging ethnic pride. Second, the process of cross-cutting pressures was operative and effective at both the cantonal-regional and federal-national levels, as language and religious affiliations overlapped rather than coincided. Thus, economic and political problems had to be resolved on the basis of economic and national self-interest rather than on the basis of ethnic pride and ethnic consciousness. Third, the Swiss tradition of tolerance, which developed over many centuries of different ethnic groups living together, encouraged political cohesion, political integration, and political stability.

In Canada, this formula has not been so successful. Yes, the constitution entrusted the provincial governments with duties, powers, and responsibilities equivalent to those of the Swiss cantons as, *de jure*, the British North America Act of 1867 specified provincial protection of minorities' rights. However, *de facto*, the practices in Canada reneged, that is, revoked those constitutional guarantees. Moreover, the theory of Cross-Cutting Pressures was inoperative and, therefore, ineffective, as ethnic pride and ethnic consciousness of religious and language affiliation exacerbated rather than ameliorated and accommodated primordial attachments. Consequently, intolerance in Canada was endemic and nurtured political disharmony, political disintegration, and political instability. Whatever success existed in 1980 was due to the astute maneuvers of an adroit Prime Minister, Pierre Elliot Trudeau, who was dedicated to preserving the Canadian union, as well as to the Quebecers themselves, who feared for their economic future if they went off on their own and pursued René Lévesque's and the Parti Québécois' fantasy of a sovereign association with the rest of Canada but outside the Federation. As a consequence, Canadians were able to preserve their Federation and enhance their political integration, at least temporarily.

In Northern Ireland, neither the law, the practice, nor the democratic process protected the Irish Catholics and guaranteed their civil rights and liberties. As Britain has no written constitution to serve as a guide, blueprint, or point of reference, ethnic minorities are dependent upon the so-called British *sense of fair play* to attain their rights and guarantee their liberties.

In the next two chapters, we shall observe Malaysia and Nigeria, two developing countries with significant ethnic problems. In both countries, the independence constitutions were intended to ensure political cohesion, political integration, and political stability. However, in both cases, political disharmony, political disintegration, and political instability have been endemic. In the developing world of former British colonial dependencies these countries, against their will, were turned into today's multi-ethnic societies: "In tropical dependencies there was no common social will to set a bar to immigration, which has been left to the play of economic forces. . . . The union is not voluntary but is imposed by the colonial power and by the force of economic circumstances; and the union cannot be dissolved without the whole society relapsing into anarchy."[4]

British imperialism had no preconceived idea or comprehensive plan for the peoples in her colonial dependencies, other than that Britain would rule them until such time when Britain's leaders decided they could rule themselves. In other words, the British believed that they had *endless time* in which to accomplish whatever they were to accomplish in their colonial dependencies, and that they, not the indigenous peoples, would decide when the time was appropriate for any change from the colonial *status quo*, i.e., when the dependencies were *ready* to govern themselves. Regrettably, the medley of indigenous peoples in colonial dependencies were not prepared for self-government either by education or with administrative experience, until the dawn of the Second World War, when Britain desperately needed their raw materials and their manpower to aid her in the immense struggle with the Axis powers not only in Europe but throughout her empire, especially in Asia. "Though in 1939 tensions between the Malays and the Chinese were still potential rather than actual, the moment was clearly not far ahead when a balance would have to be struck between the legitimate aspirations of these two peoples."[5] Thus, in 1957, when Britain granted independence to the Federation of Malaya, she did so not out of a sense of altruism but rather as a response

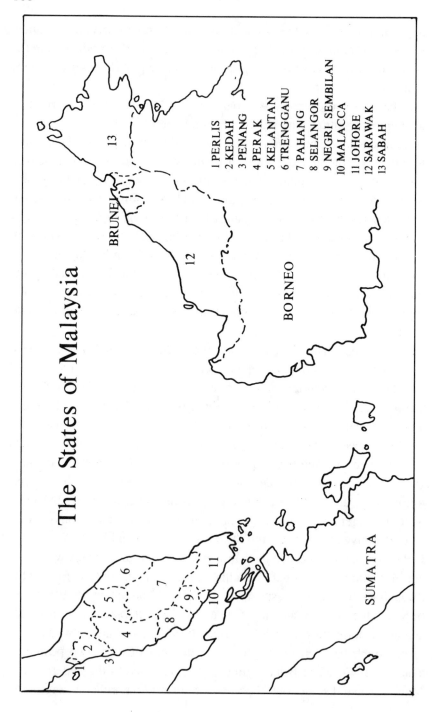

The States of Malaysia

1 PERLIS
2 KEDAH
3 PENANG
4 PERAK
5 KELANTAN
6 TRENGGANU
7 PAHANG
8 SELANGOR
9 NEGRI SEMBILAN
10 MALACCA
11 JOHORE
12 SARAWAK
13 SABAH

BRUNEI

BORNEO

SUMATRA

to expediency, as a kind of *reward* for the efforts and contributions made by the Malays, but especially by the Chinese, in Britain's war with Japan. The new Federation of Malaya contained the states of the Malay peninsula, which, today, are collectively referred to as Western Malaysia. In 1963, the Federation of Malaysia was created which, today, contains the peninsula states as well as Sabah and Sarawak in northern Borneo, which are referred to as Eastern Malaysia. Wedged between Sabah and Sarawak is the tiny oil-rich sultanate of Brunei, which was a British colonial dependency from 1888 until 1984 when it became self-governing. For economic reasons, Brunei chose not to become part of the Federation of Malaysia: "Who would get what share, when, how, of Brunei's huge oil revenues?"[6] Today, the Sultan of Brunei is reputed to be the world's richest man with an annual income, from oil, of at least $20 billion dollars. In 1987, the Sultan was reported to have donated $10 million to the Nicaraguan contras, but the subsequent *misplacement* of those funds generated much interest in the American media.

Until 1965, Singapore was a member of the Federation of Malaysia but was *ejected* from the union by the Federation Government in Kuala Lumpur for *irreconcilable differences* after less than two years of membership. The population of Singapore was 15% Malay and 77% Chinese.

> When the Federation of Malaysia was founded in 1963, more than one million Chinese of Singapore became citizens of the new state. Almost immediately, they sensed the real danger that their culture as well as their economic interest would be submerged in the larger Malay-dominated community.[7]

In 1957, when Malay gained its independence, the country did not *relapse* into anarchy, as Furnivall had predicted, although, during the first decade of self-government, the country's political stability was threatened by two sources—externally from Indonesia and internally from communism. The external threat from Indonesia, which was an aggressive foreign policy directed toward the Federation of Malaya the creation of which the Communist-inspired Sukarno regime considered a front for Western neo-colonialism, ended because Sukarno's rule in Indonesia ended and not because of diplomatic negotiations or military initiatives on the field of battle. The internal threat from communism developed before the Second World War but took on greater significance following the events in China in 1949. This period in Malayan history, often referred to as *the Emergency* and sometimes as *the War*, ended in 1960 after twelve years of guerrilla warfare.

> The British Government declared a State of Emergency. This lasted twelve years and was really a war, but since the insurance policies of the many businesses in Singapore and Malaya contained clauses suspending them in time of war, the Government throughout denied that a war was in progress. It was always *the Emergency*.[8]

The internal crisis was resolved by strategic initiatives, especially the relocation of Chinese living in Malaya under what was called the Briggs Plan: "Squatters were all to be moved into *new villages* where they could be supervised by the police and thus prevented from helping the CTs [Communist terrorists]. It was an ambitious policy that would eventually require shifting half a million people."[9] On the field of battle, Britain transferred units of its supernumerary armed forces from Palestine, as the state of Israel came into existence in 1948, to meet *the Emergency* in Malaya.

In Malaysia, the most conspicuous characteristic of its multiethnic society has been ethnic cleavage which predetermines economic roles and political allegiances. That is, the Malays, the Chinese, and the much smaller Indian community are separated by primordial attachments such as race, religion, language, and culture as well as by education, income, occupation, areas of residence, styles of living, and values of life. As each of these ethnic and social demarcations has been cumulative, ethnic fragmentation has been reinforced rather than reconciled. *Trust* is absent, and the process of *cross-cutting pressures* is non-existent.

In 1955, two years before Malaya's independence, perfidious Albion, with unctuous certainty that Britain had in no way been involved in the dichotomization of these two peoples, said of the Malays,

> Easy-going, valuing their leisure above price, they have left to others the monotonous wage-earning in tin mines and on rubber estates. The Malay prefers independence, and though liking the security of government employment, he has, in general,

remained, as his fathers were before him, a fisherman or a small farmer, tending his rice, coconuts, and vegetables, and earning a little extra by tapping his own rubber trees. . . . He has no canny sense of the value of money and too easily gets himself hopelessly in debt to money lenders. He has a reputation for indolence. . . . The Malay has been called *Nature's gentleman.*[10]

Of the Chinese, the British said,

The Chinese is well equipped to become a colonist. He is enterprising, ingenious, shrewd, economical, and not afraid of hard work. But he is no missionary; he is not interested in exploration for its own sake, or concerned with the progress or welfare of the people in the lands he travels to. His object is to make money, and to that end he will trek far into the jungle, live cheerfully in the poorest conditions, and work tirelessly for very long hours.[11]

The original inhabitants of Malaya are, today, found in the mountains and rain forests of the Malay peninsula, where, over the centuries, they were driven there by invaders from Sumatra in Indonesia.[12] In the main, when one speaks of the Malay people—the *Bumiputra*, sons of the soil—one is referring to the descendants of these invaders from Sumatra. In other words, these people are no more indigenous to Malaysia than the majority of Americans are indigenous to North America. Nevertheless, these invaders spoke a common language, professed a common religion, and adhered to a common culture. Left to themselves, they might have developed a homogeneous, agricultural society with a small minority of indigenous peoples living in the mountains and rain forests. But they were not left to themselves: first came the Portuguese, the sixteenth century's version of astronauts; then came the Dutch, and finally came the British, the nineteenth century's version of Roman conquerors.

The European powers—the Portuguese in the sixteenth century, most strikingly the Dutch in the seventeenth century, and the English after the mid-eighteenth century—were able to exploit the vulnerabilities of the individual Malay politics and to disturb the system of which they formed a part. . . . In particular, it can be argued that the European presence, increasingly superior in arms and relying especially on the exaction of commercial treaties from weaker powers, the compulsory stapling of trade in its own entrepôts, and the detachment of vassals and dependencies, contributed to the decay of the larger political units in the Malay world and to their fragmentation either into weaker states or into squabbling bands of marauders. The loss of commerce and revenue to the ruler and chiefs of a riverine Malay state produced a corresponding diminution or loss of political control—either inside the *negeri* or between it and its dependencies.[13]

What brought the British to Malaya was their quest for adventure and their entrepreneurial desire to develop and exploit Malay's tin, tea, and rubber resources.[14] This thirst for adventure also induced the British to venture into Sabah and Sarawak as developers of Northern Borneo. But the development of Malaya's tin mines, tea and rubber plantations, with cheap labor nurtured the influx of laborers, merchants, and speculators from China and India during the nineteenth century, although Chinese had been migrating to Malaya as traders, miners, and laborers for centuries. Thus, the influx of these migrants and immigrants transformed Malaya into today's multiethnic society of Malaysia.

Many Chinese arrived in Malaya poor, worked ceaselessly, and saved and drove themselves and their families until they became millionaires. Malays did no such thing. And while the Indians were mostly shipped back to India, too many Chinese, so far as the Malays were concerned, stayed in Malaya. By the end of the Second World War, of a total population in Malaya of five million, more than 38 per cent were Chinese; 50 per cent Malays; 11 per cent Indian. To the Malays, the Chinese seemed to be taking over the country.[15]

In 1990, the population of Malaysia was approximately 17 million: 59% Malays, 32% Chinese, 9% Indians.[16] Ten years earlier, the population was estimated at 13½ million: 45% Malays, 36% Chinese, 9.1% Indian, and 8% non-Malay indigenous peoples.

Islam is the state religion, although most Chinese profess Buddhism, Confucianism, Taoism, and Christianity, while the Indian and Pakistani communities are 70% Hindu, 20% Muslim, 5% Christian, and 2% Sikh. The official language is Malay (Bahasa Malaysian), although English, Tamil, and a variety of Chinese, Indian, and indigenous dialects are also spoken.

The British occupied the Malay interior not so much by choice as by happenstance, an afterthought. British adventurers considered the Malay peninsula's tropical rain forests an impenetrable jungle and not worth the effort and sacrifice to exploit. What did interest them were the Straits

Settlements of Penang and Malacca, which for centuries had been coveted for their strategic military and trade value. Initially these adventurers were not interested in Singapore, which, in the early nineteenth century, was a sparsely populated, disease-infested unhealthy island covered with swamps and inhospitable mosquitoes, however, by the mid-1820s, Singapore, hanging like a pendant at the tip of the Malay peninsula, was added to the garland of Straits Settlements and destined to become the center of British naval interests and entrepôt enterprises in Southeast Asia. Nevertheless,

When, in 1874, traders in the Straits Settlements clamoured for British protection in the Malay interior (where tin was beginning to be mined), governments in London, both Liberal and Conservative, refused to allow any money to be spent on so fruitless a venture. The Governor of the settlements, Sir Andrew Clarke, found a way to protect the traders on the cheap, by sending *Residents* to the *courts* of the petty-robber-baron Malay sultans. Thus, unknown to London, control over Malaya was acquired.[17]

The British Government eventually adopted Sir Andrew Clarke's initiative for imperial expansion. The so-called *Indirect Rule* worked like this:

In 1895 Perak, Selangor, Negri Sembilan, and Pahang were formed into the Federated Malay States. Later Kedah, Kelantan, and Trengganu in the north and Johore in the south accepted British advisers, and by 1914 the whole of Malaya had become an area of British influence, with a number of separate governments but a considerable uniformity of law, policy, and administration.[18] . . . The Malay States did not become colonies like the Straits Settlements, but remained sovereign states under British protection, through treaties signed by their Sultans.[19]

Whether they were Federated (FMS)[20] or Unfederated Malay States (UMS),

All of them in due course accepted *advisers* on the pattern of the residents of the Federated States, but with slightly reduced powers, which (reflecting the strength of the ruling elites in Kedah and Johore, and the unattractiveness of Kelantan and Trengganu to the export economy), left Malay participation in the governance of the state somewhat intact.[21]

The peoples of Sabah and Sarawak, in British Northern Borneo,[22] were deemed politically and socially less sophisticated than those of the peninsula sultanates and were, therefore, organized and developed differently from the Federated and Unfederated Malay States, although they came within the British sphere of influence with an omnipotent British Resident. Eventually, they would become part of the post-colonial Federation of Malaysia. The difference in Sabah and Sarawak, but especially in Sarawak's development, was the presence of a flamboyant, eccentric English adventurer called *Raja* James Brooke and his nephew Charles Brooke, who together created a veritable fiefdom in Sarawak. Nevertheless, both Sabah and Sarawak "were characterized by the kind of paternalism that does not hasten to see its children grow up."[23]

In 1992, perhaps a newer and harsher form of paternalism revealed itself, for in that year during a visit to Los Angeles Mrs. Rafidah Aziz, the Malaysian Minister of Trade and Industry and the highest ranking woman in the ruling party, the UMNO, was asked by an environmentalist investment adviser whether letting clients invest in Malaysian industry was conscionable, when the country had such a deplorable record of exploiting its rain forests and oppressing the indigenous peoples who lived in them.

Rafidah shot back with a blistering attack on the Penan, one of the primitive tribes who oppose logging in their habitat in the state of Sarawak. She derided the jungle dwellers for wearing loincloths, eating monkeys, worshipping at ancestral graveyards, and resisting government attempts to give them modern health care and put their children in schools. She also said it was nobody's business but Malaysia's: "Anybody who is too concerned about what happens in other countries better not venture out of their own country. . . . We don't want people to impose their human rights and values on us. These great busybodies of the world, who don't bother with their own problems, their backyards are full of dirt." This was a lively moment in an otherwise tedious investment seminar sponsored by the Malaysian government.[24]

The *Indirect Rule* by which the British ruled Malaya was for British agents to negotiate treaties with local chieftains called Sultans which placed them completely under the control, guidance, and protection of the British Government, for, at his Court, each Sultan accepted a British agent, who came to be called, in Malaya as he was in Northern Nigeria, the *Resident*. He was the Sultan's principal adviser on all matters, internal and external, that affected his sultanate, except for those of a traditional religious or cultural nature.

The role of the Malay Sultans was vital in Britain's scheme of Indirect Rule, which brought all the FMS and UMS under British suzerainty. For British agents negotiated with the Sultans the treaties of protection that legitimized the British presence in Malaya, and the Sultans accepted British Residents as advisers, "whose advice must be asked for and acted upon in all questions other than those touching Malay religion and custom."[25]

The British did not share power with the Sultans in the Federated and Unfederated Malay States, but rather the British sanctioned the co-existence of two parallel systems which, in British India, was called a *dyarchy*. Under this arrangement, the Sultans retained their traditional religious and cultural authority. In fact, the Sultans found their political powers considerably enhanced under the umbrella of British gunpowder protection against the possible encroachment from rival chieftains bent on territorial infringement. The British and the Sultans were in a symbiotic relationship which was mutually beneficial. At the vortex, however, sat the Resident, who, like a spider, controlled everything in his web of influence, i.e., all the sultanate's business except for matters deemed religious and cultural. Thus, "The fiction of the Resident's *advice* failed to obscure the reality that it was the Resident and his English bureaucracy who ruled, the sultan and his chiefs who advised and, occasionally, assisted . . . listening to proceedings conducted in a language they did not understand."[26]

Likewise, the role of the traditional Malay elite was essential to the success of the British scheme, for not only did they continue to play their customary roles in traditional society but they were the indispensable linchpin between the Malay peasants and their British overlords. For their acquiescence, the traditional Malay elite were recipients of considerable British largess.

After the turn of the century, the Malay aristocrats of the younger generation received special education and training reserved largely for the sons of the traditional elite, and were recruited into the colonial bureaucracy. Though the positions they occupied were subordinate in relation to the European civil service, the Malay administrative cadre, thus created, had a dual advantage—over their fellow Malays of peasant origin, who had not had the same educational opportunities, and over all non-Malays, who were barred, by policy, from the administrative or executive ranks of the public service. Malay officers, as they were styled, were almost invariably employed in rural administration among their own people. . . . The prestige and authority conferred by traditional social status was thus re-emphasized by administrative authority derived from the colonial regime.[27]

The traditional Malay elite acquiesced to British rule but not without some initial resistance:

The Malay ruling class in the Federated States accepted the steady extension of British control over their affairs after 1874 for a variety of reasons. In the first place, in the early stages of intervention, those who rebelled were put down by force. . . . In the atmosphere of acceptance so engendered, it made sense to settle for what one could get—a political pension commensurate with previous income from tax and toll, subordinate office in the administration as a "superintendent of *penghulus*" or a seat with early state councils, the appointive legislative assemblies of the separate states and advisory bodies to the Residents. For a sultan, acceptance of British rule entailed a reasonable income from the civil list, new and more elaborate, palaces and other proud appurtenances, and, perhaps most important of all, the sort of respect and recognition for his position as head of state that would render *de facto* within Malay society itself the authority that had in the past so often been merely *de jure*. What the protectorate system protected most of all was the shape and structure of the traditional society from the top down.[28]

Thus, the British Resident, as representative of the British Government, and the Sultan, as the intermediary between the Resident and the Malay peasants, walked in tandem. The Resident blended the intermediary role of the Sultan with that of other traditional Malay elites, with a striking absence of any role for the Malay peasants in the new mining and plantation economy, either as laborer or as entrepreneurs:

British policy in the peninsula was based on a mutually profitable alliance with the Malay ruling class, by which, in turn for the right to develop a modern extractive economy within the *negeri* by means of alien immigration labor, the British undertook to maintain intact the position and prestige of the ruling class and to refrain from catapulting the Malay people into the modern world.[29]

For three main reasons, the British Resident excluded the Malay people from the new economic order. First, to ensure the continued production of food for local consumption which was produced, almost exclusively, by the local Malay peasants. Second, to avoid the political, social, and economic consequences which they, the British, thought likely to accompany any substantial disruption of traditional Malay peasant life. Third, because of the British sentimental attachment for village life, at home and abroad, and, in the case of the Malays, the British love of simple, folkloric traditions.

In their own interest, the Sultans and the traditional Malay elite concurred with these British sentiments and objectives and, therefore, collaborated in the British stratagem of *Indirect Rule.* The problem of providing the labor force needed for exploiting, developing, and expanding the mining and plantation economy was solved by the importation of migrant workers from China and India.

The effect of these economic innovations on Malaya's social order was that under British rule: (1) the Malay peasant pursued a traditional Malay education, in the vernacular, where local values were instilled, where crafts and cottage industries were taught, and where few, if any, marketable skills were developed for the new evolving economy. (2) While the *unprotected* Chinese went not only to traditional Chinese schools, which were taught in the vernacular, they also went to Christian missionary schools where English was taught, where new values, ideas, and skills were communicated, and where Chinese pupils developed marketable skills for the new evolving economy. As a consequence of this dichotomy in development, the Malay peasant remained insulated from the mainstream of social and economic change in Malaya as well as isolated from other forces of modernity. This isolation exacerbated rather than ameliorated and accommodated ethnic cleavage between themselves and the industrious, migrant Chinese.

In other words, under British rule, the Chinese became the dominant economic factor not only in the rural mining and plantation industries, as laborers and entrepreneurs, but in the urban commercial and professional sectors, as lawyers, doctors, and businessmen. Meanwhile, the Malays remained dominant in those rural sectors where social factors such as religion and culture were staunchly protected by primordial attachments by the Sultans and the traditional Malay elite.

Even after the British departure and the Malays gained political control of their country, they remained in the backwaters of their country's economic development, because they lacked the education, the capital, and the entrepreneurial skills to compete. As a consequence of these cumulative factors, in Malaysia, national identity evolved around primordial attachments to race, religion, language, and culture, with the two major ethnic groups, the Malays and the Chinese, having almost nothing in common. To the Malays, the Chinese were ruthless, unprincipled money-mongers. To the Chinese, the Malays were lazy and incompetent. Under these circumstances, the attempt to build a sense of national integration in Malaysia has been the equivalent of trying to make bricks without straw, for *trust*, the binding ingredient for national building and political integration, has been sorely lacking in Malaysia. This situation would be well understood by John Furnivall, who said,

> They mix but do not combine. Each group holds by its own religion, its own culture and language, its own ideas and ways. As individuals they meet, but only in the market-place, in buying and selling. There is a plural society, with different sections of the community living side by side, but separately, within the same political unit.[30]

Many critics have accused the British, throughout their Empire, of having pursued a policy which was not so much Indirect Rule as Divide and Rule. By pursuing their policy, exclusive communalism was not only perpetuated but exacerbated. The British denied that their policy was to Divide and Rule. They claim that in Malaya assigning Malays to positions of authority over Chinese and Indians would have been imprudent because the Malays were incapable of moving in or understanding any society other than their own. Nevertheless, British policy in Malaya did reflect the dominant role the British had conceived for themselves: holding the balance of power between the separate and essentially different communities of multi-ethnic Malaya. This role was, to a large extent, predicated on preserving the separateness among the diverse ethnic communities. Furthermore, the British perpetuated the stereotype of the unassimilable Chinese, who were portrayed as irrevocably tied to China and disinterested in the operations of government as long as they were able to make money. True or not, the selling of this stereotype made possible the British avoidance of any responsibility for integrating even the locally born and domiciled Chinese into a larger Malayan society.

As a form of political integration, Britain did establish a Territorial Assembly and an Executive Council, whose members were appointed rather than popularly elected. The British were wedded to the preservation of the autocratic Malay sultanates. Consequently, British colonial policy left no room for substantial reforms leading to the eventual popular participation in democratic institutions. Until after the Second World War, no tradition of popular participation in territorial government or elections existed. As long as the economy remained buoyant and the British remained benevolently humanitarian toward the Chinese and Indian communities, while giving *preferential* treatment to the Malays, few complaints were heard. Demands for self-government were seldom heard, and then only in the form of gentle hints or friendly persuasion. Furthermore, in order not to diminish or jeopardize its authority, Britain tried to respond to grievances before they became too intense. In this way, Britain was *responsive to* without being *responsible for* to the peoples it ruled.

Although British colonial policy was remarkably effective in discouraging widespread political activity, Malaya did develop some associations with political objectives before the Second World War. These were not stimulated by factors inside Malaya but by nationalist movements in India and China as well as events taking place in Egypt and the Dutch East Indies. Consequently, during the inter-war period, Malay political activities were dispersed and fragmented. These early political associations tended to be oriented towards issues arising outside Malaya's borders. The diverse ethnic communities inside Malaya were not inclined to view one another as political protagonists, because their political enemies were being defined outside the arena of domestic politics. This provides an essential explanation for the relatively low level of ethnic conflict before the Second World War, despite serious communal antagonisms which were evident but submerged.

In Malaysia, national identity has evolved around ethnic concepts of race, religion, and language. These exert a powerful centripetal force toward association with others of like ethnicity inside Malaysia, and a magnetic pull toward identification with the countries which were the original source of these ethnic associations outside Malaysia: China, India, and Indonesia. Under these circumstances, developing something called a Malaysian national identity is a herculean task indeed, as so little is common to each group to use as a basis for a national identity. One is reminded, therefore, of that wise pronouncement in the nineteenth century by that French savant, Ernest Renan: "Man is the slave neither of his race, nor his language, nor his religion, nor of the windings of his rivers and mountain ranges. . . . *To forget, to get one's history wrong, are essential factors in the making of a nation.*"[31]

After the Federation of Malaya received independence in 1957, strains and tensions, arising from the lack of a common sense of national identity, were papered over by the performance of the Alliance Party. For instance, throughout the 1960s, the majority of political pundits outside Malaysia regarded the country as one of the most politically integrated states in Southeast Asia. What was enthusiastically pointed out by these pundits was the degree to which political integration was accomplished in accordance with the consociational model for democracy advocated by Arend Lijphart, that is, political bargaining by elite, ethnic leaders.[32] This consociational arrangement was manifested in a political association called the Alliance Party, where ethnic sentiments were accommodated and where centrifugal ethnic tendencies were effectively detected, deflected, and contained. However, after the events surrounding the 1969 national elections, this enthusiasm waned considerably.

The Alliance Party operated the apparatus of government for the purported benefit of all ethnic communities. Up to a point, it was successful in convincing those inside the country, as well as those outside, that the ethnic antagonisms were being slowly sublimated and subsumed within the framework of a Malaysian national identity. Therefore, an act of will was necessary to ignore the many danger signs flashing along the way, but the signs were there. They flashed most glaringly when political participation was solicited in a national election; the most monumental election of all was the federal election of 1969. In developing countries, national elections are times when ethnic antagonisms come raging to the fore, for these are times when primordial attachments soar to the forefront of the electorates' ethnic consciousness.

In 1948, when the Federation of Malaya was established, key communal arrangements were written into the constitution which were intended to prevent internal communal disruptions. Article 153 of the 1948 and subsequent constitutions was entitled "Reservations of quotas . . . for Malays."[33] This article assured Malays of political supremacy by granting them preference in all civil service jobs and in all university positions for teachers as well as for students. In order to get the Chinese to acquiesce to this arrangement, the 1948 constitution included more liberal provisions enabling Chinese to obtain Malay citizenship. Before 1948, citizenship was not national: one was a citizen of one of the Malay states, or one was a British subject, if born in the British Crown Colony then composed of Sabah, Sarawak, and Singapore. The position of the Chinese was extremely vulnerable because few Chinese enjoyed citizenship in the Malay states. Under British rule, the Chinese relied upon British largess, but what would happen when the British left? Consequently, one of the main post-war political efforts of the Chinese was directed towards acquiring more liberal laws for obtaining citizenship, in order to secure their political position and thereby protect their rights and interests in an independent Malaya.

Other arrangements were included in the 1948 Constitution, but one *bargain* did not appear in that legal document nor in the constitutions of 1957 and 1963 but was accepted as a vital part of the delicate balance negotiated in the 1940s. By this unwritten *bargain*, non-Malays, meaning the Chinese, were acknowledged to have a predominance in the country's economy.

The effects of these constitutional arrangements and political *bargains* were that in the country's political sphere the Malays were dominant, while, in the country's economic sphere, the Chinese were dominant with the Chinese given some opportunities for increasing their numbers of citizens.

Now, what was the mechanism by which all of these written and unwritten arrangements were to be worked out? Originally, the cooperation of two communal parties: the United Malay's National

Organization, the UMNO, and the Malayan Chinese Association, the MCA, were responsible. Later, the Malayan Indian Congress, the MIC, was included, and three communal parties combined to form the Alliance Party. The Alliance Party was the political coalition which led the struggle for Malaya's independence from Britain in 1957. For the next twelve years this coalition governed not only the peninsula states, but the entire Malaysian Federation when it was formed in 1962-1963.

The Alliance Party won one general election in 1955, before independence, and three other general elections after independence in 1959, 1964, and 1969. Other political parties existed, but until the elections of 1969, they did not represent a serious challenge to the supremacy of the Alliance Party. This was partly due to the mystique of the Alliance Party for having led the country to independence but was also due to the fragmented nature of the opposition parties, which could find little basis for uniting against the Alliance Party. Moreover, the Alliance Party proved to be an effective mechanism for maintaining an appeal to voters. That is, it enabled communal differences to be discussed and resolved by the elite leadership of each communal party within the confines of the Alliance. The Alliance Party was effective until the national elections of 1969, when the scheme of consociational politics became inoperative and the Federation of Malaysia was brought to the brink of a bloody communal war.

The 1969 elections were held in staggered sequence. First, they were held on the mainland, in the peninsula states. Then, several weeks later, they were held in Sabah and Sarawak. Malaysia has a tradition of staggered elections, due to the remoteness of many of its voters. On the mainland, 104 of the Federation's 144 seats in the House of Representatives were contested.[34]

In the 1969 elections, the Alliance Party lost 23 seats on the mainland, including 3 seats held by cabinet ministers. Now, it held only 66 seats, not including the still to be contested seats in Sabah and Sarawak. The Alliance Party still held enough seats to ensure control of the House of Representatives but not enough to ensure an absolute majority, as it previously could. Furthermore, as the Malays were not even a substantial minority in Sabah and Sarawak, where they had little in common with the indigenous inhabitants, a strong possibility was that the Malays might be in the numerical minority in the House of Representatives, if Sabah and Sarawak did not elect at least seven members favorable to the Malays and the Alliance Party. Given their paranoia, the Malays were in a state of panic. Even before the elections in Sabah and Sarawak, they regarded the elections as a disaster and a threat to their predominance in the country's political sphere.

The communal component of the Alliance Party which lost most heavily in the 1969 elections was the Malayan Chinese Association. For months prior to the elections, the MCA had been strongly criticized by local Chinese on the grounds that it only represented a few wealthy business men and merchants. Certainly, the greatest weakness of the Alliance Party was that the MCA increasingly lost political touch with the Chinese masses. This can be attributed to two factors: one, the lack of dynamic leadership within the MCA, and two, the willingness of the MCA leaders to defer to the Malays on matters such as special privileges for the Malays and the suppression of Chinese education rights. Although the Malays lacked the Chinese economic power, they had a predominance in the country's political arena, and they controlled the country's military and police, both of which were largely composed of Malays.

While the greatest fear among the Malays was that the Chinese might gain political hegemony by gaining control of the government apparatus, the ordinary Chinese feared that the Malays might use their political and armed power to strip them of their economic gains as well as their citizenship rights, and then drive them from the country. By 1969, the ordinary Chinese were deeply worried that the MCA leaders were doing little to protect these interests.

In the 1969 elections, the MCA won only 13 of the 33 seats it contested on the mainland. Chinese voters moved in large numbers from the MCA to moderate Chinese parties which, in previous elections, had won only a very few seats. Having tasted real political success for the first time, the supporters of these moderate Chinese parties celebrated their minor victory with noisy parades. Imprudently, the parades made their way through Malay neighborhoods in the capital city of Kuala Lumpur. Even more unwisely, the paraders waved red banners, as they were celebrating with the Chinese color of joy, but to the Malays, who were not enamored of communists, the color red had another meaning. This was the spark which set off the ensuing violence, when a Malay political rally broke up with frustrated, angry, and paranoid Malays going on a rampage of violence through Chinese neighborhoods.

The 1969 elections and the extreme communal violence which accompanied them marked the end of the Alliance Party, as originally organized. In their wake came a twenty-one-month suspension of the Constitution with rule by decree, and although Parliament was reconvened in February of 1971, full democracy was not. For example, a constitutional amendment was adopted which made even talking about matters relating to race a crime. To discuss any subject deemed "likely to arouse racial feelings and endanger racial peace in the country"[35] became an Act of Sedition, punishable by a fine and imprisonment.

The Alliance Party, as such, died in 1969. However, it reappeared in a greatly altered state in the guise of the National Front Coalition which, in 1974, won 120 seats in the 154 member House of Representatives, while the moderate Chinese Democratic Action Party, the CDAP, won only 9 seats. In 1978, the National Front Coalition again won by a wide majority, and in the 1982 elections, the National Front Coalition of eleven Malay, Chinese, Indian, and indigenous peoples parties had already won 110 of the 154 seats in parliament, even though Sarawak with 24 and Sabah with 16 had not yet voted. When these two states did vote, the overwhelming majority of their votes went to the National Front Coalition, which increased the number of seats it held in the House of Representatives from 130 to 140 out of 154 seats. Still, the National Front coalition was built on shifting sand, for the struggle continued between the Malays, who consider themselves the rightful owners of Malaya, although they are the descendants of invaders from Indonesia, and the Chinese, who owned 90% of the country's commercial outlets, who occupied an overwhelming majority of the positions in the country's professional fields such as law, medicine, engineering, and architecture,[36] and who possessed an energy and drive that the graceful, deliberate, and deeply religious Malays did not admire.

After the 1969 elections, the Government of Malaysia instituted a 20-year program of affirmative action on behalf of the Malays. The key to the affirmative action or Positive Discrimination plan, as it was referred to in Malaysia, was the so-called New Economic Policy enacted in 1970 that aimed to give Malays 30% ownership of all Malaysian companies, heavy preference in public employment, and put pressure on private companies and organizations to employ more Malays. In short, the plan for Positive Discrimination was a legal device for giving the Malays a larger share of the country's economic pie by 1990. As a result, the Chinese and Indian communities, while largely accepting that, economically, some Positive Discrimination in favor of mainly rural Malays was unavoidable, felt that they were not allowed to be as Malaysian as the government urged them to be. The leader of the Chinese Democratic Action Party was quoted as saying, "The present policy gives the non-Malays the sense that they don't really belong." As a form of positive action, "In Malaysia, discrimination is the law of the land and segregation the way of life," all of which is sanctioned by "one of the most radical affirmative-action programs ever implemented by a government."[37]

Ethnic animosity plagues Malaysia. Illustrative of this animosity was the reaction of the Malays to the heavy tide of refugees from Vietnam, known as boat people, who came to Malaysian shores in 1978 and 1979. Although the government temporarily accommodated thousands of these refugees, many Malays forced other refugees back into the sea, where hundreds, probably thousands, drowned. Almost all of these refugees were Chinese and, therefore, were perceived by the Malays as a threat were they to stay in Malaysia. On the other hand, had the boat people been Muslims instead of Chinese, they probably would have been treated differently. For instance, at the same time as the boat people were Chinese refugees from Vietnam, 92,000 Muslim refugees arrived in Sabah from the Philippines, and the Malays made no fuss about them. However, the Malaysian government did make a fuss about the boat people and inaugurated a policy for dealing with them, which was to get rid of them fast and preferably to the United States. As the Malaysian Minister of Home Affairs was quoted as saying, "Who could appreciate the problem of the Boat People better than the descendants of the Mayflower?"[38]

Today, political pundits are more cautious about predicting Malaysia's future. Some fear that Malaysia may be a time bomb that could explode at any time into a violent ethnic confrontation, as it did in the summer of 1969.   They look to the disaster in Sri Lanka as a frightening demonstration model.   Nevertheless, Malaysia's territorial integration, which was once threatened by China and Indonesia, now seems secure with no immediate fear from those near neighbors.   On the other hand, its national integration *its sense of common identity* as well as its political integration *its sense of a common set of loyalties* seem much less secure given the volatile changes, the uncertain vicissitudes, which seem to be endemic in multi-ethnic developing countries.

Notes

1. Barry Newman, "Ethnic Upheaval: Malaysia Torn by Drive for More Malay Rights at Expense of Chinese," *New York Wall Street Journal*, 8 May 1978.

2. Karl Deutsch, *Political Community at the International Level* (Garden City, NY: Doubleday, 1954), 33-45, and Karl Deutsch, *Political Community and the North Atlantic Area* (Princeton, N.J.: Princeton University Press, 1957), 5-7.

3. See Swiss Chapter One.

4. Furnivall, 306-307.

5. Great Britain Colonial Office, *British Dependencies in the Far East, 1945-1949* (London: His Majesty's Stationery Office [HMSO], May 1949), 2.

6. R. S. Milne, "Malaysia: A Federation in the Making," *Asian Survey* 3, no. 2 (February 1963): 80.

7. Kurt Glaser and Stefan Possony, *Victims of Politics* (New York: Columbia University Press, 1979), 139-140.

8. Brian Lapping, *End of Empire* (New York: St. Martin's Press, 1985), 166.

9. Ibid., 174.

10. British Colonial Office and Central Office of Information, *Introducing the Eastern Dependencies* (London: HMSO, 1955), 14.

11. Ibid., 21.

12. Ironically, it was the descendants of slaves and indentured servants from Indonesia, whom the Boers imported to South Africa, who became known as the original Cape Coloured.

13. David Joel Steinberg et al., *In Search of Southeast Asia* (Honolulu: University of Hawaii Press, 1986), 77. The word *negeri* translates in English to mean state.

14. Rubber trees were not indigenous to Malaya but were imported there by the British from Kew Gardens in London from specimens gathered in the rain forests of Brazil.

15. Lapping, 154.

16. *The World Almanac 1992* (New York: Pharos Books, 1991), 781.

17. Lapping, 149.

18. The year 1914 was also momentous for Nigeria, for in that year all of Nigeria was united under a single British administration with a system of *Indirect Rule* evolving in the North with a more direct, less subtle administration in the South, especially in the Southeast among the Ibos.

19. British Colonial Office, *Eastern Dependencies*, 32.

20. The Federated States were Perak, Selangor, Negri Sembilan, and Pahang. The Unfederated States were Kedah, Kelantan, Johore, and Trengganu.

21. Steinberg, 190.

22. In addition to their conflict with the Chinese, the Malays are also in conflict with the indigenous inhabitants of Northern Borneo, with whom they are not ethnically allied.

23. Steinberg, 191.

24. Karl Schoenberger, "Malaysia's Trade Minister Exhibits a True Grit," *Los Angeles Times*, 15 June 1992.

25. Lapping, 153. Significantly, the British Colonial Office, in its publication, chose to omit the clause "must be asked for

and acted upon" (British Colonial Office, *Eastern Dependencies*, 32).

26. Steinberg, 188, 189.

27. Ibid., 323.

28. Ibid., 189. The pattern of accommodation and collaboration that was developed between the Resident and the traditional ruling class was repeated in Northern Nigeria between the Resident, the Emir, and the traditional elite. The word *penghulus* refers to traditional Malay headmen.

29. Ibid., 322.

30. Furnivall, *Colonial Policy and Practice*, 304.

31. Ernest Renan, "What Is a Nation?" in *Modern Political Doctrine*, ed. Alfred Zimmern (London: Oxford University Press, 1939), 205 and 190. Italicized by the author for emphasis.

32. Arend Lijphart, *Democracies: Patterns of Majoritarian and Consensus Government in Twenty-One Countries* (New Haven: Yale University Press, 1984), xiv.

33. Malaysian Government, *The Federal Constitution* (Kuala Lumpur: Government Printer, 1964), 97.

34. At the time, Malaysia had a bicameral parliament consisting of a Senate and a House of Representatives. The Senate was composed of 58 members: 32 Senators were appointed by the Head of State and 26 were elected by state assemblies; all served for a 6-year term. The House of Representatives consisted of 154 members: 114 from the mainland and 24 from Sarawak and 16 from Sabah; they were elected for a 5-year term.

35. James Sterba, "Malaysia is About to Amend Constitution to

Declare Discussion of Racial Issues a Crime," *New York Times*, 2 March 1971.

36. For instance, in 1980, of 5,099 engineers 527 were Malays; of 3,058 doctors 218 were Malays; of 1,129 lawyers 147 were Malays; and of 502 architects 45 were Malays. The majority of those who were not Malays were Chinese.

37. Margaret Scott, "Where the Quota Is King," *New York Times Magazine*, 17 November 1991.

38. "Sought Aid for Refugees," *New York Times*, 11 January 1982.

Chapter Six
Nigeria: A Geographical Expression, An Historical Accident, or a Nation?

Nigeria, Africa's colossus, is an enigma. What is it, and what does it want to be: a unified nation or a collection of autonomous, balkanized states?

In 1947, Chief Awolowo, one of the candidates in Nigeria's 1979 presidential election and one of the titans of twentieth century Nigerian politics, crystallized this salient dilemma when he dropped the following verbal bomb-shell. He said,

> Nigeria is not a nation. It is a mere geographical expression. There are no *Nigerians* in the same sense as there are *English*, *Welsh*, or *French*. The word *Nigerian* is merely a distinctive appellation to distinguish those who live within the boundaries of Nigeria from those who do not.[1]

Chief Awolowo made this statement at a time when his primary concerns were twofold: Nigeria's political independence from British rule and the political advancement of the Yoruba, his own ethnic group. Nevertheless, since independence, Nigeria has been haunted by the belief of many political observers, in and outside the country, and by the events which have occurred over the past thirty years that perhaps Nigeria is merely a geographical expression, a historical accident.

Nigeria is a huge country of about 380,000 square miles, smaller than Alaska but twice the size of California.[2] Evidence of its ethnic diversity is the 250 different languages and dialects spoken within its boundaries as well as the myriad religious practices, ranging from Islam to Christianity to the traditional, which are commonly professed within its borders. As a consequence, Nigeria's basic problem of political integration has been to create a nation out of its vast multiplicity of ethnic groups: to attain unity despite diversity. Hindering this task, however, is the failure of the country's leaders and its peoples to engen-

The Nigerian States in 1991

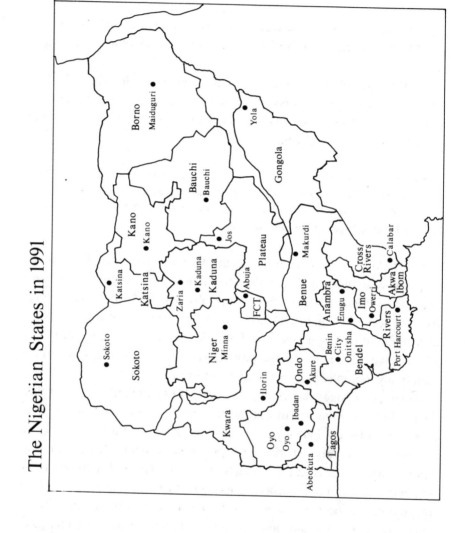

der, within themselves, a sense of national identity and national unity.

Nigeria is not alone in having to face this predicament. The United States, a vast country with a multitude of ethnic groups, faced a similar dilemma and, like Nigeria, was subjected to a violent civil war in pursuit of a solution. Furthermore, all the new states of Sub-Saharan Africa are faced with enormous ethnic diversity in their populations. Nevertheless, Nigeria is worthy of special attention because of its size, its population, and its other sources of economic and political power.

Nigerians outnumber Britons or Frenchmen. Just how many Nigerians there actually are has always been a matter of political controversy. For instance, in the 1953 census, which was the last one taken before Nigeria gained its independence from Britain in 1960, the population was determined to be 30.5 million people. Ten years later, in 1963, it was estimated to be 55.5 people: plus 25 million. Ten years after that, in 1973, it was estimated to be 80 million people: again, plus 25 million. Six years later, for the 1979 presidential election, it was again estimated to be 80 million people. Six years after that, in 1985, Nigeria's population was estimated to be 91,200,000 million people. Then, in March of 1992, in a startling revelation—after closing its borders, after sending 700,000 census takers to scurry the countryside, after ordering all factories closed and tens of millions of people to stay home for the week, and after weighing the political risks involved—the Nigerian Government released its head count for the last national census taken in November of 1991. So what was the figure arrived at: a mere 88.5 million people, which confirmed Nigeria as the most populous state in Africa but was far below recent estimates. For instance,

> The United Nations Population Division estimated that the population was 95.7 million in mid-1985, growing at 3.4 percent a year, and that it had reached 105 million by mid-1988. The World Bank came up with a mid-1988 estimate of 110 million. By comparison, the Nigerian Government's estimate of the 1987 mid-year population was 112.3 million.[3]

Why this wide discrepancy? Whatever the actual figure, probably one out of every five Africans is a Nigerian,[4] although Professor Jean Herskovits sets the figure at one out of every four.[5] The problem, of course, is that no one has the foggiest notion of how many Africans are on the whole continent. Nonetheless, the November 1991 Nigerian head count was the most thorough census in the country, although many essential questions were left unanswered, because they were not asked. For example, aware of the political ramifications, the turbulence, and the ethnic rivalries that census taking engenders in Nigeria, the census takers, on instructions from the military regime, avoided asking ethnic questions about linguistic affiliation, religious profession, or *tribal* allegiance.

Thus, population figures are *the* hot political issue in Nigeria, where political wisdom dictates that every ethnic group inflates its own *numbers* in order to benefit from higher allocations from the Federal Government's treasury as well as greater representation in federal and state assemblies. Therefore, every head count in Nigeria invites conflict, tension, and corruption because, in a democracy, *numbers* matter, as they determine who gets what portion of the political and economic pie. In an uncertain democracy, General Olusegun Obasanjo, a former Nigerian Head of State, has described the census in Nigeria as a cemetery: a place where government are buried.

A possible solution for resolving Nigeria's penchant for ethnic politics and extricating the country not only from its ethnic morass by developing a truly politically integrated society with a sense of national identity would be to encourage the development of a responsive and responsible middle class. In Aristotle's *Politics*, the Greek philosopher and his translator, Ernest Barker, set out a program for utilizing the strengths of the middle class for these purposes that seem ideal for developed nations and developing nations alike. Barker begins:

> We are here concerned with the best constitution and way of life for the majority of men and states. Goodness itself consists in a mean; and in any state the middle class is a mean between the rich and the poor. The middle class is free from the ambition of the rich and the pettiness of the poor: it is a natural link which helps to ensure political cohesion.[6]

Aristotle concludes:

> In all states there may be distinguished three parts, or classes, of the citizen-body—the very rich; the very poor; and the middle class which forms the mean.

Now it is admitted, as a general principle, that moderation and the mean are always best. . . . Community depends on friendship; and when there is enmity instead of friendship, men will not even share the same path. A state aims at being, as far as it can be, a society composed of equals and peers [who, as such, can be friends and associates]; and the middle class, more than any other, has this sort of composition. It follows that a state which is based on the middle class is bound to be the best constituted in respect of the elements [i.e., equals and peers] of which, on our view, a state is naturally composed. . . . It is clear from our argument, first, that the best form of political society is one where power is vested in the middle class, and, secondly, that good government is attainable in those states where there is a large middle class—large enough, if possible, to be stronger than both the other classes, but at any rate large enough to be stronger than either of them singly.[7]

The Aristotelian prescription would, of course, turn Marxist theory on its ear: from a negative view of the middle class as oppressive to a positive realization of the middle class as a vital ingredient in political integration. Thus, what James Madison refers to as a vigilant, diligent, informed citizenry rather than a factional ethnicity would become the determinant of group and individual allegiance based on enlightened self-interest. This, of course, can only happen in a free and open society: one in which all citizens are able to express their opinions and join associations without fear of intimidation, persecution, or death.

Nigeria demands special attention because its power comes from various sources including its population, which is large, articulate, well-educated, and politically savvy. It has a substantial middle class which lacks the freedom to assert itself due to numerous government constraints.

It was, however, the Nigerian military that first attracted international attention to the country's power, although various estimates had been given as to its size and efficiency. In 1978, the *New York Times* reported,

Nigeria has an army of 250,000, the largest in black Africa. But according to some military attachés, the force is badly equipped and trained. One observer called it "the largest outdoor welfare organization in the world." Many units have not been on training maneuvers for more than five years and the few crack units are said to be required at home to protect against coups and civil unrest.[8]

In 1980, the Nigerian military received higher praise: "Nigeria has an army of 160,000, and is the only black African nation with the capacity to transport large numbers of soldiers over long distances."[9] In 1985, however, the African military, in general, was given a scathing evaluation:

> In much of Africa, it seems, the warrior caste has evolved into a ruling class. Soldiers, policemen, and militias have become members of a privileged elite, free to inflict will or whim on the citizenry. They are fed and clothed while peasants starve and dress in rages. They are issued guns and bullets while farmers lack hoes and seeds. And in many countries they are accountable to no one—not to politicians, not to the press, not to the public they are pledged to serve. Africa's armies are one of the few colonially imposed institutions that have not only survived but also have grown and even prospered since independence. However, the discipline and professionalism that the English and French demanded of men in uniform has often been lost. Beyond that, the vast majority of African soldiers have never mounted or halted an invasion. Indeed, most troops have never fired a shot at a soldier of another nationality. By and large, African forces are deployed only against their own people in their own countries. . . . It is difficult to imagine how the future will be different. Africa's armies receive some of the first world's most advanced technology. MIG fighter planes soar over fields plowed by oxen. Tanks seem to be more common than tractors.[10]

Finally, in 1988, a reliable reference source stated that in Nigeria, "Total armed forces numbered 94,000, and the military service was voluntary," with the figures broken down to include 80,000 army, 5,000 navy, and 9,000 air force.[11] Whatever its size and efficiency, Nigeria's massive instrument for destruction was mobilized for the Biafran Civil War, which lasted from mid-1967 to January of 1970 and which was an abnormal deviation from the normal course of government and politics in a democracy; in other words, it was an aberration.[12]

The first military takeover in Sub-Saharan Africa took place in The Sudan, in 1957, when the military seized control the year after the country's independence. In 1960, a group of military men attempted a coup in Ethiopia, during the Emperor's absence, but that attempt failed when Haile Selassie returned. However, a later coup succeeded, in 1974, even with the Emperor in residence. In 1965, Colonel Joseph Mobutu, a tough, Israeli-trained paratrooper, ended the chaos that had plagued The

Congo since its independence from Belgium in 1960, when he seized power, changed his name to Mobutu Sese Seko and the country's name to Zaire, and made himself president. Today, Zaire again seems to be on the brink of chaos and anarchy.

The year 1965-1966 is known as *the Year of the Generals* because "between June 1965 and February 1966 no less than seven African governments were overthrown by their armies," including the coup which removed Kwame Nkrumah from power in Ghana, which in March of 1957 had become the first Sub-Saharan African dependency to gain its independence.[13]

The role of the military in African government and politics has three distinct stages. The first stage, that of relative passivity and abstention on the part of the military from political interference, is confined to the immediate post-colonial period. During this stage, the military still remained under European control with European officers, which precluded or, at least, made more difficult African military involvement in government and politics. In the second stage, African soldiers' resentment of European officers and African political leaders erupted into mutinies. These outbursts were not intended, at least not directly, to unseat the civilian government in power, but rather, they were aimed at forcing the civilian government to adopt certain policies that would be beneficial to the military such as better pay and higher pensions and the immediate Africanization of the officers' corps. The third stage was characterized by the political coup d'état. The occupants of presidential palaces were removed from office and sometimes executed. Into their office moved the officers who had initiated the coup with the aim, they said, of redeeming the nation and restoring normalcy.

A fundamental principle of Western democracy has been the supremacy of civilian authorities over the military. Nevertheless, throughout history the military has always been involved in government and politics, in the West as well as in Africa.[14] The military has often acted as a pressure group attempting to influence political decisions. Sometimes civilian groups have themselves urged the military to intervene. Often the military has intervened of its own accord, because it regards itself as the most honest, the most efficient, and the most accomplished organization in the country. As a consequence, the military has turned out civilian governments it believes are corrupt, misguided, and inefficient. For example, in the 1984 coup which brought down Nigeria's second civilian government since independence in 1960, "The coup was announced in an early morning radio broadcast by Brigadier Saleh Abacha, who said the military had taken power because of the country's economic difficulties, and accused the Shagari administration of being *inept and corrupt*."[15] Finally, the military may intervene, when the country's instability seems to have resulted from irreconcilable differences between competing political personalities, or continued political or economic crises, or when the country has been humiliated in a military encounter with a neighbor or with foreign troops or mercenaries.

By early 1966, the armies of Africa clearly had emerged as perhaps the most significant factor in the political arena. Nevertheless, in 1963, Rupert Emerson, Harvard University's distinguished professor of African history and politics, predicted,

Because they are so young, inexperienced, and, in many instances, almost nonexistent, the military forces, which have played so large a role in other nations, cannot be expected to be of much significance in Africa for some time to come.[16]

In 1992, as Nigeria celebrated its 32nd anniversary of independence from Britain, the country had only known 9 years and 5-1/2 months of civilian government; all the remaining years were under military regimes.

During the 1960s, public order in Nigeria broke down culminating in the Biafran Civil War of 1967.[17] Political integration, political cohesion, and political stability had disappeared. The political process was characterized by centrifugal primordial ethnic loyalties taking precedence over a centripetal politically integrated Nigeria. In 1966, a military regime came to power, but, in 1979, the country's second civilian government was installed. Would it last? In 1980, Senator Shitta-Bey, who represented the new state of Lagos, said,

This federal-style Constitution is ideal for a country like Nigeria, which is so spread out and so ethnically and culturally diverse. . . . If our new system fails, it won't be out Constitution that failed us but the people who failed themselves.[18]

One summary judgment was that "the new Constitution, based on the American model, is a gem. Clearly, then, it was the Nigerians themselves who let Nigeria down."[19]

In December of 1983, under the leadership of Major General Mohammed Buhari, the military once again replaced an elected civilian government. Then, in August of 1985, General Buhari was overthrown in a bloodless coup led by Major General Ibrahim Babangida, who later proclaimed himself the country's president. In July of 1987, General Babangida unveiled a formula for the installation of a civilian government in 1992 that would terminate the specter of military rule in Nigeria.

To understand Nigeria flirtation with civilian government and democracy, one should think of a man who has been married several times, with each marriage ending in failure. Nevertheless, he is keen to try again, because his faith in the institution of marriage remains unshaken. In fact, with each failure, his enthusiasm intensifies, because his inner self propels him to try harder in the belief that next time he will succeed. Unfortunately, Nigeria's flirtation with civilian government and democracy has not been very successful; nevertheless, the romance goes on.

Nigeria is a natural leader and role model for the rest of Africa, because of its size, its resources, and the talents of its people. The ethnic discord, which continues to prevent Nigeria from attaining its great potential, does not bode well for the rest of the continent, which is not so richly endowed with human talents and natural resources but is as ethnically diverse.

This brings us to the third source of Nigeria's power that most impressed foreigners and Nigerians alike, which was the revenue the country obtained from the sale of its oil, one of the primary causes of the Biafran Civil War.[20] Nigeria is a member of OPEC, and, from 1974 through 1978, Nigeria's revenues from crude oil exports averaged above $9 billion annually.[21] In 1979, it jumped to over $15 billion and, in 1980, soared to $25 billion.[22] At the time, oil revenue accounted for 90% of all export earnings and 80% of the Federal Government's total income.[23] Furthermore, Nigeria was the second largest supplier of oil to the United States, after Saudi Arabia. Today, it is probably the fourth or fifth largest supplier, but, during the boom period, from 1979 through

1981, Nigeria exported approximately $9.5 billion worth of crude oil annually to the United States.[24] Nigeria's premium *sweet oil* was preferred by American refiners for processing into gasoline, because it released less sulfur and nitrogen oxides into the air, thereby causing less pollution.

Then, in 1982, a 30% decline in Nigeria's oil revenues occurred, and, after 1983, the glut of oil on the world market and the resulting lower prices paid for oil seriously affected Nigeria's oil income: "After years of unfettered spending, Nigeria's leaders are seeking to lower the expectations of their citizens, and have warned that the economic future can no longer be computed on high oil production levels or high oil prices."[25] By 1989, Nigeria's oil revenues had dropped to $6 billion. Moreover, the decline in oil revenues and oil prices revealed that the country's basic economic infrastructure had been realigned, and oil was seen as the culprit.

These days, around 70 percent of Nigeria's 80 million to 100 million people still live on the land, but the country cannot feed itself and spends $2.4 billion a year importing food: You can buy a frozen chicken here that has come from Alabama, and American rice to go with it. When Nigeria became independent from Britain in 1960, its agricultural products were the prime source of export earnings and subsistence farming fed many. But, along with drought, disease and war, there have been changes. Above all, oil. It brought a boom that lured young men from the land to seek riches in the cities of black Africa's most populous and wealthy nation. Migration to the cities, inspired by sudden wealth from a single commodity, is not uncommon in Africa. Zaire and Zambia experienced a similar flight from the land, and from adequate food production, because of copper booms. Eventually, the copper price collapsed, but agriculture did not revive.[26]

The bubble that burst in Nigeria's oil balloon caused the country's leaders to apply draconian measures not only to its own citizens but to the millions of foreign African workers who had been encouraged to come to Nigeria, when the times were good:

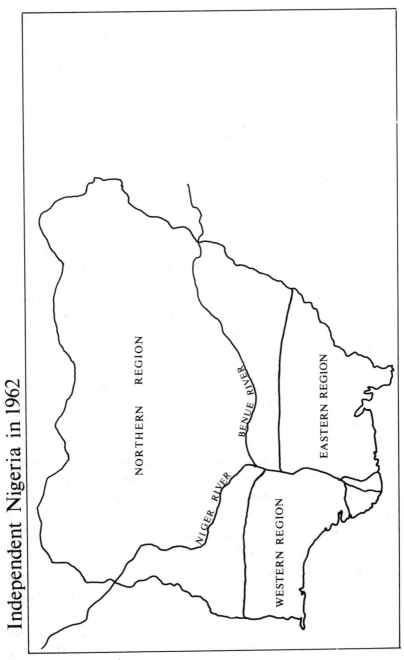

Independent Nigeria in 1962

NORTHERN REGION

BENUE RIVER

NIGER RIVER

EASTERN REGION

WESTERN REGION

About 1.2 million West Africans have left Nigeria since the Government ordered the expulsion of foreign workers four weeks ago, Internal Affairs Minister Ali Baba said today. The Minister said at a news conference that about 700,000 were from Ghana, 180,000 from Niger, 150,000 from Chad and 120,000 from Cameroon. Mr. Baba blamed Ghana for any suffering that had occurred during the exodus because of what he called its refusal to open its borders until three days before the expiration of Nigeria's two-week deadline for the departure of unskilled and unemployed people.[27]

The expulsion of foreign African workers, especially those with Ghanaian citizenship, severely hurt Nigeria's self-image and international prestige, especially in Africa. For example, almost a million Ghanaians were forced to leave Nigeria within two weeks and most were labeled *illegal aliens*, a term, until then, unheard of in reference to other Africans.

This herding of people into panicked flight is grim and cruel. It recalls Ghana's equally deplorable expulsion of thousands of Nigerian workers in 1969. But not only are Nigeria's laborers treated as disposable, they are being chased with xenophobic zeal. Always resented as competitors, they are also being blamed for increased crime and for fundamentalist rioting by Hausa-speaking Moslems. With elections impending, the aliens make a tempting political target for a government that has been forced to scale down its development goals.[28]

When oil was king, however, the revenues from oil gave Nigeria a power base that was unique among developing countries. Other developing countries claimed to be *non-aligned*, but often their economic base was too weak to support their rhetoric, and their commitment to non-alignment was compromised by East and West. But this was not so with Nigeria, for Nigeria non-alignment meant neither East nor West had preferred status. Good relations were sought with both, but a preferred status was reserved for African states and African interests.

While some African states had long waited for Nigeria's continental hegemony to emerge, others had feared it. What held Nigeria back was its lack of political integration.

Before the Biafran Civil War, which was a monstrous manifestation of Nigeria's political disintegration, three large regions were commonly spoken of as Nigeria, and their four largest ethnic groups as Nigerians. For instance, the north was said to be inhabited by the Hausa and the

Fulani, the southwest by the Yoruba, and the southeast by the Ibo (also spelled Igbo). We know now, as we should have known then, that this description was over-simplification and grossly misleading. For instance, in the southeast, the Ijaw and the Ibibio were only two of several large and distinct ethnic groups which resented and resisted Ibo hegemony. While in the north, in addition to the Hausa and the Fulani there were at least 100 other ethnic languages and dialect groups which were highly regarded by other Africans for their resistance to Hausa-Fulani hegemony. Ironically, the light-skinned Fulani subjugated the dark-skinned Hausa, who, in turn, incorporated the Fulani into their social and political systems, thus the Hausa-Fulani union.

In any case, in the north, southeast, and southwest, the Hausa-Fulani, Ibo, and Yoruba, respectively, were the dominant groups in those regions. Nevertheless, those regions were not closed preserves, spheres of influence, allocated solely to those four ethnic groups. This was one of the major false assumptions made by the British during their colonial adventure in Nigeria, thereby ignoring the considerable number of ethnic minorities, who would clamor for recognition and power before and after independence.[29]

After independence and before the Biafran Civil War, following a political crisis in the Western Region within the Yoruba ruling party, the Action Group, a fourth region, the Midwest Region, was carved out of the Western Region in 1962. In 1967, at a conference entitled *Leaders of Thought* a trend toward autonomy had emerged among the northern emirs. The views of northern minority tribe leaders and minority elements in the army added to the new sense of localism that prevailed, and explain the surprising call for creation of new states which come from the meeting of the northern *Leaders of Thought*.[30]

In May of 1967, the same month in which Biafra was declared an independent republic, the military regime issued its *12-state decree*, which abolished the former four regions and created 12 new states: 6 were carved out of the Northern Region, 3 out of the Western and Midwestern Regions, and 3 out of the Eastern Region. This began a process, which has continued up to the present, that was intended to allay the fears of minority ethnic groups of being dominated by the three major ethnic groups (the Ibo, Yoruba, and Hausa-Fulani) and would eventually lead to

The Nigerian States after 1967

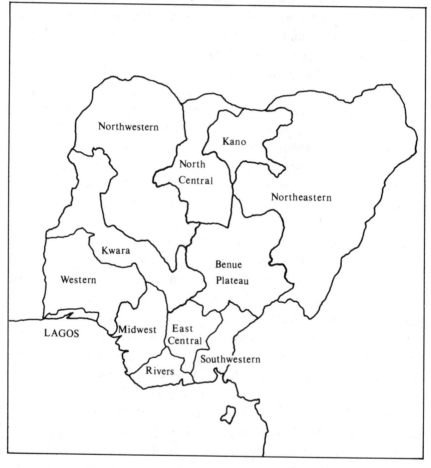

the creation of more than twenty states. In addition, the federal capital shifted from Lagos in the south to Abuja in the center of the country to allay the fears of northerners that southerners would dominate political affairs, if the capital remained in Lagos.

The subjugation or, to use the British euphemism, *pacification* of Nigeria to British rule was not easy. For instance, in the southeast, the Ibo of decentralized, middle-size societies were bitterly resentful and hostile to all forms of alien and centralized rule. Therefore, their *pacification* took many years and cost many lives. In fact, in 1914, when, in theory, all of Nigeria came under a centralized British administration, many Ibos were still fighting in the forest to avoid British attempts at their *pacification.* At this time the name Nigeria was given to the whole territory. Flora Shaw is credited with coining the name *Nigeria.*[31] She was the famous and very influential colonial editor of the *London Times* and the wife of Frederick Lugard, the British Resident in the north, the "birthplace of the concept of Indirect Rule,"[32] although this has been disputed:

> [Sir Frank Swettenham] had been one of the first and most successful of the British Residents sent in the 1870s to *advise* the Malay sultans—*advice* which, as the Colonial Office blandly admitted, *could not be disregarded.* . . . Thanks to the Lugards [Frederick and Flora Shaw], Northern Nigeria had now [1906] become a prestigious posting. . . . Northern Nigeria could now take its place, [Flora Shaw] suggested, as a model of successful English autocratic rule in the tropics beside India and Egypt. She described in detail her husband's pioneering method of indirect rule which retained the native authority of the emirs in partnership with their British rulers. . . . Old Malay hands like Swettenham and [Hugh] Clifford must have snorted—they believed they had pioneered the method [Indirect Rule in Malaya] twenty years before.[33]

In Northern Nigeria, the British came to realize, very early, that only by giving formal recognition to the existing political institutions, called emirates, could they hope to exercise even a modicum of control over so vast a region. Therefore, out of expediency and for pragmatic reasons, Frederick Lugard, the British Resident in the Northern Region, devised his scheme of Indirect Rule on which, in theory, British colonial policy in Africa came largely to be based, although the Northern Nigerian model was only repeated in Uganda, where the British Resident was Frederick Lugard.

Probably, Lugard, born in 1858 and died in 1945, who as a young soldier had served in Malaya and, therefore, was familiar with the system of Indirect Rule that had been imposed there, did not foresee that his arrangement with the Emirs of Indirect Rule would rigidify the political and social structures of Northern Nigerian society making them impregnable to modern influences. As a result, in the political sphere, the power of the Emirs was aggrandized under the umbrella of British *protection* and the system of Indirect Rule. While, in the social sphere, especially with regards to modern education, in the Muslim north, the masses stayed out of the mainstream of modern education and ideas, while in the south, Christian missionaries came, opened schools, and the floodgates were opened to new ideas and development.

In 1914, when the Northern Region and the Southern Region were united under a single, centralized system of British administration (in 1939, the Southern Region was further divided into the Western and Eastern Regions with Lagos as a separate colony), these contradictory developments became obvious.[34] The north entered the union as a closed autocratic society, dominated by the Emirs, without the trained personnel familiar with the operations of a modern participatory system of government and a modern system of public administration. The bureaucrats and technocrats needed to operate such a system had to be imported from the south and were mainly Ibos who had absorbed modern ideas and education like a sponge.

Political change came last to the north, for not only was it the last region to train its own modern civil service, but, until the 1950s, the north had no vocal opposition to British rule. The first and for many years the only Western-educated northers were the sons of titled aristocratic families whose place in the political and social structures of the emirates was ascribed and, therefore, assured, while northern peasants seemed passive and apathetic under the heavy weight of dynastic autocratic feudalism. In other words, the northern elite seemed born to wealth and power, while the northern masses seemed destined to a life of subjection and subordination. In contrast, in the south, social and political mobility were much more fluid and flexible.[35]

Thus, at Independence in 1960, as at its birth in 1914, Nigeria was a country divided between a modernizing south and a tradition-bound north, a dichotomy that also existed at Independence in Malaya between the Chinese and the Malays. Moreover, at Independence, Nigeria possessed the facade of a federal system of government, which many political pundits outside Nigeria took for the real thing. They, and the Nigerians themselves, were in for a traumatic shock, when the truth of the situation became obvious during the unsettling decade that followed, culminating in the chaotic Biafran Civil War.

Between 1946 and 1954, British and Nigerian leaders deliberated, negotiated, and operated a series of constitutions in pursuit of a mutually acceptable formula for an independent Nigeria. Both sides recognized that Nigeria could only achieve its great political potential if it remained intact, that is, a single, unified polity. As a consequence, between 1946 and 1954, British and Nigerian leaders concluded three separate constitutions with this aim in mind.

First came the Richards Constitution of 1946 named after Nigeria's governor, Sir Arthur Richards, which emphasized limited regionalism with advisory regional councils and remained the law of the land until 1951.

The 1946 Constitution set up Regional Assemblies to channel demands to a federal LegCo [Legislative Council] in Lagos. One reason for this decision was that the poor command of the English language by most northerners would work to their disadvantage, if the single federal LegCo were merely enlarged to include the North. Since these Regional Councils for Eastern, Western, and Northern Nigeria had only advisory functions, it would not be true to say that Nigeria had become a federation by virtue of the 1946 Constitution. The governor retained the balance of power at the center, though the countryside was administered according to the levels of development of each of Nigeria's Regions. In essence, the Richards Constitution instituted a system of advisory councils that would make policy recommendations at more local levels.[36]

Second came the MacPherson Constitution of 1951, named after Richards' successor, Sir John MacPherson. Richards, an unpopular governor who resigned, "had acquired the stigma of being antinationalist."[37]   The MacPherson Constitution added greater *bite* to regional power.

> Vigorous Nigerian anticolonialism forced a shortening of the projected operation period for the Richards Constitution. The colonial government had intended to make any revisions that proved necessary after nine years. However, three years of strong criticism, coupled with the resignation of Governor Richards, brought plans for a new constitutional formula. The new colonial administrator, Governor Sir John MacPherson, proved more open to Nigerian opinion. His government found that Nigerians generally favored more devolution of policy making into Regional hands. Consequently, the 1951 constitution transformed the regions, which had been merely administrative divisions, into complete political and governmental systems with executive councils and legislative assemblies. In addition, direct election to the central legislature was ended: The regional legislatures would provide the federal delegates. . . . Soon after the 1951 Constitution went into effect, the assumption that it was only temporary, coupled with a series of crises, made the system unworkable.[38]

Third came the Lyttleton Constitution of 1954 named after Oliver Lyttleton, the British Colonial Secretary, who later received a peerage and became Lord Chandos. The Lyttleton Constitution was the final formula for an independent Nigeria and became known as Nigeria's first federal constitution.

> The Lyttleton Constitution of 1954 [was] the first truly federal system since *Nigeria* came into existence in 1914. . . . In some of its major features, the Lyttleton Constitution was rather like the United States Constitution's Tenth Amendment. Powers not specifically bestowed on the federal government [were] the province of the states. However, the list of concurrent powers was impressive, and many observers hoped the Nigerian Federal Government would achieve the growth in central power that had occurred in the United States, particularly in view of the stated desires of Nigerian politicians for rapid economic development. These trends were anticipated from another point of view as well. Strong central initiative would have aided the growth of a sense of *Nigerian* identity and common purpose.[39]

Actually, the Lyttleton Constitution of 1954 de-emphasized a strong central government and emphasized regional guarantees against central government encroachment:

The revised Constitution of 1954 gave the regions greater autonomy in the Federation of Nigeria, and made Lagos the federal capital. Thus, accidents of historical acquisition together with the changing imperatives of administrative convenience were among the determinants of the present division of Nigeria into three regions.[40]

Under the Lyttleton Constitution of 1954, the central government retained only those powers thought necessary to maintain Nigeria as a single, unified polity, such as power over defense, customs, foreign affairs, and the country's common currency, the naira. On the other hand, the Lyttleton Constitution gave to the regions power over those matters that most vitally affected the emirates as political institutions such as power over regulation and recruitment of the regional civil service as well as power over rules regulating election to the regional parliament.

Under the provisions of the Lyttleton Constitution, the blueprint for an independent Nigeria, four separate civil services were created: a federal one for Lagos, the capital, and one for each of the three regions. Immediately, each regional administration recalled the ablest of its civil servants back to their region of origin. This deprived the central government of experienced Nigerians capable of operating the federal administration of a vast independent state. Furthermore, each of the leaders of the three major ethnic groups (the Ibo, the Yoruba, and the Hausa-Fulani) disappeared into his region of origin where he became the Regional Premier, while his second in command was sent to Lagos as his surrogate representative in the central government's administration. Inevitably, this made the central government, with its predominantly non-Nigerian, British civil service, function as the agent of the regional governments.

At its inception in 1960, independent Nigeria possessed the facade of a federal system of government. A facade which many pundits took for the real thing. In fact, neither foreign observers nor Nigerians themselves should have been surprised by the Nigerians' failure to make the system work. First, they had no experience with a federal system of government nor had their mentors, the British colonial administrators.

At independence, the British passed on to the Nigerians a quasi-unitary, parliamentary system of government, much like their own

Westminster model, and tried to pass it off as federalism. Merely dividing a state into regions or provinces does not constitute a federal system of government. For instance, where were the checks and balances in the Lyttleton independence constitution, with the executive, legislative, and judicial independent of each other but intimately connected each with the others? No, what the British decreed to the Nigerians, which they accepted, having no experience with any other Western system, was the British model of parliamentary democracy, and called it federalism. The government was a hybrid with bits of a unitary system attached to bits of a federal system. If anything, it was closer to a confederation than to a federation.

Second, even if the British passed on to the Nigerians a parliamentary system under the guise of federalism, they failed to instill in the Nigerian politicians a basic element that makes Britain's parliamentary democracy function so effectively: the concept of the *loyal opposition*. In the Westminster model, as practiced in Britain, the loyal opposition is prepared to take the helm of government at a moment's notice, whenever the party in power fails to maintain its majority in the House of Commons by receiving a *no-confidence* vote, thus requiring immediate new elections which could bring the loyal opposition with its *shadow cabinet* into power. No such procedure was established in Nigeria by the Lyttleton independence constitution. More importantly, the idea of a loyal opposition was never instilled into the psyche of Nigerian politicians during the era of British rule, nor during the years after 1922 when Africans were allowed to be elected members of the Legislative Council (LegCo) was the educative role of loyal opposition instilled into those who were in the minority. For example, in the Legislative Council (LegCo), the African majority had the assistance of the colonial administration's advisers and civil servants to aid it in answering questions raised by the African minority. On the other hand, the African opposition had no such bureaucratic assistance. Thus, a winner-take-all mentality was developed in LegCo and has remained a significant part of the Nigerian politician's psyche and the country's political culture.

LegCo was a forum where the zero-sum game was played out and where ethnic allegiance was enhanced and exaggerated. LegCo was not a proving ground for trust and tolerance, nor was it an incubator for developing federal minded politicians. Regionalism and ethnicity were what LegCo embraced and the Lyttleton independence constitution enhanced.

In 1986, General Ibrahim Babangida promised to return Nigeria to civilian government under an American inspired, federal constitution with only two parties competing for the presidency instead of the more than fifty political parties which started out competing in the 1979 presidential election but which were reduced to a mere five by the Nigerian Election Commission. But Babangida's two party system was an odd mix indeed. Despite the trappings of electoral involvement, Babangida's *Transitional Program* was tightly controlled by him. For instance, he decreed that all former politicians were banned from participating in the process, and the two-party model he imposed ran counter to Nigeria's multiparty political culture. Furthermore, when none of thirteen potential parties gained his approval, Babangida decided to *create* two new parties of his own: one party *a little to the left* and the other *a little to the right*. Babangida was setting pre-conditions for attaining political cohesion, political integration, and political stability with a citizenry famous for its independent-mindedness. Nonetheless, with the prospect of a new civilian government, two perpetual questions remained foremost in the minds of the very ethnically oriented Nigerians: would it succeed and how long would it last? Only time would tell, but this we know for certain: instant democracy is a myth.

Nigeria has had a long and bloody history of ethnic conflicts, emphasizing *tribal* affiliation, going back at least to the months preceding the Biafran Civil War. In late 1966, thousands of Ibos working in the north were slaughtered by northerners with more than a million surviving Ibos fleeing for their lives to the Eastern Region, their homeland.

In more recent times, the ethnic conflicts have centered on religious animosity. For instance, on October 17, 1991, at the time of the 1991 national census, the *New York Times* reported,

Muslims pursued their hunt for Christians today in religious rioting in the northern city of Kano. . . . President Ibrahim Babangida cut short his visit to Zimbabwe for the meeting of Commonwealth nations to return to Lagos tonight. . . . Government troops have failed to contain the violence which began when thousands of Muslims took to the streets to protest the granting of police permission for a Christian revival meeting. . . . Deadly clashes between Muslim and Christian zealots are frequent in the north of Nigeria. . . . Muslims are believed to outnumber Christians, but the question is so sensitive that a national census will not ask people to identify their religion. Three previous attempts to conduct a census were abandoned because of religious and ethnic manipulation of the count. Much of the violence was centered on Kano's Sabongari neighborhood, which has a large population of Christians.[41]

Although regionalism is less a threat to Nigeria's political integration, religious animosity, which has often been at the core of regional affinity, continues to hold sway and severely threatens the country's territorial integration and sense of a common national identity. The north is overwhelmingly Muslim; the southwest and southeast have been strongly influenced by Christianity. Specific figures are difficult to come by, and none was solicited for the 1991 national census, but estimates are that 50% of all Nigerians are Muslim, while 40% are Christian. The religious carnage has usually taken place in Northern Nigeria and rarely, if ever, in the south. This suggests that religious animosity may result in an eventual division of a country that was stitched together, for the convenience of the British, along sectarian lines. Nigeria is not alone in having to face this dreadful dilemma, for the Muslim/Christian cleavage in Sub-Saharan Africa has played an essential role in the distrust of fellow citizens between northern Muslims and southern Christians in Chad as well as in the on-going civil war in The Sudan. In Nigeria, until this religious quagmire is nullified, the country may remain a geographical expression, an historical accident, but not a nation, and may never attain its much vaunted potential as an international as well as a continental superpower.

Summary

After nearly a decade of military rule, Nigeria held its first free presidential elections on June 12, 1993, against a backdrop of social unrest and disillusionment. The exhilaration many Nigerians felt in 1986, when General Ibrahim Babangida promised a swift return to elective civilian government, were supplanted by rising anger and anxiety over the sluggish pace of political change.

About 39 million Nigerians were eligible to vote for candidates from two new parties, which the military rulers created for the presidential elections. Both men were wealthy businessmen, Mashood Abiola of the center-left Social Democratic Party, and Bashir Tofa of the center-right National Republican Convention. Both men are reputed to have spent millions of dollars of their own money in the contest for a four-year term. Furthermore, both Mr. Abiola and Mr. Tofa are Muslims, which was said to worry many Christians. Mr. Abiola, who comes from the mostly urban southwest, which is dominated by the Yoruba ethnic group, traveled extensively in the North. Mr. Tofa, whose natural base is the North, which is mostly Hausa-Fulani, spent much of his time in the South. For his part, General Babangida repeatedly assured the country that his commitment to hand power back to elected civilian officials on august 27, 1993, was irrevocable. Nevertheless, Nigeria's planned return to civilian government was suspended, when a commission appointed by the military rulers, i.e., General Babangida set aside the results of the presidential election on the grounds that they were rigged. At the time, there were growing indications that the candidate of the Social Democratic Party, Mashood Abiola, was well on his way to a resounding victory over his rival, Bashir Tofa of the National Republican Convention.

Ending months of speculations, General Ibrahim Babangida resigned on August 26, 1993, and a new interim civilian leader was sworn in, Ernest Shonekan, a 57-year-old Harvard-educated businessman *was appointed* by General Babangida to head the interim government. But Mr. Shonekan's commitment to democratic rule was questioned by the political opposition and even by some neutral analysts. They cited his virtual silence and acquiescence to General Babangida's decision in June 1993 to annul Nigeria's first civilian presidential elections in nearly a decade. Mr. Shonekan announced that the next presidential elections would be held on February 19, 1994. In the interim, however, a military coup replaced Mr. Shonekan and his regime, which consisted almost entirely of either close friends or longtime political allies of General Babangida. *Plus ça change, plus c'est la même chose.*

Notes

1. Obafemi Awolowo, *Path to Nigerian Freedom* (London: Faber and Faber, 1947), 47-48.

2. *The Hammond Almanac* of 1982 says 379,628 square miles, while *The World Almanac* of 1992 says 356,667 square miles. As with all things statistical concerning Africa, the numbers are often inconsistent.

3. Kenneth Noble, "Nigeria Reveals Census' Total, 88.5 Million, and Little More," *New York Times*, 25 March 1992.

4. Larry Diamond, *Class, Ethnicity and Democracy in Nigeria* (Syracuse, NY: Syracuse University Press, 1988), xi.

5. Jean Herskovits, "Democracy in Nigeria," *Foreign Affairs* (Winter issue 1979/1980): 314.

6. Aristotle, *Politics*, 179.

7. Ibid., 180-181, and 182.

8. Michael Kaufman, "In Africa, When Lagos Speaks Everybody Else Listens," *New York Times*, 2 July 1978.

9. Pranaye Gupte, "Civilian Leader Quickly Puts His Stamp on Nigeria," *New York Times*, 19 August 1980.

10. Clifford May, "Africa's Men in Khaki Are Often a Law unto Themselves," *New York Times*, 6 October 1985.

11. "Nigeria: Bold Initiatives for the Future: Military Rule until 1992," in Colin Legum, ed., *Africa Contemporary Record 1986-1987* (London: Africana Publishing Company, 1988), 19:B115.

12. John de St. Jorre, *The Nigerian Civil War* (London: Hodder and Stoughton, 1972) and Michael Mok, *Biafra Journal: A*

Personal Report on a People in Agony (New York: Time-Life Books, 1969).

13. John Shingler and F. Seth Singleton, *Africa in Perspective* (New York: Hayden Books, 1967), 274. Concerning Ghana, Vice President Richard Nixon was the United States representative at Ghana's independence celebrations. Upon his return to Washington, Mr. Nixon sent the following memorandum to President Eisenhower: "We cannot talk equality to the peoples of Africa and Asia and practice inequality in the United States. In the national interest, as well as for the moral issues involved, we must support the necessary steps which will assure progress toward the elimination of discrimination in the United States." "Memorandum from the Vice President to the President of the United States," *State Department Bulletin* (22 April 1957).

14. At least since Napoleon, the French have utilized the military, especially the army, as an integrative instrument: from the highest to the lowest citizen, all must serve for the *gloire* of France, which instilled and enhanced a sense of a common national identity. In Africa, this has not been the case, for the military, in colonial as well as post-colonial times, has been served by men from specific ethnic groups, where the loyalty to their own ethnicity has not only been enhanced but often been exaggerated.

15. Reuters, "Army Seizes Control in Nigeria Coup," *Los Angeles Times*, 1 January 1984.

16. Rupert Emerson, "Nation-Building in Africa," in Karl Deutsch and William Foltz, eds., *Nation-Building* (New York: Atherton Press, 1963). 115.

17. "Prior to its politicization in 1966, the Nigerian army had been predominantly composed of a curious mixture of minority tribe troops, mostly Tiv and other middle belt northerners, and Ibo officers. The slaughters of July 1966 changed the ethnic texture of the army drastically. Ibo troops and officers were killed or left in the North; northerners deserted units located

in the east. Most units in the Western Region were manned by northerners, since few Yoruba had shown much interest in military life. By March 1967, it was only Ojukwu's East Region that was rebelling against the new Gowon regime." John Ostheimer, *Nigerian Politics* (New York: Harper and Row, 1973), 69-70.

18. Pranaye Gupte, "Nigeria, a Year Away from Military Rule, Struggles to Build a U.S.-Style Democracy," *New York Times*, 17 August 1980.

19. John de St. Jorre, "Nigeria's Unhappy Prospects," *New York Times*, 7 January 1984.

20. Oil had just been discovered off the shores of the Eastern Region, and Ibos, who considered the region their preserve, resented what they considered excessive shares of the oil revenues from their region going to northern projects. Thus, after the Ibo military leader, Colonel Ojukuwu, failed to attain autonomy for the Eastern Region, in May of 1967, he withdrew the Eastern Region from the federal union and declared Biafra an independent republic. Soon after, an all-out civil war began which was fought almost entirely in the Eastern Region. "The *de facto* secession of the Eastern Region dates from October 1966, after which time no effective federal power was exercised there." Ostheimer, 65.

21. Carey Winfrey, "Oil and Nigeria's Economy," *New York Times*, 8 July 1979.

22. Clifford May, "Nigeria's Oil Export Earnings," *New York Times*, 8 January 1984.

23. The non-petroleum products that were once so important for Nigeria's export market have either entirely disappeared, as in the case of peanuts, once the staple of the colonial north, where sacks of them were stacked in pyramids ten storeys high, or have declined drastically, as in the case of tin, rubber, cocoa, and palm oil.

24. Alan Cowell, "Nigeria's Oil Exports to the U.S.," *New York Times*, 26 November 1982.

25. Ibid., "World Oil Glut Cramps Nigeria's Development," *New York Times*, 26 November 1982.

26. Ibid., "Nigeria, Rich with Oil, Is Dependent on U.S. and Other Nations for Food," *New York Times*, 15 August 1981.

27. "Nigeria Says 1.2 Million Have Been Expelled," *New York Times*, 15 February 1983.

28. Editorial, "Moving Misery in Africa," *New York Times*, 3 February 1983.

29. British Colonial Office, *Nigeria: Report of the Commission Appointed to Inquire into the Fears of Minorities and the Means of Allaying Them* (London: HMSO, July 1958).

30. Ostheimer, 70.

31. Flora Shaw was one of two women who had a considerable influence in the development of British colonial policy in Nigeria: Shaw, through her position as the London Times journalist and as the wife of Frederick Lugard, the first Resident in Northern Nigeria, and Margery Perham, an astute student of Nigerian political development about which she wrote continuously, from her position as an Oxford University professor but also from her relationship with Lugard, for they were close friends, and she was his biographer. During the interwar period, Perham was considered progressive in her thinking about Nigerian political development, but by the end of the Second World War, her thoughts were considered anachronistic, at least they were by the Africans. In 1946, she wrote, "I do not mean by this that the British Government will or should in the immediate future hand over the final responsibility for this vast region with its still unintegrated groups of peoples to the first small group of African officials and professional men who emerge at the centre." Awolowo,

Path to Nigerian Freedom, 15. Fourteen years later, Nigeria gained its independence from Britain.

32. Gwendolen Carter, ed., *National Unity and Regionalism in Eight African States* (Ithaca, NY: Cornell University Press, 1966), 4.

33. Valerie Pakenham, *The Noonday Sun: Edwardians in the Tropics* (London: Methuen, 1985), 25, 34.

34. L. Diamond, *Class, Ethnicity and Democracy in Nigeria*, 28.

35. Okwudiba Nnoli, *Ethnic Politics in Nigeria* (Enugu, Nigeria: Fourth Dimension Publishers, 1978).

36. Ostheimer, 23.

37. James Coleman, *Nigeria: Background to Nationalism* (Berkeley: University of California Press, 1958), 309.

38. Ostheimer, 24.

39. Ibid., 27-28.

40. Coleman, 48.

41. Throughout the 1980s, the *New York Times* continuously chronicled Nigeria's religious massacres. For example, "At Least 1,000 People Are Killed as Nigeria Crushes Islamic Sect" (12 January 1981), "Flames of Islamic Fervor Unsettle Nigeria's North" (29 April 1982), "300 Believed Killed in Religious Rioting in Nigeria" (30 October 1982), "Nigerian Toll Put at 452 in Religious Riots" (1 November 1982), "An Outburst of Cult Strife Tests Nigeria's Civil Rule" (16 November 1982), "30 Die in Nigeria as Islam Militants Brawl" (28 February 1984), "1,000 Are Reported Dead in North Nigeria Clashes" (5 March 1984), "Religious Frictions Heat Up in Nigeria" (12 August 1984), "A Burst of Moslem Fervor in Nigeria: The North Stirs and the South Frets" (21 February 1986).

Chapter Seven
South Africa: The Decline and Fall of Apartheid

In 1948, the Afrikaners came to power as the National Party under a slogan termed apartheid. The Afrikaners, who for centuries were known as *Boers*, a Dutch word meaning farmers or peasants which most of them were well into the third decade of the twentieth century, have taken to calling themselves Afrikaners, a word that *sounds* African. They have done so to justify their presence on the African continent, in general, and in South African, in particular, by implying that they are as much indigenous to the African continent as are the Africans themselves. It is part of a propaganda ploy to give their presence in South African some semblance of legitimacy.

In 1964, Brian Bunting, an English-speaking white South African born in Johannesburg, wrote,

> The tragedy of the South African situation is that the Nationalist government has adopted a position from which it cannot retreat without destroying the very basis of its power.[1]

Today, the National Party is retreating from its position of almost half a century as the result of changes instituted by President F. W. de Klerk with much of the cohesive organizational structure of the Party and its tight control over members in disarray, as the National Party and its leaders flounder in their attempts to retain the reins of power in the face of determined African demands for the ultimate in dramatic political change: majority rule. At the same time, Afrikaner reactionaries reject any actions on the part of the National Party and its leaders that indicate a change from the *status quo*: white supremacy. From what are African nationalists demanding a change, and from what are Afrikaner reactionaries refusing to retreat? The answer for both is the system of apartheid.

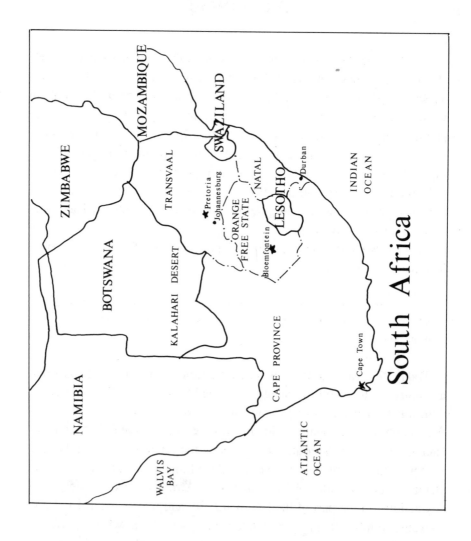

The system of apartheid is not new in South Africa. It is a modification of a policy which is as old as the Dutch presence in South Africa. The earlier policy was known as *Baasskap*, which in Dutch meant mastery, domination, white supremacy.[2] The modification under the system of apartheid meant an increase in the degree of racial separation and racial subjugation, with white domination extended to all aspects of the Africans' social, economic, and political life.

Put succinctly, *Baasskap* kept the races separated and subjugated by custom, while apartheid accomplished this feat *by statute*. In other words, white domination has been a way of life in South Africa for almost 350 years, but, since 1948, the customary system of *Baasskap* has been formalized, institutionalized, and extended, *by law*, under the system of apartheid. *Law*, which is the cornerstone of a democratic system of government, has been used fraudulently for the purposes of white supremacists not for justice but for domination of the Africans.

This system of domination has been called many things, but it is clearly a *plural society* in John Furnivall's usage of the term, although he did not think so, for Furnivall did not formulate his theory of the plural society with the African majority in South African given even a scintilla of consideration. His only concern was with the white minority of European origin:

> Outside the tropics society may have plural features, notably in South Africa, Canada and the United States, and also in lands where the Jew has not been fully assimilated into social life; in other countries also there are mixed populations with particularist tendencies. But in general these mixed populations have at least a common tradition of Western culture, and, despite a different racial origin, they meet on equal terms and their relations are not confined solely to the economic sphere. There is a society with plural features, but not a plural society.[3]

In order to give some semblance of legitimacy to their system of apartheid, the Afrikaners devised a theory for the practice, and, for this purpose, a propaganda machinery was developed.

The Afrikaners claimed that between the seventeenth and nineteenth centuries most of South Africa was empty of human inhabitants. They claimed that during this period, Europeans settled in regions that were devoid of human habitation, which, therefore, became their by right of first occupancy. At the same time, so claimed the theory, African migrants from north and central Africa were settling in other uninhabited regions, which became theirs by right of first occupancy. Nothing was said about the right of first occupancy by the nonmigrant, indigenous Africans, such as the San and the Khoikhoi, whom the whites referred to as Bushmen and Hottentots respectively.[4] "Neither the Black nation nor the White nation have a prior claim to all of South Africa except to those territories which they settled by right of first occupation."[5] By this tidy theorizing, the white minority took 87% of the land for itself and allocated the remaining 13%, most of which was inhospitable if not uninhabitable, to the Africans.

The theory of apartheid admitted that racial domination and separation had been a way of life, since the first Dutch Protestants and French Huguenot settlers arrived in the seventeenth century. The theory claimed, however, that customary *Baasskap* was a static system of social degradation, economic deprivation, and political subjugation, while apartheid was a dynamic system providing for the emancipation of the Africans into their own self-governing homelands.

The so-called homeland system of independent African states within, but separate from, the South African Republic was the theory's way of meeting international criticisms of the policies and practices of apartheid, while, at the same time, an attempt to placate Africans' impatience, frustration, and fury over the absence of any fundamental changes affecting their daily lives. The so-called homeland system was, however, not only not a fundamental change; it was no change at all. It was merely a switch in nomenclature and a shift in tactics. The *reserves*, to which the Africans had been consigned, since 1913, were metaphorically converted into so-called homelands thereby maintaining the long-term strategy, and the fundamental basis of the entire system of apartheid, of continued white supremacy:

The Native Land Act of 1913:   This legislation prohibited Africans from purchasing land outside designated native reserves and even from entering into sharecropping arrangements in the *white* agricultural areas. Its larger implication, made clearer in subsequent legislation, was that the reserves were the only places where Africans could reside except to the extent that the interests and convenience of the whites required them to be elsewhere. African laborers were needed on farms outside the reserves, but their status was to be that of contract wage laborers or labor tenants rather than sharecroppers or *squatters*. Similarly their presence was required in urban-industrial areas, where they became the majority of the work force; but the principle was established in the 1920s that the influx should be limited, as much as possible, to those who were absolutely essential to the economy.[6]

The theory of apartheid claimed that Africans in South Africa were not a homogeneous ethnic group but rather a heterogeneous group of separate nations and that the ethnic divisions among them was so fundamental and so deeply felt that they could not possibly unite to form a single nation. Some Afrikaners referred to the early nineteenth century internecine *Mfecane* of Africans massacring one another to justify this claim:

> Known in Sotho as the *Difaqane* ("hammering"), and in Nguni languages as the *Mfecane* ("crushing," implying something like the idea of total war), it was a cataclysmic event, *one of the great formative events of African history . . . , which positively dwarfs the Great Trek*. In terms of geographical range and numbers of people involved, this assessment is undoubtedly true, for the *Mfecane* scattered African chiefdoms in fragments across half the continent of Africa.[7]

Therefore, under the disguise of self-determination and independence for the so-called homelands, the theory of apartheid sought to prevent the unification of Africans against the system. In dividing up 13% of the country's poorest land into so-called homelands, the theory stressed African ethnicity, that is, the separateness and incompatibility of African ethnic groups. Thus, under the guise of avoiding potentially devastating conflicts among Africans of different ethnic groups, the theory claimed that the system of apartheid would separate each ethnic group and allot to each its own so-called homeland, which was its by right of first occupancy.

Notwithstanding, the South African regime's protestations to the contrary, until the so-called homeland system came into existence, probably no region in South Africa which was inhabited by only one African ethnic group. In other words, the so-called homeland system was a draconian ploy to abate African unity and its long-developing African nationalism. It was a manifestation of the colonial policy of divide and rule.

Why did the Afrikaners go to such lengths to try and legitimize the system of apartheid with a theory? Because at the heart of the Afrikaner theory of apartheid was *fear*. On the one hand, the Afrikaners *feared* that if the Africans were to unite, this would seriously threaten white supremacy and white domination. In other words, the Afrikaners *feared* African *revenge* for centuries of unmitigated abuses. Some of the literati probably recalled Becky Sharp's remark in Thackeray's *Vanity Fair* that *revenge* was normal. On the other hand, and just as important, the Afrikaners *feared* their loss of cultural identity. They *feared* that once the door was opened to political integration, then social integration and eventually cultural assimilation would follow, and then they would be swallowed up by the African ethnic majority. This possibility was plainly stated, in 1955, in the *Tomlinson Report*: "The choice is clear: either the *challenge* must be accepted, or the inevitable *consequences* of the integration of the Bantu and the European population groups into a common society, must be endured."[8]

While the Afrikaners persuaded themselves that the system of apartheid was in the best interest of the Africans, they also persuaded themselves that separate development was the only way to avoid their own cultural assimilation and subsequent extinction. The theory of apartheid, therefore, claimed that total separation of blacks and whites was necessary, with Africans returning to their so-called homelands, which, although small, would, in time, become viable economic entities, with temporary African labor complementing permanent white labor in South Africa itself. In theory, therefore, the centerpiece of the system of apartheid was to be the establishment of the so-called homelands as viable political and economic entities. In fact, they were nothing of the sort.

The *Tomlinson Report*, which was the most comprehensive analysis of the potential for developing the so-called homelands, declared that for these regions to support, after 25 or 30 years, even an African population of seven million (today, there are more than 28 million Africans representing 78.3% of the total population),[9] would require an immediate expenditure of $70 million and $300 million over the first 10 years:

The extent of the financial requirements must be regarded as a function of the seriousness of the problems as revealed in the previous chapters. The problems include, among other things, the destruction of resources, the poverty and ignorance of the Bantu, the unproductive utilization of human resources, the concentration of industrial activities in a small number of places of which the Bantu are flocking, with undesirable social consequences. In view of the fact that in the initial stages of development of any under-developed country, difficult problems of adjustment have to be handled, the commission does not wish to submit an over ambitious programme. A ten-year period was regarded as the most appropriate commencing period and expenditure over this initial period is estimated [at] £104,486 (millions).[10]

The regime's response was,

The Government's attitude towards the recommendations of the Tomlinson Commission were made known in a White Paper, published in April, 1956. . . . The Government acknowledges the valuable work done by the Commission in collecting factual data. It commends the Commission for the unequivocal rejection of a policy of integration and for the acceptance of the policy of Apartheid or Separate Development. While it will pay heed to the Commission's recommendations on the administrative and other measures necessary to attain the objects in view, it must also consider views based upon much wider practical experience of administrative affairs, the existing machinery, and the country's financial resources. . . . The Government agrees that it is essential that large sums be expended in the development of the Bantu Areas. The extent and rate of development cannot be accurately determined in advance, and the Government, therefore, does not deem it advisable to fix, at this stage, the amount needed for the various projects.[11]

The paucity of the regime's expenditures and the resulting poverty of the so-called homelands made impossible the productive use of their human resources. This poverty underwrote the Africans' migration into white areas in search of work, for survival, while consigning to the so-called homelands the old, the infirmed, and the women with children. However, the most fundamental objection to the apartheid policy of so-called homelands was that African preoccupation with and participation in this draconian ploy distracted and drained African energies from what should have been the primary objective of their political activities: their full participation in the political, social, and economic life of the Republic of South Africa and not in some client or satellite state.

On March 18, 1985, Pik Botha, South Africa's Foreign Minister, appeared on American television's *ABC News Nightline* and proclaimed that South Africa was the only country on the African continent where the press daily and openly criticized the regime. Some media experts acknowledged this license to criticize. For example, Frank Barton concluded that South Africa's press, "which though also bound by the ruthless philosophy of apartheid, still has more freedom than newspapers in any other part of the continent."[12] But why is a critical press, which is a vital ingredient in a democratic society, allowed to flourish in a political system which is categorically undemocratic in principle and in practice? The answer is that a critical press is an essential part of the ultimate aim of the apartheid regime's propaganda machinery which is to maintain white rule in South Africa.

For instance, a critical press enhances the regime's legitimacy in the eyes of sympathetic Western leaders and image makers and the appearance of commitment to the democratic principle of freedom of expression. Moreover, the South African regime perceives a critical press as a safety valve for releasing, nonviolently, some of the country's tensions, frustrations, and dissatisfactions. Furthermore, South Africa's critical press is a legacy from the Dutch and British tradition of an active and vigorous press. Therefore, the regime, for propaganda purposes, would not like to appear to be usurping that tradition. Finally, in conjunction with a critical press, the regime maintains an extensive propaganda machinery, which disseminates counter-information to counteract adverse criticisms from the critical press. In short, the South African regime allows a critical press to exist and to flourish in order to achieve its own undemocratic ends.

Propaganda is a form of communication, a deliberate manipulation of attitudes and opinions by the use of symbols rather than by the use of force, which could be counter-productive, for the use of force could lead to the use of counter-force. Therefore, the skill in the implementation of propaganda, which the South African regime learned by emulating Nazi Germany, was one of the most effective means for white supremacists to attain and retain power, for the ultimate aim of the regime's propaganda machinery was to maintain white domination in South Africa.

The South African regime institutionalized its propaganda machinery with the establishment of the Department of Information, which was created in the image of Nazi Germany's propaganda machine, and which was subdivided into the State Information Service, for external image-making propaganda, and the Ministry of Information, for internal purposes. Internal consumption meant placating and co-opting the white minority by making it aware that the regime's aims were to maintain the status quo and secure white supremacy.

An example of the external and internal usages of the regime's propaganda for dual purposes are two diametrically opposed statements by the same man, Hendrik Verwoerd, to two separate audiences, with two different messages. First, on April 2, 1961, in an interview with the *London Sunday Times*, the Prime Minister of South Africa said, "Apartheid is widely identified with race prejudice, whereas its very purpose, is to remove prejudice and create harmony."[13] Then, speaking in the South African House of Assembly to an all-white audience on January 25, 1963, Prime Minister Verwoerd proclaimed, "We want to keep South Africa White. . . . Keeping it White can mean only one thing, namely, White domination, not leadership, not guidance, but control—supremacy."[14]

In South Africa, the Department of Information was the regime's major instrument for perpetuating its propaganda purposes. *Information* was the preferred term for communication rather than *propaganda*, because of the suspicion the latter would arouse. But whether termed information or propaganda, the process of communication was highly selective: the material chosen or the ideas put forth were intended to elicit a specific and desired reaction in attitudes and opinions.

The tone of the South African propaganda was not defensive. The refusal to seem defensive stemmed from the belief that such a posture would imply that something was unjust about the apartheid system's policies and programs. Therefore, the South African regime always chose *security* from outside instigators and inside agitators as the primary goal of its *information* policies and programs. Outside instigators were portrayed as communists, while inside agitators were designated African nationalists.

The image that South African propaganda sought to project was one of a highly developed, exceedingly well-administered industrial state with a rich Western heritage of art and culture, scientific knowledge, and generous philanthropy; all developed in a country that was well endowed with animal, human, and mineral wealth. South African propaganda sought to create an image of white intelligence and generosity in contrast to African stupidity, incompetence, ingratitude, and greed: an image of white civilization constantly threatened by African primitivism.

A favorite device of South African propaganda was to answer a question that had not been asked, while leaving unanswered a question that had been asked thereby diverting the questioner's attention away from the original question. For example, to the question, "Do Africans receive a fair share of the regime's financial allotments for education, literacy programs, health, social services, and other necessities and amenities," the regime's spokesman replied,

> The standard of education and the degree of literacy in the Republic are not equalled by many other countries in Africa. . . . South Africa's peoples enjoy social services of which the quality and scope are nowhere better in Africa and perhaps only rarely elsewhere. . . . The largest hospital in Africa is the Baragwanath near Johannesburg. It caters exclusively for Non-Whites. . . . South Africa's per capita food consumption is by far the highest in Africa.[15]

What was left unanswered was how much financial assistance was specifically allotted to the needs and amenities of the Africans. The response was typical of the diversionary tactics employed by the Department of Information.

A major aim of the South African regime's propaganda machinery had always been to *sell* the system of apartheid to an outside world which was becoming more critical and impatient with its segregation policies and discrimination programs; not because such policies and programs were not in existence in other countries but because they were being instituted and heinously implemented by whites against Africans on the continent of Africa itself. Furthermore, the outside world was gradually agitating for equality, justice, and majority rule in South Africa. This challenge required considerable ingenuity on the part of South Africa's image makers. Thus, the propaganda machine sought to define the system of apartheid in terms that would appeal to Western liberal and democratic ideals, because its propagators realized that the term apartheid, which had been coined by Dr. Malan during the 1948 election but had been alluded to in 1895 by a journalist in an English language newspaper, had become anathema to the outside world, which the regime was endeavoring to cultivate, with no government openly prepared to condone it. Apartheid, therefore, was first defined as *separate development*. It then became *separate freedom* with the emphasis on the word freedom. Soon the word *separate* was decided to have negative connotations and, therefore, raised unwanted problems, and so apartheid was redefined as *parallel development*, which implied that African society would progress at the same rate as white society and would receive from the regime comparable financial assistance. Eventually, apartheid would be used to mean *plural democracy*, which implied new social and political rights for all, including Africans.

This constant redefinition of apartheid was accompanied by a replacement for *Baasskap*, meaning white domination, with *Buurskap*, meaning neighborliness. But whatever the terminology or the definition, the regime's policy remained the same: white supremacy.

In 1977, for a twelve-month period, Barbara Rogers itemized the budget of South African propaganda agencies in the United States alone and arrived at the figure of $1,301,465 million. She added, "This total *excludes* many items, e.g., SAA promotion, South African Government Embassy, Missions to international organizations and consulates, and the cost of support operations (including sponsored tours) in South Africa."[16]

During the 1970s, as its system of apartheid became more and more odious to the international community, the South African propaganda machinery sought to declare itself opposed to racism and racial discrimination. In 1976, for example, Dr. C. Mulder,[17] proclaimed,

Race discrimination is being done away with and in its place a positive alternative is offered which allows for the development of all national groups in South Africa and acknowledges and respects the human dignity of each individual.[18]

Positive alternative referred to the so-called homelands, which, at an earlier stage in nomenclature development, were referred to as *Bantustans.* The South African regime now proclaimed, "The development of the Bantu should be based not on an extension of political rights in competition with the Whites but on the traditional authority and order of their own national groups."[19] The apartheid regime now emphasized that its policy was to promote the "self-determination of its tribal nations and proposes to provide sovereign states for each different nation in its historical homeland."[20]

At this juncture, an analysis of the decline and fall of apartheid must take into account the decline and fall of liberalism in South Africa, for the Afrikaners were not alone but had a collaborator in London: the British Liberal Party Government.

In today's usage, the term liberalism is a much abused, misused, and misunderstood terminology. In fact, much of what is termed conservatism in today's parlance was termed liberalism in the nineteenth century, when the term was first coined in Spain and later employed by the English Enlightenment to legitimize the industrial revolution, the rise of capitalism, and the new-found freedom of the individual. In the nineteenth century, liberalism evolved as an antithesis to the centralization of authority and ideas: whether as conceived by Marx as totalitarianism or practiced by the Roman Catholic Church as authoritarianism.

Throughout the nineteenth century, the *locus operandi* of liberalism was in Protestant thought and institutions. Even in the twentieth century, ideas and institutions that are accustomed to centralized control have rarely, if ever, been comfortable with the concept of liberalism, for the essence of nineteenth century liberalism was non-violent, non-revolutionary, evolutionary change. At its center was the freedom of the individual to think and act in accordance with his own conscience, while tolerating the ideas and actions of others which were not in accord with his own.

Today, the term liberalism has taken on myriad meanings depending upon who uses the expression and the substance of the user's political agenda. As used in this study, liberalism pertains to the duties, rights, and responsibilities of individual citizens.

In modern political systems, two basic types of citizens have evolved: (a) *consumer citizens*, whose main concern is what the political system can do for them in terms of rewards and services, and (b) *participatory citizens*, whose main concern is what can they do to improve the political system in order to make life more commodious for themselves and their fellow citizens. In all political systems, of whatever size, whether families, class, states, or nations, the linchpin of societal organization and the most vital status of the individual is that of citizen. It was this status the Boers and the British denied the Africans.

Liberalism was not indigenous to South Africa but rather, in theory and in practice, liberalism was a concept imported to South Africa via the Atlantic Revolution, emanating from the American and French revolutions. Moreover, during the Dutch Administration of South Africa from 1652 to 1795, South Africa was not ruled by the Dutch Government but rather by the Dutch East India Company. This was also the case with India during its formative colonial years, when India was ruled not by the British Government but by the British East India Company until the Indian mutiny of 1857-1858, after which the British East India Company ceased to exist, and the British Crown, with Victoria as Empress, took over the Company's duties and treaty responsibilities in the subcontinent. In both instances, in India and in South Africa, these chartered companies were less interested in liberal, democratic government than in achieving sizable profits for their stockholders by the most expeditions and least expensive means possible.

In 1602, the Dutch East India Company was founded with the intention of exploiting and developing the spice riches of what, today, is called Indonesia, but then was known as Java and sometimes as Batavia. This Company was given extensive political, judicial, economic, and military authority by the Dutch Government. Thus, it became one of the chief organs of Dutch imperialism in places as disparate as Cape Colony, South Africa, and Jakarta, Indonesia.[21] In 1619, the Dutch East India Company became ensconced at Batavia. Later, in 1652, it established a kitchen garden at the Cape for the purpose of supplying its ships on the way to Batavia, around the Cape of Good Hope, with fresh fruits and vegetables to prevent their sailors from developing scurvy: a disease resulting from the body's deficiency of vitamin C.

In 1795, the British navy, under an agreement with the Dutch House of Orange, seized the South African Cape Colony to prevent it from falling into the hands of French imperialists, who were losing their hope of a global empire after losses to Britain in India and in Canada. The transfer of the Cape Colony from the Dutch East India to the British Crown took place in three stages. First came Britain's temporary occupation of the Cape Colony in 1795, the same year that the French invaded Holland, and proclaimed it the Batavian Republic. Second came the repossession of the Cape Colony by the Dutch in 1803, but the Dutch occupied the Cape for less than three years, when, in 1806, the British reoccupied the Cape Colony. Again, the impetus for this seizure was a rambunctious French army rampaging through Europe. However, this second tenure, by the British, was undertaken with some idea of permanent occupation, for now the British recognized the strategic importance of the Cape for the protection of the route to India, long before the shorter route through the Suez Canal was built. Third and finally, Britain was granted permanent possession of the Cape Colony by the victorious powers at the Congress of Vienna, in 1814-1815, which divvied up the spoils of the Napoleonic Wars.

Against this historic background we must now determine the significance of liberalism in South Africa.

Both Afrikaner reactionaries, such as the Conservative Party, and extreme African nationalists, such as the Pan-Africanist Congress, deeply resent the rhetoric of liberalism. Why this deep antipathy by both groups? For their part, Afrikaner reactionaries, as manifested in their Conservative Party, view liberalism as suicidal for whites in South Africa, because of its advocacy of universal civil rights and a common franchise for all citizens regardless of ethnicity. These Afrikaner reactionaries pine for the *good old days* of *Baasskap*, when the white minority was unquestionably the Boss. They regard such notions as liberalism as naïve, and the proponents of such ideas as communist deceivers masquerading under the disguise of majority rule.

For their part, extreme African nationalists view as irrelevant the liberalists' insistence on nonviolent change and the evolutionary reform of a system which all African nationalists denounce as illegal and immoral, for the exclusion of the African majority from any meaningful political participation in the country of their birth and the land of their ancestors. Extreme African nationalists no longer plead for admission into a white dominated system whose legitimacy they deny. Furthermore, they demand the exclusion of all whites from any meaningful role in the political system which they predict will inevitably replace the apartheid autocracy.

This, then, is a critical moment in South Africa's political history, which was anticipated by the wise Alexis de Tocqueville, when he wrote of the decline and fall of the Bourbon monarchy:

> Patiently endured so long as it seemed beyond redress, a grievance comes to appear intolerable once the possibility of removing it crosses men's minds. For the mere fact that certain abuses have been remedied draws attention to the others and they now appear more galling.[22]

De Tocqueville's axiom holds true for South Africa, with two added corollaries. First, if the demands of African nationalists for majority rule are not met, social unrest may follow in the form of ethnic violence, and, perhaps, even a civil war. Second, if their demands are met, regional autonomy may become alluring, and, perhaps, even the establishment of separate states. The latter would indeed by ironic, for, by turning the tables, the African nationalists might take for themselves the 87% of the land, which the whites claimed belong to them by right of first occupancy, and turn over to the whites the remaining 13% of desolate land allocated to the Africans as a whites-only homeland.

In South Africa, however, liberalism has always been associated not with the idea of separate homelands but with the ideal of a *unitary state*. That is: (1) a *unitary state* in which all citizens, regardless of ethnicity, would enjoy equal political rights based on universal suffrage; (2) a *unitary state* in which political equality would be supplemented by equality of opportunity and a system of social security to ameliorate the lives of the disadvantaged, regardless of ethnicity; (3) a *unitary state* in which a comprehensive program of progressive, developmental education and social welfare would be inaugurated in an attempt to compensate for the effects of past discrimination and segregation; and (4) a *unitary state* in which the judicial system would be used to guard against ethnic discrimination and segregation with the establishment of a judiciary that was independent of the executive and legislative branches of government, and a Bill of Rights to protect both group and individual rights and privileges, regardless of ethnicity.

With what Hannah Arendt would call all these high-minded principles, why has liberalism failed in South Africa? For one thing, liberalism has never existed for the South African majority, the Africans, except temporarily and conditionally for a selected few non-whites in the Cape Province. For another, liberalism has not always existed for those whites commonly referred to as English-speaking.

Between 1652, when the first Dutch sailors arrived at the Cape, and 1833-1834, when Britain abolished slavery throughout its empire, the settlement at the Cape was a stratified, multiethnic, slave-owning colony. Upon arrival, these Dutch sailors had no intention of establishing a permanent settlement at the Cape but merely of developing a refreshment garden to produce fresh fruits and vegetables for sailors sailing between Holland and the Dutch colonies in the East Indies. But within five years, by 1657, due to the Cape's strategic location between the Netherlands and East Indian and Asian commerce, the decision had been made to encourage Dutch farmers, artisans, and burgers to immigrate to the Cape and establish a permanent settlement. This decision was not made by the Dutch Government but by the Dutch East India Company. Moreover, within the same five years, the decision had been made to import peoples, *as slaves*, from as near as Angola, Mozambique, and Madagascar and from as far away as West Africa and East Asia to supply the farm labor which the San and Khoikhoi could not or would not provide. Thus, South Africa is unique in Sub-Saharan Africa, for it is the only country that systematically imported peoples, *as slaves*. Furthermore, these peoples, their descendants, and others, who were the consequences of miscegenation between white settlers and non-whites, became known as Cape Coloureds.

As the whites were not indigenous to South Africa, they arrived in four distinct and gradually increasing waves. First, came a handful of Dutch seamen, in 1652, followed by Dutch immigrants. Next, came several hundred French Huguenot refugees escaping religious persecution in Catholic France in 1689. Then, in 1820, after the Napoleonic Wars came

4,000 British colonizers. Finally, following the discovery of diamonds in 1867 and gold in 1886, came tens of thousands of prospectors, speculators, and entrepreneurs from around the globe. The first two waves, the Dutch sailors and immigrants and the Huguenot refugees, came to be joined together as Boers probably because they intermarried but just as likely because of their religious affinity, as they were both adherents of Calvinism, the Reformed religion. The last two waves, whom the Boers referred to as *uitlanders*, meaning foreigners or outsiders, were predominantly of British origin and came to be known as the English-speaking South Africans. This designation was, however, deceptive. For instance, in the 1990s, among the English-speakers were approximately 120,000 Jews whose ancestors emigrated from wherever Jews were persecuted, and whose mother-tongue might have been Polish, Russian, Lithuanian, or Yiddish but certainly not English.

The dominant European ethnic group was and has remained the Boers and their descendants, whose disposition toward the African majority was predetermined by the Calvinist doctrine of predestination, that is, the division between those who were Saved and those who were eternally Damned. As the Africans were perceived, by the Boers, to be not only not Christians but pagans, they were obviously the Damned. Nevertheless, predestination concerned the purpose of God: His inscrutable will.

> By His Will some are chosen to be the elect, and called to salvation; and others, by what Calvin called an irreprehensible but incomprehensible judgement, are condemned to reprobation. . . . Every issue was a moral issue. . . . If every moral issue was also a religious issue, and every religious issue involved reference to the will of God and to the Bible which revealed His will, it followed that the Bible became the obligatory canon of the whole life. [It is] a stringent form of theocracy.[23]

The ideological revolution, which erupted on opposite sides of the Atlantic (the Atlantic Revolution) in America in 1776 and in France in 1789, was basically a revolution of the human spirit which embraced in its areas of concern a variety of under-dogs such as the Protestant victims of French religious persecution, i.e., the Huguenots. The inspiration for this ideological revolution was derived: (a) partly from the rationalism of the French Philosophes such as Voltaire, Diderot, D'Alembert, and Montesquieu; (b) partly from the humanitarianism of the English Evangelicals such as William Wilberforce; and (c) partly from the enthusiasm for democracy from the disciples of John Locke and Jean-Jacques Rousseau.

The Huguenot refugees, who arrived from France by way of Switzerland and Holland, helped to give the Cape Colony its Calvinist intensity and doctrinaire commitment. Together, the Boers and the Huguenots developed a defensive mind-set to keep intact the caste structure of their isolated slave-owning society. Before the liberalism of the *Atlantic Revolution* could permeate the Cape Colony, these Calvinist settlers had become intellectually isolated from the new ideas of individual rights and freedoms, which were the essence of the eighteenth century's Age of Enlightenment; that is, they had become intellectually isolated from these ideas, except where these rights and freedoms pertained to themselves.

These Calvinists settlers, most of whom survived on solitudinous rural farms, made their own adjustments to the rigors of frontier life and the inconvenience of the Africans they happened to come upon on the basis of their doctrinaire commitment to the orthodoxy of the Saved and the Damned. They lived within the confines of a closely knit family laager and a firmly held biblical theology, which they believed equated them with the wandering Israelites. After 1814, to these Calvinist settlers, rule by the British became as odious as rule by the Dutch East India Company had been, as these new rulers began to tamper with the Boers' sacred trinity of land, labor, and security, which the Boers translated to mean abundant land, free access to slave-labor, and absolute security from any African encroachment.

What was particularly repugnant to the Boers was the British liberal rhetoric with regard to non-white civil rights. For instance, in 1828, under pressure from the Reverend John Philip and other humanitarians, the British Government gave to all peoples of color who lived at the Cape the same civil rights as those enjoyed by whites who lived at the Cape. This was the beginning of what came to be called the Cape Colony's liberal tradition. The Reverend John Philip was the Superintendent of the London Missionary Society in South Africa, from 1819 to 1851, and he, more than any other single person, gave life to the rhetoric of liberalism at the Cape. Moreover, like William Lloyd Garrison in America, Reverend Philip was an avid and active opponent of the institution of slavery.

The abolition of slavery was the life-long endeavor of the British, Methodist philanthropist and politician William Wilberforce, who, in 1833, lay on his death-bed as the Bill for the emancipation of slaves worked its way through the final stages of passage in the British Houses of Parliament. The British abolitionists' movement against slavery was aimed, primarily, at the practice of slavery in the British West Indies, but the Cape Colony, as part of the British Empire, was also the recipient of this liberal, humanitarian munificence.

But for the Boers, the abolition of slavery was *the last straw*: not only because they felt inadequately compensated for this loss of property but also because the British placed no legal restrictions on the movements of these freed persons. Thirty years later, in the American South, Abraham Lincoln would be vilified for the same reason. The Boers' fury would be vividly expressed in the diary (some sources say a letter) of Anna Steenkamp, a niece of one of the trekboers, who made the Great Exodus from the Cape Colony, after 1834, into the vast wilderness of frontier isolation. Anna wrote,

> The reasons for which we abandoned our lands and homesteads, our country and kindred, were the following: (1) the continual depredation and robberies of the Kaffirs,[24] and their arrogance and overbearing conduct: and the fact that, in spite of the fine promises made to us by our Government, we nevertheless received no compensation for the property of which we were despoiled (2) the shameful and unjust proceedings with reference to the freedom of our slaves: and yet it is not so much their freedom that drove us to such lengths, as their being placed on an equal footing with Christians, contrary to the laws of God and the natural distinction of race and religion, so that it was intolerable for any decent Christian to bow down beneath such a yoke; wherefore we rather withdrew in order thus to preserve our doctrines *in purity*.[25]

What this excerpt reveals and the Boer Exodus signifies is that in turning their backs on the liberalism of the Cape, the Boers were turning their backs on all that was positive, progressive, and enlightening in the

Atlantic Revolution, which was the culmination of two centuries of Western culture's endeavors to raise the human spirit and improve the human condition. Instead, the Boers took with them into the vast, isolated wilderness of the veld the social backwardness of an aggressive, frontier mentality, sustained by a Calvinist orthodoxy and the doctrinaire commitment to their own predestined salvation and the Africans' eternal damnation.

After the Exodus of the 1830s, the Boers, in their efforts to escape British imported liberalism at the Cape, tried to establish new settlements as independent Boer republics. But wherever the Boers went, the British were soon to follow. For instance, in the case of Natal, the first of these independent Boer settlements, the British were firmly against any independent Boer settlements with access to Indian Ocean harbors that could be used by adversaries to threaten India. Therefore, in 1843, the British annexed Natal to the Cape Colony. Two other poor, landlocked Boer settlements did not represent a similar threat. Therefore, in the early 1850s, Britain recognized the independence of the Transvaal and the Orange Free State. These two Boer settlements established the intransigent serf society which, in time, would engulf the whole of South Africa. The basic characteristics of these serf societies were landless Africans, land-owning whites, and laws that institutionalized racial segregation and discrimination. Among Western democracies, only the United States institutionalized racial segregation and discrimination, by statute.

Significantly, at the beginning of the nineteenth century, British rule in South Africa was responding, in a vacillating fashion, to three conflicting British domestic pressures: evangelicalism, spreading the Word of God; liberalism, spreading the word of freedom and enlightenment; and economic interests, spreading the word of capitalism and individualism. In the final analysis, economic interests won out, especially after the discovery of diamonds in 1867 and gold in 1886.

Furthermore, Boer settlers, in their two landlocked Boer settlements, played almost no role in the diamond and gold industries as they developed, although many of the richest mines were located in Boer regions. Why not? First, the Boers were unalterably enamored with the land, as farmers. Second, the Boers lacked the skills needed to operate the mines. Third, the Boers lacked the capital to invest in the mines that was needed to develop them. In terms of the latter, capital formation, rural, impoverished Boers were indifferent to capital accumulation for mining investment and industrial development. As a consequence, for capital investment, South Africa relied almost entirely on foreign speculators and entrepreneurs, especially British and American investors, who became the owners and managers of South Africa's means of mining exploration and industrial production, i.e., the country's new economy. In terms of the former, new technology, the Boers were not interested in developing the necessary skills. Thus, to operate the mines and develop the new industrial economy, foreign workers were imported, mainly from the English-speaking world of Britain, North America, and Australia. Other migrant and immigrant laborers included Jews from Eastern Europe, who formed a separate and distinct minority. Today, the descendants of these nineteenth-century workers are referred to, collectively, as English-speaking South Africans, to distinguish them from the descendants of Calvinist settlers, who are, predominantly, Afrikaans-speaking, which was formerly known as *Cape Dutch*.[26]

The discovery of diamonds and gold resulted in a rapid change in the South African economy. From the Boers' perspective, this rapid economic change brought in a flood of white migrant and immigrant workers. Moreover, virtually none of these white workers spoke Dutch or tried to learn the language. Why should they: the Dutch speakers toiled in the soil, while the new workers labored in the mines and industries where English was king. The Boers perceived a new threat to their *doctrine in purity* from these uitlanders. The threat the Boers perceived to their survival *in purity* from the Africans was different from the threat they perceived from the white workers. That is, the Africans were a threat to their physical survival, while the uitlanders were a threat to their cultural survival, and, to the Boers, the latter was more ominous, because that threat was associated with the ballot box: the basic instrument of political liberalism and the democratic principle of majority rule.

Put succinctly, the Boers feared that some day the ballot box might give the uitlanders the political power to dominate them, if they became the white, numerical majority, and this was no phantom fear. For instance, in 1853, Johannesburg had only 50 white inhabitants. By 1934, however, Johannesburg had a population of 380,000 of whom 200,000 were whites and the majority of these were uitlanders. As a consequence, in the nineteenth century, the electoral laws of the Transvaal, where Johannesburg is located, were so arranged that uitlanders could not receive full voting rights until they had been resident there for 14 years, and only then, after having gone through an elaborate procedure for voting registration not unlike that required in most southern states, until recently, for African Americans.

Frustrated by such tactics, the uitlanders turned to armed conspiracy in order to secure their political rights. In 1895, such action led to the abortive Jameson Raid to overthrow the Transvaal's government and, ultimately, to the Boer War of 1899-1902. In fact, one of the immediate causes of that war was the Boers' rejection of British attempts to alter the regulations governing uitlanders' voting rights.

In 1899, the uitlanders went to war in order to secure their political rights from an intransigent Boer majority, but what, if any, were their concerns for the political rights of the African majority? An indication of how the white, English-speaking South Africans viewed the African majority in the matrix of South African politics can be gleaned from an article published in 1895, the same year as the Jameson Raid, in the *Cape Times*, a newspaper that was referred to as the mouthpiece of the British party. This article, written by Edmund Garrett, was a harbinger of what, in 1948, would be the nucleus of the theory of apartheid: separate development.

> Say not that we are superior and they are inferior, but simply that we are different, and that the difference involves, as a matter of practical comfort and convenience for both colours, a certain amount of keeping to ourselves. Of course, we shall go on thinking ourselves the superior race.[27]

Several years later, in 1917, in a London speech in which he tried to give legitimacy to the theory of apartheid by justifying the Native Land Act of 1913 which had laid down the principle of territorial segregation, Jan Christiaan Smuts said,

We have realised that political ideas which apply to our white civilisation largely do not apply to the administration of native affairs and so a practice has grown up in South Africa of creating parallel institutions. Instead of mixing up black and white in the old haphazard way, which instead of lifting up the black degraded the white, we are now trying to lay down a policy of keeping them apart as much as possible in our institutions.[28]

So much for the myth that, in theory and practice, apartheid came into existence in 1948 with the electoral victory of the National Party and was solely the result of Afrikaner attitudes and not of English-speakers' racial attitudes as well.

From 1814, the date of Britain's permanent occupation of the Cape Colony, until 1948, when the Afrikaners gained undisputed power in the whole of South Africa, whites, inside as well as many outside South Africa, viewed the great ethnic conflict as between those who were Afrikaans-speaking and those who were not. The crucial relationship between the Africans and all whites was viewed solely as a labor issue, that is, the continued supply of cheap African labor. In other words, liberalism, as had apartheid, had relegated Africans to the status of an economic factor: an economic commodity. In short, to be a political person one must have rights, duties, and responsibilities, i.e., citizenship, and for almost 350 years the rights of citizenship have been denied to Africans, by both liberalism and apartheid, in the Republic of South Africa itself.

In November of 1983, a referendum was held among the white electorate on a new constitution. The results gave Prime Minister Pieter Willem Botha a mandate to embark upon what, only a few years before, would have been regarded as heresy and a betrayal by the Afrikaner *volk*, because it allowed for Asians and Coloureds to share power with whites. The debate over power-sharing, and the constitutional amendment which resulted from it, brought to light in vivid focus a long smoldering, fundamental cleavage within the Afrikaner *volk*.

Over several decades this cleavage had been developing under the terms *verligte* and *verkrampte*, which entered the South African political vocabulary to refer to the so-called *liberal* and *conservative* wings of the Afrikaner *volk*. Generally, however, these terms were taken to represent nothing more than the manifestations of an in-family quarrel between the young and the old, but not a fundamental cleavage as to their collective means and ends for South African society. Then, in 1982, when an ultrareactionary wing of the National Party broke away to form the ultra Conservative Party, the feeling arose, among many observers of National Party machinations, that although the Afrikaner *volk* might be united as to their collective *ends* for South African society—white supremacy and African subjugation—a fundamental disagreement might exist as to the *means*, which could spell doom for the entire system of apartheid.

A fundamental cleavage had developed, with regard to the means for achieving the collective Afrikaner goals of white supremacy and African subjugation, between the urban Afrikaner who, in a modern industrial environment, had taken on new, one might even say modern, values, and the rural Afrikaner who still retained the frontier values and laager mentality, which had accompanied his forefathers into the isolation of the veld. On the one hand, the urban Afrikaner had been touched by the enlightenment which often accompanies change and evolving individualism. On the other hand, the rural Afrikaner was consumed by ultraconservatism and a brooding collectivism. Their great enemies, however, were not the Africans, whom they could probably overwhelm with their superior armaments, but time and change, which they could not hold back. The urban Afrikaner said, *Compromise in order to survive*, while the rural Afrikaner enjoins, *No compromise at any price*. The pragmatic urbanite seemed to have won out.

What we have witnessed, over at least the past decade in South Africa, is a contest of values not between different ethnic peoples but within the same ethnic people. This contest has led to the self-destruction not only of Afrikaner solidarity but will eventually lead to the downfall of the National Party, as Brian Bunting predicted, and the collapse of its mystique of invincibility. Max Weber pointed out in *The Protestant Ethic and the Spirit of Capitalism* that life itself is a contest between conflicting values. Ironically, his model linked elements of Calvinism with those of capitalism, which have been two of the most significant forces at play in South African politics.

Politics has two basic forms of government: majority rule or minority rule. South Africa has experienced the latter, and the former is inevitable. But given the country's past history of the rise and fall of apartheid after almost 340 years and the decline of liberalism after 100 years, the transformation will not be easy.

In 1991, the South African regime and the African nationalists agreed to begin talks about negotiating a new constitution relevant to a democratic South Africa. In 1992, these talks were suspended as each side, and the factions within each side, maneuvered for a position that would be most beneficial to the constituency which each represents. The crux of the matter is how, in a political democracy, to secure the right of the African majority to determine who rules, while protecting the right of the Afrikaner minority to exist and participate in the same political system. Under *normal* circumstances the solution would be simple: a just constitution and an enforceable bill of rights. But nothing about South African politics is or ever has been normal. Nevertheless, after the political jockeying has been played out, the determination of South Africa's political future will be solely in the hands of the African majority. They will be asked to be magnanimous. But how can a people forget and forgive four centuries of unmitigated cruelty? Can they ever trust the white minority? From past history, they have no reason to do so. Nonetheless, one tiny ray of hope is present: the religious factor.

Christianity has had an enormous influence on all Africans in Sub-Saharan Africa. Its impact has probably not been greater anywhere in that region than among Africans in South Africa. How else can one try to explain their centuries of anguish? When all else failed, including liberalism, it was the hope that their Christian beliefs gave them that allowed the Africans to persevere, survive, and ultimately to triumph. It is truly a biblical saga. But one recalls that the Boers misused Christianity to divide; can the Africans use Christianity to unite? That is The BIG question, and a leader with the stature of Moses is needed to lead them.

Finally, the year 1936 is generally regarded as the date of the demise of liberalism in South Africa. That, however, is incorrect. The correct date is 1910. In 1936, Africans in the Cape Province were removed from the common electoral roll that included all ethnic groups and were placed on a separate communal roll for Africans *only*, thus ending the Cape Province's so-called *liberal tradition* and thereby signifying the death of liberalism in South Africa. After 1936, those Africans—in the Cape only—who met certain stringent financial and economic requirements were allowed to elect three white representatives to the Provincial Assembly's Lower House and four white representatives to the Provincial Assembly's Upper House. At no time in its history were Africans ever allowed to elect representatives to South Africa's National Assembly. Furthermore, during the halcyon days of the Cape Province's so-called liberal tradition, when non-white voters from a common roll could elect representatives to the Cape's Provincial Assembly, no non-white—African or coloured—was ever knowingly elected to that legislative body.

The Settlement of 1936, as the arrangement at the Cape Province was called, lasted until rescinded in 1960. In 1960, Africans had no voting rights anywhere in South Africa, except in local African townships and in so-called African homelands.

In 1955, coloureds were also removed from the Cape Province's common electoral roll—after a long, heated, and bitter debate among the white electorate, especially among the Afrikaners themselves, who had coloured relatives and, some said, coloured blood—and placed on a separate communal roll for coloureds only. In 1968, this coloured communal roll was also abolished. Today, coloured voters are eligible to participate in the tripartite system, established by the 1983 constitution, which also includes Asians but excludes Africans.

The correct date for the demise of liberalism in South Africa is not 1936 but 1910. During the negotiations for the post-Boer War constitution of 1910, the Boers demonstrated their abhorrence for the Cape's so-called liberal tradition by adamantly refusing to have such a tradition spread to the other three provinces of Natal, the Transvaal, and the Orange Free State. The British acquiesced: they called it being magnanimous to the defeated Boers. In other words, the Boers lost on the battlefield, but they won at the negotiation table.

In 1910, the Union of South Africa was formed, which united the four provinces into a single polity under Boer leadership. By this arrangement, Britain gave to the white minority absolute power over all aspects of the country's internal policy-making, and what was the first thing that the Boer regime accomplished: the Native Land Act of 1913, which laid down the principle of territorial segregation, the cornerstone of the system of apartheid. As this self-government, with its abuse of power, became anathema to the international community, the white minority was forced to withdraw South Africa from the Commonwealth, which it did in 1961, when the Republic of South Africa was formed. This completed the Great Exodus away from British imported liberalism, which had begun after 1834, to preserve the Boer doctrine *in purity*. By this withdrawal from the Commonwealth, the white minority severed all political ties with Britain: *now the Great Trek was truly complete*.

Ironically, Britain had introduced liberalism to the Cape in order to benefit the non-whites, but Britain also was instrumental in the death of liberalism in South Africa. For with the Settlement of 1910, which established the Union of South Africa and internal self-government, Britain not only abandoned liberalism at the conference table; she also abdicated her responsibilities—moral and physical— for the African majority's future political and economic development as well as their social welfare. By this forfeiture of responsibility, democratic Britain left the future of the disenfranchised African majority in the hands of their most feared and most hated adversary, the enfranchised Boer minority, thereby abandoning a primary principle of political democracy: majority rule.

Ironically, this despicable deed took place under the aegis of a Liberal Party Government in London. To compound this irony is the paradox that although they lost the war, the Boers won everything else, especially their sacred trinity of abundant land, free access to cheap African labor—with the reserves and later the so-called homelands serving as repositories—and absolute security, with the might of the state firmly in Boer hands. The Boer police and military would be able to thwart any African nationalists' attempts at self-determination, which the Boers had just attained from the British.

Today, white and black leaders in South Africa are in the process of trying to rectify four centuries of social injustice, economic depravation, and political inequality. The task will not be easy, but the alternative is unthinkable. The first bold step must be the institution of a color-blind constitution; one that fulfills the ideals of political liberalism and the leadership to put it into operation and make it work.

Summary

In October 1993, the Nobel Foundation awarded the Nobel Peace Prize to South Africa's two most eminent leaders—F. W. de Klerk, President of the Republic of South Africa, and Nelson Mandela, President of the African National Congress—in recognition of their efforts to end the system of apartheid by a negotiated political solution rather than by violence. However, other principal performers in this drama, such as Eugene Terre Blanche, Andries Treurnicht, and Zephania Mothopeng have tried to thwart their valiant efforts.

Eugene Terre Blanche, "in Hitlerian tones, preaches [Afrikaner] survival through racial exclusivism." He is a "farmer and former policeman, demagogue of the far right . . . and self-appointed custodian of Afrikanerdom's soul [with] messianic visions of Afrikaner nationalism. . . . Terre Blanche's group calls itself the Afrikaner Resistance Movement."[29] In Afrikaans the group's name translates to Afrikaner Weerstandsbeweging (AWB). In August 1991, however, a violent confrontation erupted between the AWB and the state police, many of whom were Afrikaners, in the Transvaal town of Ventersdorf where President de Klerk was speaking to supporters of the National Party. This violence left three men dead and fifty-seven other people wounded, including seven police officers. Moreover, it seriously damaged the image of the Afrikaner Resistance Movement, which was becoming recognized as a neo-Nazi paramilitary group of thugs: "The incident at Ventersdorf is forcing many Afrikaners to review their loyalties." Professor David Welsh, of the University of Cape Town, added, "Large numbers of ordinary Afrikaner people have not got terribly much stomach for violent confrontation."[30]

Perhaps more damaging to the image of the Afrikaner Resistance Movement occurred in August 1992, with the public ridicule of its leader, Eugene Terre Blanche:

> Afrikaners, who pride themselves on their rectitude, have been cringing at the tabloid tales featuring one of the stars of the gunslinging Afrikaner right, Eugene Terre Blanche, leader of the Afrikaner Weerstandsbeweging, the Afrikaner Resistance Movement. The stories flowed from London, where Jani Allan, a Johannesburg newspaper columnist, was suing a British television company over

a documentary alleging she had been Mr. Terre Blanche's lover. For weeks, all other news was dwarfed by the reports of Mr. Terre Blanche moaning forlorn love messages into Ms. Allan's answering machine, by stories of him cavorting drunkenly in a pair of tattered green underpants, and by her roommate's description of his *large white buttocks* glimpsed above Ms. Allan through a bedroom keyhole. She lost her lawsuit, but has prolonged "the insult" by lending her taped voice to a phone service. For $2 per minute, callers can hear her *tell all* about Mr. Terre Blanche.[31]

Andries Treurnicht, a virulent advocate of apartheid, "In 1982, alarmed by Prime Minister Botha's talk of *sharing power* and proposed concessions to South Africans of mixed race and of Asian descent (but not Africans) . . . quit the National Party and formed a new one."[32] In 1983, Treurnicht formed the right-wing Conservative Party, taking 23 National Party members of Parliament with him, but, unlike the Afrikaner Resistance Movement, the Conservative Party continued to function within formal politics as the official opposition in the *white* chamber of the three chamber Parliament. On April 22, 1993, however, Andries Treurnicht—a former cabinet minister in the National Party government, a newspaper editor of *Die Kerkbode*, the voice of the largest of the Dutch Reformed churches, the Nederduits Gereformeerde Kerk (NGK), a minister of the Dutch Reformed church, and a high official of the Broederbond, the powerful, elite, secret Afrikaner society—died after heart bypass surgery: "His death poses new uncertainties for his party, over who will succeed him as leader and what policies the Conservatives will press as the country drafts a new national constitution."[33] In fact, even before his death, the Conservative Party was beginning to splinter. In August 1992, "The Conservative Party, which claims to be the heir of the *big idea* of a racially pure and independent Afrikaner state, suffered the defection of five Conservative members of Parliament."[34] Furthermore, the Conservative Party's relatively respectable image and credibility among Afrikaners was badly damaged, "with the arrest of a Conservative Party leader, Clive Derby-Lewis, and his wife Gaye, for questioning about the assassination of Chris Hani, a popular, militant leader in the African National Congress."[35] Since December 1991, Chris Hani had been the General Secretary of the South African Communist Party. He replaced the ailing Joe Slovo, who was battling cancer of the bone marrow and who with his wife, the assassinated Ruth First, were the most prominent white members of the African National Congress. Finally, in May 1993, leaders of most of South Africa's white separatist groups formed the Afrikaner People's Front to demand that a white *homeland* be carved from the northeastern province of the Transvaal as a refuse for those sharing their language, culture, and ideology. "Under the leadership of four retired generals, almost all of South Africa's white separatist political parties, labor unions, farm organizations, and paramilitary groups have coalesced for a last ditch resistance to black rule."[36] One of the most illustrious of the retired generals,

> Constand Viljoen, the chief of the South African Defense Force from 1980 to 1985, who is revered by many whites for his swashbuckling leadership of front-line troops against Cuban soldiers in Angola [said], "I feel personally the climate for violence, the climate for revolution, is running so high at the moment I don't think one can even talk about negotiations."[37]

But will these white separatists fight till the last man? The same bravado was heard from white settlers in Southern Rhodesia on the eve of Zimbabwe's independence in April of 1980.

Zephania Lekoane Mothopeng, before his death in October 1990, was the President of the Pan-Africanist Congress (PAC), which advocated the return of South Africa to its indigenous people and supported African take over by armed struggle. At the time of his death, however, the PAC seems to have reconsidered its militant and aggressive stance against any cooperation with whites and adopted a more conciliatory posture in terms of negotiating with whites and the African National Congress.

> A radical black rival to Nelson Mandela's organization said today that it was ready to join him in a united front to work for a multiracial democracy in South Africa. [Clarence Makwetu] the acting president of the Pan-Africanist Congress . . . which broke from Mr. Mandela's African National Congress in 1959, told a conference of African leaders in [Mbabane] Swaziland's capital that he favored a joint approach to President F. W. de Klerk's program of political change. "I promise this house that the PAC is ready for such a united front," said . . . Clarence Makwetu, who spent more than 10 years in prison with Mr. Mandela.[38]

There remains one major obstacle to the de Klerk-Mandela agenda: Chief Gatsha Buthelezi, who could not make up his mind how to play the game of life and politics after apartheid. Chief Buthelezi, however, is too powerful and prominent a figure to be ignored. In 1990, in a tacit challenge to the African National Congress, Chief Buthelezi, the principal leader of the largest single ethnic group in South Africa, the Zulus, converted his ethnic movement, Inkatha, into a multi-racial political party called the Inkatha Freedom Party. His principal and avowed aim is to prevent the African National Congress from claiming to represent the African majority in South Africa. Inkatha's transformation into a multi-racial political party seems unlikely, however, to attract many members from other ethnic groups because it remains so closely identified with the Zulus. Moreover, Chief Buthelezi has a not so secret *hidden agenda*: who will succeed Mandela, if the old gentleman is elected president in 1994. Obviously, Chief Buthelezi envisions himself as Mandela's successor.

F. W. de Klerk's and Nelson Mandela's mutual quest for a multi-ethnic, non-racial, participatory democracy, and a color-blind constitution are South Africa's best hope for peace and reconciliation without violence. Buthelezi is a wild card and a maverick in this drama, but he is too astute a politician to leave himself completely out of the new South Africa's political arena.

In the last week of April 1994, South Africa, for the first time in its history, held a national election that included all races. One week before the Presidential election, Chief Buthelezi agreed to have his Inkatha Freedom Party included on the election ballot. His reasoning was that the ANC was a tyrannical party whose progress he aimed to thwart. Nevertheless, the African National Congress won 63 percent of the national vote thereby capturing 252 of the 400 seats in the National Assembly. Moreover, the ANC emerged as the majority party in seven of the nine provincial legislative elections, which were held at the same time as the National Assembly and Presidential elections. The ANC gained more than 75 percent of the votes in four provinces. With these elections, the so-called homelands ceased to exist. None of the competing parties, de Klerk's National Party nor Buthelezi's Inkatha Freedom Party, offered a leader with the popularity and charisma of

Nelson Mandela, "In many part of South Africa, black people voted for Mandela, rather than the ANC."[39]

The new South Africa has been blessed with the leadership of two astute politicians: President de Klerk and the newly elected President Nelson Mandela. The task before them, however, is a daunting one filled with countless pitfalls. Nevertheless, the leadership exhibited thus far, especially by President Mandela, is of the caliber advocated in the *Discourses* by Machiavelli.

Notes

1. Brian Bunting, *The Rise of the South African Reich* (London: Penguin Books, 1964), 401.

2. Jean Branford, *A Dictionary of South African English* (Cape Town: Oxford University Press, 1980), 13.

3. Furnivall, 305.

4. "The names Bushmen, Hottentots, and Bantu are unsatisfactory for several reasons: (a) Hottentots and Bantu have acquired pejorative connotations and are rejected by present-day black South Africans; (b) though Bushmen and Hottentot may be regarded as ethnic terms, Bantu is essentially a linguistic term; and (c) it is a serious oversimplification to regard the precolonial population as consisting of three clear-cut types distinguished by ethnic, linguistic, and economic factors; these three factors are independent variables." Leonard Thompson and Andrew Prior, *South African Politics* (New Haven: Yale University Press, 1982), 21.

5. "Separate Development: South Africa and the European Example," *South African Scope*, September 1975/January 1976, 10. Originally, the theory of apartheid claimed that white settlers not African migrants arrived first in South African; later that claim was changed to say that both arrived simultaneously but in their own separate regions.

6. George Fredrickson, *White Supremacy: A Comparative Study in American and South African History* (New York: Oxford University Press, 1981), 241-242.

7. T. R. H. Davenport, *South Africa: A Modern History* (Toronto: University of Toronto Press, 1977), 10.

8. D. Hobart Houghton, *The Tomlinson Report: A Summary of the Findings and Recommendations in the Tomlinson Commission Report*, (Johannesburg: *The South African Institute of Race Relations*, 1956), 59.

9. *South Africa 1992* (Johannesburg: The South Africa Foundation, 1992), 9-10.

10. Ibid., 56.

11. Ibid., 75-76.

12. Frank Barton, *The Press of Africa* (New York: Holmes and Meier Publishers, 1979), 185.

13. John Laurence, *The Seeds of Disaster: A Guide to the Realities, Race Policies and World-wide Propaganda Campaigns of the Republic of South Africa* (London: Victor Gollancz, 1968), 81.

14. Ibid., 82. Dr. Malan, the first editor of the newspaper *Die Burger*, and Dr. Verwoerd, the first editor of the newspaper *Die Transvaler*, were the two primary forces who were instrumental in the creation of the South Africa's propaganda machinery. Both men later became prime ministers.

15. South African Department of Information, *This Is South Africa* (Pretoria: Department of Information, 1971), 43, 49, and 52.

16. Barbara Rogers, "Sunny South Africa: A Worldwide Propaganda Machine," *Africa Report* 22, no. 5, September-October 1977, 7.

17. Dr. Mulder's name is given as *Connie* in most reference sources, but, not knowing whether this was a diminutive or a nickname, I have used his initial so as not to confuse him with a woman. By 1978, Connie Mulder, in accordance with the new definition of apartheid, *plural democracy*, had become Minister of Plural Relations and Development, which was a tactical change from Bantu Administration and Development. Gwendolen Carter and Patrick O'Meara, editors, *Southern Africa: The Continuing Crisis* (Bloomington: Indiana University Press, 1979), 112.

18. Dr. C. Mulder, quoted in "Watershed Years for South Africa," *South African Digest*, September 10, 1976: 5.

19. W. J. de Koch, *The History of South Africa* (Pretoria: Department of Information, 1971), 47.

20. "Separate Development: South Africa and the European Example," *South African Scope*, December 1975-January 1976: 10.

21. It was the Dutch West India Company, which, in 1621, was given a monopoly for trade in the Americas, that founded and settled New Amsterdam, i.e., the island of Manhattan.

22. de Tocqueville, 177.

23. Ernest Barker, *Church, State, and Education* (Ann Arbor: The University of Michigan Paperbacks Press, 1957), 112 and 117.

24. *Kaffir*, the Arabic word meaning infidel, was, until recently, in common use in South Africa among whites to identify an African. Its English equivalent would be *nigger*.

25. Leonard Thompson, *The Political Mythology of Apartheid* (New Haven: Yale University Press, 1985), 149.

26. Branford, 4.

27. G. H. Le May, Black and White in South Africa: *The Politics of Survival* (New York: American Heritage Press, 1971), 43.

28. Ibid., 51.

29. Alan Cowell, *New York Times Magazine*, 23 November 1986.

30. Christopher Wren, *New York Times*, 14 August 1991.

31. Bill Keller, *New York Times*, 16 August 1992.

32. Bruce Lambert, *New York Times Obituary*, 23 April 1993.

33. Ibid.

34. Bill Keller, *New York Times*, 16 August 1992.

35. Bruce Lambert, *New York Times Obituary*, 23 April 1993.

36. Bill Keller, *New York Times*, 6 May 1993.

37. Ibid.

38. *New York Times*, 25 November 1990.

39. Patrick Laurence, "Election Results Analyzed," *African Report*, July-August, 1994, 18.

Conclusion

In 1958, Kwame Nkrumah of Ghana, when he was advocating a nationalist agenda for those colonial dependencies that were not yet free,[1] predicted that once colonialism had been removed and the Political Kingdom of Independence had been attained, all else would follow. He was wrong.

That a country can mount a united anti-colonial movement is no guarantee that it will be able to maintain national solidarity once the common enemy, the colonial power, is displaced. A more basic sense of national cohesion is necessary, if national solidarity is to endure, and that sense of belonging together—through the experience of a common history and a set of common goals—is something no state can create overnight. For the Swiss, it took over 500 years. In other words, nationalism, by itself, is not the panacea for a country's malaise. Therefore, rather than being viewed as the *end* of a process, nationalism should be recognized as the *beginning* of a new and more difficult task, which is the political integration of disparate groups with divergent interests. This primary objective of nation-building is all the more arduous, if there is no catalytic agent, such as a common will to unify these different groups, once the common enemy has disappeared with the demise of colonialism.

Today, modernizing elite leaders in developing states have found that one of their most awesome tasks is to control internal divisiveness. Many of these leaders blame this legacy of ethnic disharmony on the colonial policy of *Divide and Rule*. But internal divisiveness is a malaise that also afflicts developed nations. Thus, for whatever reasons, the major causes of internal divisiveness are internal factors, because most modern states contain ethnic groups, many of whose chief loyalties are to primordial attachments rather than to national solidarity and political integration. Thus, centrifugal ethnicity—moving away from a state's primary objective of national solidarity and political integration—is in conflict with centripetal nationalism—moving towards national solidarity and political integration. Even after the attainment of the Political Kingdom of Independence, nationalism can continue to have a positive influence, if the goal is national unity, that is, when centripetal nationalism is dominant and the emphasis is on nation-building loyalties. On the other hand, nationalism, in its ethnic disguise, can have a devastatingly negative effect on all attempts at nation-building, if the goal is ethnic exclusivity, that is, when centrifugal ethnicity is dominant and the emphasis is on ethnic loyalties. Therefore, when these two dynamic forces, centrifugal ethnicity and centripetal nationalism, are in conflict, ethnic loyalty may rival the state for power, loyalty, and legitimacy and result in the use of force and violence, as has been the case in Yugoslavia and other states in Eastern Europe and the former Soviet Union, with the demise of the totalitarian, Communist empire.

Today, the popular press makes no distinction between state and nation, as it makes no distinction between race and ethnicity but uses these terms loosely to accommodate their journalistic objectives. Such usage has been the cause of much confusion in both the popular press and in scholarly writing. Some scholars, however, do make a distinction between state and nation. These scholars use the term state, when referring to the existence of a central authority with the capability and responsibility to enforce its will upon citizens in a specific geographic territory, i.e., a country, and they use the term nation, when referring to the loyalty of citizens to each other, to the state, and to the laws and political system by which all citizens are governed. Nation-building states, therefore, are perceived of as being in the process of becoming nations, as they have not yet achieved the national solidarity and political integration that older and more established nations have attained, such as Britain and France. In such developed nations, customs, traditions, and institutions have evolved which grant legal and political protection to ethnic groups and allow these and all other groups, individuals, and minorities to exercise a meaningful function in the political system and its processes through the instrumentality of the nation's constitution. In developed nations, tolerance is a tradition built upon the past and its experiences, while in developing nations, tolerance and a viable constitution are in the most embryonic stages of evolution.

Machiavelli, in the fifteenth century, made the distinction between state and nation in his work *The Prince and The Discourses*. In *The Prince*, Machiavelli provided his political formula for establishing the state in *Troubled Times*; in *The Discourses*, he presented his political solution for developing the nation in *Settled Times*.[2] Machiavelli speaks of "ordinary means" for *Settled Times* and "extraordinary measures" for *Troubled Times*.[3] However, in both works, he was primarily concerned with the political solidarity and political integration of the political community:

> There is a striking similarity between the Italy of the *cinquecento* and today's developing nations. In both worlds, the chief characteristics are internal fragmentation with little or no community of interest, the all-too-frequent rise and fall of political regimes, a disharmonious relationship between government and the governed, and the absence of meaningful direction. Flux and volatility are the all-pervasive features.[4]

In *Troubled Times*, when civility and civil duty and responsibility were lacking or totally absent, Machiavelli believed that what was needed was a leader of great vision and small scruples, who was prepared to do whatever was necessary to bring disparate groups together and establish unity out of disunity and create order out of chaos.

> As in Italy nearly five hundred years ago, the immediate goal to be pursued in the contemporary developing nation, beset as it is by deep internal cleavages, is creation of order and stability; for no further goal, however noble, can be promoted and pursued if the prevailing conditions are chaos, violence, and discord. Expectations of the establishment of a *democratic political system* in new nations have been repeatedly betrayed. Law as a method of suasion, which Machiavelli considered to be the means whereby men would stabilize their conduct and regulate their mutual relationships, has indeed failed and led to lawlessness. Today, then, is witness of the very paradox to which Machiavelli pointed: the subversion and destruction of *the end* by the very *means* which purport to promote and protect it. The other alternative for the creation of order and stability is violence, the method of combat of "beasts." Dictatorship is often justified as inevitable and here, too, a similar paradox emerges: *violence*, instead of achieving *the end* for which it is used, often becomes a permanent institution and substitutes itself for *the end* sought. The predicament of political leadership in contemporary developing society is, therefore, identical with that of the prince of the *cinquecento*: he confronts flux and pervasive fragmentation from which he must create order and stability.[5]

My analysis of leadership, which follows, is based upon Taketsugu Tsurutani's critique of Machiavelli's role of the prince. In his conclusion,

Tsurutani says, "The real responsibility of the prince, therefore, is anything but what many a superficial critic of Machiavelli finds by reading *The Prince* alone."[6]

> The catalytic role of political leadership is important not because of its almost aesthetic dimensions but rather because of what it can ultimately promote. The ultimate duty of the prince, as is clear in *The Discourses* and is universally expected in today's world, is the development of his society into an environment of civility so that man may at last pursue his agelong dream of a life that is not solitary but fraternal, not poor but abundant, not nasty but harmonious, not brutish but humane, not short but full and long. This is the ultimate task Machiavelli assigned to the prince, and, without doubt, it is this same task that we expect the leader of today's developing nation to perform. Specifically, Machiavelli's most profound concern was to create the kind of environment for men in which civility and rule of law should prevail and where violence need not be invoked as the normal method of suasion and combat. In short, he wanted the prince *to reduce the area in which man must act the animal.* While implicitly envisioning a nobler duty of the prince and the loftier goal of human society, Machiavelli was a clear-eyed realist—the very fact that has since given rise to his notoriety.[7]

In Settled Times, the goals Machiavelli envisaged were achieved by the slow process of discussion, cooperation, and participation through the gradual education of citizens to care about each other—as well as their own enlightened self-interests, to care about the state—as well as its enlightened interests, and thus to create a civil society with a sense of civic responsibility and public spiritedness.

Put succinctly, *The Prince* is Machiavelli's leadership model for establishing the state, while *The Discourses* are his blueprints for the leadership to follow in developing the nation, with the concurrence of the citizens' participation. In both instances, the linchpin, the key factor, was effective and committed leadership. Leadership that was effective in galvanizing the disparate parts into a whole; leadership that was committed not to self-aggrandizement but to the glory, stability, and continuity of the state, and to the prosperity and well-being of its citizens. The end product of this process was loyalty to and knowledge of the state, its political system and processes, and mutual trust among its citizens, for the purpose of achieving political cohesion, solidarity, integration, and civility.

For Machiavelli, essential to the role of leadership were good laws to which the leader himself was subjected and, unlike the Leviathan of Thomas Hobbes, was not above:

> Let not princes complain of the faults committed by the people subjected to their authority, for they result entirely from their own negligence or bad example. In examining the people who in our day have been given to brigandage and other vices of that kind, we see that these arise entirely from the faults of their rulers, who were guilty of similar abuses.[8]

For Machiavelli, the good example of the leader combined with good education and good laws were to have the favorable effect of producing good leaders and good citizens: "For good examples are the result of good education, and good education is due to good laws."[9] Taketsugu Tsurutani injects,

> He believed that probity [honesty, uprightness] in princely conduct had an educative function in inculcating civility in society. The permanence of the tradition of civility Machiavelli sought is manifest in his notion of a circular and complementary relationship of habit, education, and good law. . . . There is almost a perfect identity between Machiavelli's idea of a tripartite relationship of these three ingredients of civil society and Aristotle's contention about moral virtue, education, and rule of law.[10]

Today, the failure of *political democracy*—the environment in which men hope to flourish and the environment every nation, developed and developing, aims to attain—is not due to the circumstances in which we live but the circumstances in which we are forced to live. The leaders, the decision-makers who govern, have the power to reverse circumstances, but many have forgotten that their power and authority are a responsibility and not a right. Power and authority are not for self-aggrandizement or for the enhancement of a special interest or particular group but for the general interest and welfare of all. Often, the general interest may translate to the majority interest, but this must not preclude those with power and authority from recognizing their responsibility to the needs and interests of the minority. Power and authority are a *trust*, and their use connotes trusteeship which is applicable not only to the leaders of developing nations but to leaders of developed nations as well.

All this Machiavelli recognized almost 500 years ago and made clear in *The Discourses*.

When power and authority are abused, and this *trust* is violated, then the people—as sovereign—have the right and the responsibility to withdraw their consent to be governed by those to whom they have delegated power, authority, and trust. The concept of the people, as sovereign, is based upon the belief that ultimately power rests with a country's citizens. Power is delegated, but not given up, to the people's representatives. In a *political democracy*, which all modern states claim to be, this transference of power from the people, *as sovereign*, to their leaders, *as representatives*, is accomplished through the legitimacy of the ballot box. Where no peaceful and legitimate means exist for redressing abuses, the people, *as sovereign*, have the right and the responsibility to resist authority, even if resistance entails the use of force and violence, or, in the words of Machiavelli,

> A licentious and mutinous people may easily be brought back to good conduct by the influence and persuasion of a good man, but an evil-minded prince is not amenable to such influences, and therefore, there is no other remedy against him but cold steel.[11]

Since the end of the Second World War, no government has claimed that its political system was not a democracy. Obviously, democracy means different things to different peoples and governments, for democracy has a variety of meanings, dimensions, and connotations. Moreover, no single definition of democracy can adequately encompass the vast history which the concept connotes, for it has changed its meaning and its significance in time and place.

For instance, in the fifth century B.C., in the era of Plato and Aristotle, democracy meant *rule by the masses*, which, to Greek intellectuals, was indeed an unsavory prospect. In the eighteenth century, James Madison, with an admonition toward Jean Jacques Rousseau's idea of "direct democracy," wrote, "A pure democracy, by which I mean a society consisting of a small number of citizens, who assemble and administer the government in person, can admit of no cure for the mischiefs of faction."[12] As a form of government, modern states are too large for *direct democracy* to be applicable, for many states often of millions of citizens, several have hundreds of million, while at least one state has over a billion citizens with another rapidly approaching that mark. In the nineteenth century, John Stuart Mill, in *On Liberty*, said that democracy proceeds and benefits from discussion, and discussion entails the use of reason and self-control. Mill's point was that democracy requires both maturity and restraint. Where no established democratic tradition exists, the populace has a greater willingness to submit to the dictatorship of the one, the few, or the many, but where the spirit of democracy has long been awake, the movement toward dictatorship has not often succeeded. Switzerland is a prime example of democracy's success in a nation with an established tradition of discussion, maturity, and restraint.

In the twentieth century, for some scholars, democracy is a way of life, *social democracy*, while for others, democracy is a form of government, *political democracy*. But however one views the concept of democracy, a political system that claims to be a democracy cannot ignore the principles of citizens' consent, the rule of law, the respect for the rights of the individual, and the right of individuals and groups to organize in order to articulate their grievances and aspirations.

Henry Mayo has argued that, as a form of government, political democracy has at least four closely knit set of principles, which he says are characteristic of a modern participatory democracy. Mayo emphasizes that none of these four principles should be taken singularly but collectively as characteristic of a modern participatory democracy. They are: popular control of policy makers, political equality of citizens, effective choice of candidates, and majority rule.[13] (1) Popular control of policy makers refers to frequent and honest elections. (2) Political equality of citizens means that each citizen's vote will carry the same weight and that no citizen will have more than one vote. (3) Effective choice of candidates means that a free selection of candidates will be taken from a broad spectrum of the electorate. (4) Majority rule means that in free and open elections the decision of the majority of voters must prevail, for the alternative to majority rule is minority rule, which, for centuries, has been the basic characteristic of government in South Africa. According to Mayo, political democracy means that citizens are willing to accept the results of fair and open elections, which have provided a numerous assortment of candidates, because the will of the electorate, freely and fairly ascertained through the ballot box, is supreme in determining Who Governs. Thus, the ballot box gives legitimacy to the democratic process and to political democracy as a form of government.

Robert Dahl gives the view that in the expression *pluralist democracy* the term pluralist refers to multiple, cross-cutting associations.[14] Dahl concludes that a state is a pluralist democracy, if it contains multiple associations and if these associations are voluntary and have a reasonable amount of independence. "Political decisions are reached, it is argued, as a result of numerous groups exerting pressure at different levels of the system. It is the object of a group to attempt to influence the policy of the government in such a way as to benefit the members of that group."[15] Alexis de Tocqueville had earlier remarked on the presence in the American political system of the many and varied voluntary associations as a hallmark of that country's form of political democracy.[16]

The significance of free and multiple associations is that their presence ensures and relieves the political system of the ethnic entrapment that characterized the plural society of colonial dependencies as well as the fear and fragmentation that is characteristic of the multi-ethnic developed and developing nations in this current analysis. Fear and fragmentation rather than trust and tolerance have not only hampered the political integration of these states but have severely jeopardized their economic growth and prosperity. The equation is clear: ethnic fear leads to suspicion, intolerance, revenge, and violence, while trust leads to tolerance, cooperation, compromise, and accommodation. "The ultimate resolution of ethnic conflicts depends most fundamentally on the implementation of democratic norms of equal political rights and opportunities, and pluralistic accommodation of the demands of contending groups."[17]

Notes

1. On March 6, 1957, Ghana celebrated its independence, as the first Sub-Sahara African country to gain its freedom from European colonial bondage.

2. Niccolo Machiavelli, *The Prince and The Discourses* (New York: Random House, Modern Library College Editions, 1950).

3. *The Discourses*, Book I, Chapter XVIII, Ap. 170-171).

4. Taketsugu Tsurutani, "Machiavelli and the Problem of Political Development," *Review of Politics* 30, no. 3 (July 1968), 147.

5. Ibid., 317.

6. Ibid., 325.

7. Ibid., 320-21.

8. *The Discourses*, Book III, Chapter XXIX, 495.

9. Ibid., Book I, Chapter IV, 119.

10. Tsurutani, 324.

11. *The Discourses*, Book I, Chapter LVIII, 265.

12. *Federalist Paper Ten*, 92.

13. Henry Mayo, *An Introduction to Democratic Theory*, 166.

14. Robert Dahl, *Dilemmas of Pluralism Democracy* (New Haven: Yale University Press, 1982), 2.

15. David Nicholls, *Three Varieties of Pluralism* (New York: St. Martin's Press, 1974), 2.

16. Alexis de Tocqueville, *Democracy in America*, New York: The New American Library, 1956, Book I, Chapters 10 and 11.

17. Ted Robert Gurr, "Speaking about Democracy and Peace," *Journal of the United States Institute of Peace* 3, no. 2 (June 1990), 3.

Appendix

Table I

Percentage Distribution of Swiss Citizens by Mother Tongue, 1986

	German	French
Total	73.5%	20.1%
ZH (Zurich)	94.4%	1.8%
BE (Berne)	90.0%	8.5%
LU (Lucerne)	97.7%	0.7%
UR (Uri)	98.6%	0.3%
SZ (Schwyz)	98.1%	0.4%
OW (Obwald)	98.7%	0.5%
NW (Nidwald)	98.1%	0.6%
GL (Glaris)	97.4%	0.4%
ZG (Zoug)	96.3%	1.1%
FR (Fribourg)	34.1%	64.9%
SO (Soleure)	96.7%	1.5%
BS (Bale Campagne)	92.8%	3.5%
BL (Bale Ville)	95.1%	2.4%
SH (Schaffhouse)	96.8%	0.8%
AR (Appenzall Rhodes-Ext.)	98.1%	0.4%
AI (Appenzall Thodes-Int.)	99.2%	0.1%
SG (St. Gall)	97.6%	0.4%
GR (Grisons)	64.8%	0.5%
AG (Argovie)	96.9%	1.1%
TG (Thurgovie)	97.5%	0.5%
TI (Tessin)	12.7%	2.2%
VD (Vaud)	9.7%	87.5%
VS (Valais)	34.8%	64.0%
NE (Neuchatel)	9.1%	88.1%
GE (Geneve)	11.8%	82.6%
JU (Jura)	6.7%	92.2%

German-speakers outnumber French-speakers in 73.1% (19/26) of the cantons.

French-speakers outnumber German-speakers in 23.1% (6/26) of the cantons.

NOTE: All figures in Tables I through VI are based on statistics received from the Swiss Federal Statistical Office in August of 1986 and are based on the 1980 Swiss census.

Appendix

Table II

Percentage Distribution of Swiss Citizens by Religious Affiliation, 1986

	Protestant	Roman Catholic
Total	50.4%	43.6%
ZH (Zurich)	63.1%	29.2%
BE (Berne)	82.3%	12.9%
LU (Lucerne)	13.3%	83.7%
UR (Uri)	5.8%	92.6%
SZ (Schwyz)	10.3%	88.1%
OW (Obwald)	4.9%	94.1%
NW (Nidwald)	10.9%	87.3%
GL (Glaris)	61.5%	36.8%
ZG (Zoug)	18.9%	78.0%
FR (Fribourg)	14.2%	83.7%
SO (Soleure)	40.7%	53.0%
BS (Bale Campagne)	51.2%	31.3%
BL (Bale Ville)	61.6%	31.5%
SH (Schaffhouse)	70.1%	22.6%
AR (Appenzall Rhodes-Ext.)	71.4%	24.0%
AI (Appenzall Thodes-Int.)	7.1%	91.8%
SG (St. Gall)	37.2%	60.0%
GR (Grisons)	50.0%	47.8%
AG (Argovie)	51.3%	42.8%
TG (Thurgovie)	60.8%	36.0%
TI (Tessin)	8.6%	86.8%
VD (Vaud)	67.1%	25.9%
VS (Valais)	4.8%	93.5%
NE (Neuchatel)	63.1%	26.5%
GE (Geneve)	40.2%	43.7%
JU (Jura)	14.4%	83.0%

Protestants outnumber Catholics in 46.2% (12/26) of the cantons.

Catholics outnumber Protestants in 53.8% (14/26) of the cantons.

Appendix

Table III

Percentage Distribution of Swiss Citizens by Mother Tongue and Religious Affiliation, 1986

	Protestant		Roman Catholic	
	German	French	German	French
Total	40.6%	9.0%	29.0%	9.5%
ZH (Zurich)	61.4%	0.9%	26.1%	0.7%
BE (Berne)	76.5%	5.4%	9.5%	2.5%
LU (Lucerne)	12.9%	0.2%	82.0%	0.4%
UR (Uri)	5.6%	0.1%	91.5%	0.1%
SZ (Schwyz)	10.0%	0.1%	86.6%	0.2%
OW (Obwald)	4.7%	0.1%	93.1%	0.3%
NW (Nidwald)	10.5%	0.2%	86.0%	0.4%
GL (Glaris)	60.8%	0.2%	35.1%	0.2%
ZG (Zoug)	18.2%	0.4%	75.4%	0.6%
FR (Fribourg)	10.3%	3.7%	23.0%	59.8%
SO (Soleure)	39.8%	0.7%	51.0%	0.7%
BS (Bale Campagne)	49.2%	1.4%	27.6%	1.4%
BL (Bale Ville)	59.4%	1.1%	28.9%	1.1%
SH (Schaffhouse)	69.0%	0.5%	21.1%	0.2%
AR (Appenzall Rhodes-Ext.)	70.7%	0.2%	23.1%	0.1%
AI (Appenzall Thodes-Int.)	7.0%	0.02%	91.2%	0.1%
SG (St. Gall)	36.6%	0.2%	58.4%	0.2%
GR (Grisons)	40.2%	0.3%	22.9%	0.2%
AG (Argovie)	50.4%	0.5%	41.4%	0.4%
TG (Thurgovie)	60.2%	0.3%	34.4%	0.2%
TI (Tessin)	6.2%	0.7%	5.4%	1.3%
VD (Vaud)	6.5%	60.0%	2.6%	21.6%
VS (Valais)	1.8%	2.9%	32.6%	59.9%
NE (Neuchatel)	5.9%	56.7%	2.4%	22.1%
GE (Geneve)	6.3%	33.1%	4.1%	36.1%
JU (Jura)	3.5%	10.8%	2.8%	79.3%

Protestants outnumber Catholics in 46.2% (12/26) of the cantons.
—German-speakers outnumber French-speakers in 83.3% (10/12) of the Protestant cantons.
—French-speakers outnumber German-speakers in 16.7% (2/12) of the Protestant cantons.

Catholics outnumber Protestants in 53.8% (14/26) of the cantons.
—German-speakers outnumber French-speakers in 64.3% (9/14) of the Catholic cantons.
—French-speakers outnumber German-speakers in 28.6% (4/14) of the Catholic cantons
—One canton, Tessin, 7.1% (1/14) of the total Catholic cantons, is Italian-speaking.

German-speakers outnumber French-speakers in 73.1% (19/26) of the cantons.
—Protestants outnumber Catholics in 52.0% (10/19) of the German-speaking cantons.
—Catholics outnumber Protestants in 47.4% (9/19) of the German-speaking cantons.

French-speakers outnumber German-speakers in 23.1% (6/26) of the cantons.
—Protestants outnumber Catholics in 33.3% (2/6) of the French-speaking cantons.
—Catholics outnumber Protestants in 66.7% (4/6) of the French-speaking cantons.

Table IV

Percentage Distribution of Swiss and Foreigners by Mother Tongue, 1986

GermanFrench

	German	French
Total	65.0%	18.4%
ZH (Zurich)	82.9%	1.7%
BE (Berne)	84.4%	8.2%
LU (Lucerne)	90.9%	0.7%
UR (Uri)	93.3%	0.3%
SZ (Schwyz)	91.0%	0.4%
OW (Obwald)	94.0%	0.5%
NW (Nidwald)	93.6%	0.6%
GL (Glaris)	83.3%	0.4%
ZG (Zoug)	86.8%	1.2%
FR (Fribourg)	32.3%	61.4%
SO (Soleure)	87.0%	1.5%
BS (Bale Campagne)	80.7%	3.4%
BL (Bale Ville)	85.1%	2.4%
SH (Schaffhouse)	85.3%	0.7%
AR (Appenzall Rhodes-Ext.)	89.6%	0.4%
AI (Appenzall Thodes-Int.)	92.9%	0.1%
SG (St. Gall)	88.5%	0.4%
GR (Grisons)	59.9%	0.6%
AG (Argovie)	85.6%	1.0%
TG (Thurgovie)	86.7%	0.5%
TI (Tessin)	11.1%	1.9%
VD (Vaud)	8.6%	75.1%
VS (Valais)	32.1%	60.0%
NE (Neuchatel)	8.0%	77.1%
GE (Geneve)	9.5%	64.7%
JU (Jura)	6.3%	85.9%

German-speakers outnumber French-speakers in 76.9% (20/26) of the cantons.

French-speakers outnumber German-speakers in 23.1% (6/26) of the cantons.

Table V

Percentage Distribution of Swiss and Foreigners by Religious Affiliation, 1986

	Protestant	Catholic
Total	44.3%	47.6%
ZH (Zurich)	54.7%	35.4%
BE (Berne)	76.8%	17.5%
LU (Lucerne)	12.9%	82.4%
UR (Uri)	5.9%	91.0%
SZ (Schwyz)	10.0%	86.6%
OW (Obwald)	5.3%	92.1%
NW (Nidwald)	11.0%	86.1%
GL (Glaris)	51.7%	43.0%
ZG (Zoug)	18.4%	75.3%
FR (Fribourg)	13.6%	83.2%
SO (Soleure)	36.5%	54.9%
BS (Bale Campagne)	44.4%	35.5%
BL (Bale Ville)	54.3%	36.3%
SH (Schaffhouse)	60.5%	27.7%
AR (Appenzall Rhodes-Ext.)	64.1%	28.7%
AI (Appenzall Thodes-Int.)	6.8%	90.5%
SG (St. Gall)	33.5%	61.0%
GR (Grisons)	45.2%	51.0%
AG (Argovie)	45.1%	46.5%
TG (Thurgovie)	53.1%	41.0%
TI (Tessin)	7.6%	87.1%
VD (Vaud)	55.7%	35.7%
VS (Valais)	4.7%	92.8%
NE (Neuchatel)	53.0%	36.2%
GE (Geneve)	30.6%	51.5%
JU (Jura)	13.3%	83.6%

Protestants outnumber Catholics in 38.5% (10/26) of the cantons.

Catholics outnumber Protestants in 61.5% (16/26) of the cantons.

Table VI

*Percentage Distribution of Swiss and Foreigners by Mother Tongue
and Religious Affiliation, 1986*

| | Protestant | | Roman Catholic | |
	German	French	German	French
Total	35.4%	7.8%	26.0%	9.0%
ZH (Zurich)	52.7%	0.8%	23.9%	0.7%
BE (Berne)	71.2%	5.0%	9.4%	2.5%
LU (Lucerne)	12.3%	0.2%	75.9%	0.4%
UR (Uri)	5.5%	0.1%	86.3%	0.1%
SZ (Schwyz)	9.6%	0.1%	80.0%	0.3%
OW (Obwald)	4.9%	0.1%	87.9%	0.4%
NW (Nidwald)	10.4%	0.2%	81.5%	0.4%
GL (Glaris)	50.9%	0.2%	30.9%	0.2%
ZG (Zoug)	16.9%	0.3%	67.1%	0.7%
FR (Fribourg)	9.8%	3.5%	21.8%	56.5%
SO (Soleure)	35.5%	0.6%	45.9%	0.7%
BS (Bale Campagne)	42.1%	1.2%	24.5%	1.5%
BL (Bale Ville)	52.3%	1.0%	26.5%	1.2%
SH (Schaffhouse)	59.3%	0.4%	19.8%	0.2%
AR (Appenzall Rhodes-Ext.)	63.2%	0.2%	22.1%	0.2%
AI (Appenzall Thodes-Int.)	6.7%	0.02%	85.2%	0.1%
SG (St. Gall)	32.7%	0.2%	53.2%	0.2%
GR (Grisons)	36.2%	0.3%	22.1%	0.3%
AG (Argovie)	43.9%	0.5%	36.6%	0.4%
TG (Thurgovie)	52.3%	0.2%	31.5%	0.2%
TI (Tessin)	5.3%	0.5%	4.7%	1.1%
VD (Vaud)	5.6%	48.5%	2.4%	21.0%
VS (Valais)	1.8%	2.7%	30.0%	56.1%
NE (Neuchatel)	5.1%	47.2%	2.2%	21.5%
GE (Geneve)	4.9%	23.2%	3.3%	30.3%
JU (Jura)	3.3%	9.9%	2.7%	73.9%

Protestants outnumber Catholics in 38.5% of the cantons.
—German-speakers outnumber French-speakers in 80% (8/10) of the Protestant cantons.
—French-speakers outnumber German-speakers in 20% (2/10) of the Protestant cantons.

Catholics outnumber Protestants in 61.5% (16/26) of the cantons.
—German-speakers outnumber French-speakers in 75% (12/16) of the Catholic cantons.
—French-speakers outnumber German-speakers in 25% (4/16) of the Catholic cantons.

German-speakers outnumber French-speakers in 76.9% (20/26) of the cantons.
—Protestants outnumber Catholics in 40% (8/20) of the German-speaking cantons.
—Catholics outnumber Protestants in 60% (12/20) of the German-speaking cantons.

French-speakers outnumber German-speakers in 23.1% (6/26) of the cantons.
—Protestants outnumber Catholics in 33.3% (2/6) of the French-speaking cantons.
—Catholics outnumber Protestants in 66.7% (4/6) of the French-speaking cantons.

Bibliography

General

Adam, Thomas. *Government and Politics in Africa South of the Sahara.* New York: Random House, 1965.

Andreski, Stanislav. *The African Predicament: A Study in the Pathology of Modernisation.* London: Michael Joseph, 1968.

Akintoye, S. A. *Emergent African States.* London: Longman, 1976.

Bell, Wendell and Walter Freeman, eds. *Ethnicity and Nation-Building.* Beverly Hills, CA: Saga Publications, 1974.

Bendix, Reinhard. *Nation-Building and Citizenship.* New York: John Wiley and Sons, 1964.

Blaustein, Albert and Gilbert Flanz, eds. *Constitutions of the Countries of the World.* Dobbs Ferry, NY: Oceana Publications, 1992.

Blondel, J., ed. *Comparative Government.* Garden City, NY: Anchor Books, 1969.

Bonacich, Edna. "A Theory of Ethnic Antagonism: The Split Labor Market." *American Sociological Review* (October 1972).

Brass, Paul. *Ethnicity and Nationalism: Theory and Comparison.* Newbury Park, CA: Sage Publications, 1991.

_____. "Ethnicity and Nationality Formation." *Ethnicity* (1976).

Carr, E. H. *What Is History?* Middlesex, England: Pelican Books, 1964.

Cashmore, Ellis, and Barry Troyna. *Introduction to Race Relations.* London: Falmer Press, 1990.

Castles, Stephen. *Here for Good: Western Europe's New Ethnic Minorities.* London: Pluto Press, 1984.

Chege, Michael. "Remembering Africa." *Foreign Affairs* (January 1992).

Connor, Walker. "Nation-Building or Nation-Destroying." In *Race, Ethnicity, and Social Change*, edited by John Stone. North Scituate, MA: Duxbury Press, 1977.

_____. "A nation is a nation, is a state, is an ethnic group is a . . ." *Ethnic and Racial Studies* (October 1978).

Cross, Malcolm. "On Conflict, Race Relations and the Theory of the Plural Society." In *Race, Ethnicity, and Social Change*, edited by John Stone. North Scituate, MA: Duxbury Press, 1977.

Curtis, Michael. *Comparative Government and Politics.* New York: Harper and Row, 1968.

Dahl, Robert. "Pluralism Revisited." *Comparative Politics* (January 1978).

Dahl, Robert, ed. *Political Oppositions in Western Democracies.* New Haven: Yale University Press, 1966.

Deutsch, Karl. "The Growth of Nations: Some Recurrent Patterns of Political and Social Integration." *World Politics* (January 1953).

Diamond, Larry, Juan Linz, and Seymour Martin Lipset, eds. *Democracy in Developing Countries: Africa.* Boulder, CO: Lynne Rienner Publishers, 1988.

Dinnerstein, Leonard, and David Reimers. *Ethnic Americans.* New York: Harper and Row, 1988.

Douglass, William. "A Critique of Recent Trends in the Analysis of Ethno-Nationalism." *Ethnic and Racial Studies* (April 1988).

Enloe, Cynthia. *Ethnic Conflict and Political Development.* Boston: Little Brown, 1973.

Esman, Milton. "Ethnic Politics and Economic Power." *Comparative Politics* (July 1987).

Ethnic Studies in North America: A Catalog of Current Doctoral Dissertation Research. Ann Arbor, MI: University Microfilms International.

Frye, Timothy. "Ethnicity, Sovereignty and Transitions from Non-Democratic Rule." *Journal of International Affairs* (Winter 1992).

Gurr, Ted and Vaughn Bishop. "Violent Nations, and Others." *Journal of Conflict Resolutions* (March 1976).

Hanke, Lewis. *Aristotle and the American Indians: A Study in Race Prejudice in the Modern World.* Chicago: Regnery Company, 1959.

Hechter, Michael. "The Political Economy of Ethnic Change." *American Journal of Sociology* (March 1974).

Horowitz, Donald. *Ethnic Groups in Conflict.* Berkeley: University of California Press, 1985.

_____. "Three Dimensions of Ethnic Politics." *World Politics* (January 1971).

Howard, Rhoda. *Human Rights in Commonwealth Africa.* Totowa, NJ: Rowman and Littlefield, 1986.

Huntington, Samuel. "The Clash of Civilizations." *Foreign Affairs* (Summer 1993).

Isaacs, Harold. "Nationality: End of the Road?" *Foreign Affairs* (April 1975).

Jacob, Philip, and James Toscano, eds. *The Integration of Political Communities.* Philadelphia, PA: J.B. Lippincott, 1964.

Jenkins, Richard. "The Politics of Ethnicity." *Government and Opposition* (Spring 1987).

Katznelson, Ira. "Comparative Studies of Race and Ethnicity: Plural Analysis and Beyond." *Comparative Politics* (October 1972).

Kuper, Leo and M. G. Smith, eds. *Pluralism in Africa.* Berkeley: University of California Press, 1969.

Lijphart, Arend. "Religious vs. Linguistic vs. Class Voting: The Crucial Experiment of Comparing Belgium, Canada, South Africa, and Switzerland." *The American Political Science Review* (June 1979).

Lofchie, Michael, ed. *The State of the Nations: Constraints on Development in Independent Africa.* Berkeley: University of California Press, 1971.

Markovitz, Irving. *Studies in Power and Class in Africa.* New York: Oxford University Press, 1987.

Meadwell, Hudson. "Cultural and Instrumental Approaches to Ethnic Nationalism." *Ethnic and Racial Studies* (July 1989).

Morris-Hale, Walter. "From Empire to Nation." *Studies in History.* Smith College, 1975.

Nagael, Joane and Susan Olzak. "Ethnic Mobilization in New and Old States: An Extension of the Competition Model." *Social Problems* (December 1982).

Neuman, Stephanie, ed. *Small States and Segmented Societies: National Political Integration in a Global Environment.* New York: Praeger Publishers, 1976.

Nevitte, Neil and Charles Kennedy, eds. *Ethnic Preference and Public Policy in Developing States.* Boulder, CO: Lynne Rienner Publishers, 1986.

Nielsen, François. "Toward a Theory of Ethnic Solidarity in Modern Societies." *American Sociological Review* (April 1985).

Nordlinger, Eric. *Conflict Regulation in Divided Societies.* Cambridge: Center for International Affairs, Harvard University Press, 1972.

Paden, John, ed. *Values, Identities, and National Integration: Empirical Research in Africa.* Evanston, IL: Northwestern University Press, 1980.

Palmer, Monte. *Dilemmas of Political Development: An Introduction to the Politics of Developing Areas.* Itasca, IL: F. E. Peacock Publishers, 1989.

Peil, Margaret. *Consensus and Conflict in African Societies.* London: Longman, 1977.

Potholm, Christian. *The Theory and Practice of African Politics.* Englewood Cliffs, NJ: Prentice-Hall, 1979.

Rabushka, Alvin and Kenneth Shepsle. *Politics in Plural Societies: A Theory of Democratic Instability.* Columbus, Ohio: Charles Merrill Publishing, 1972.

Richmond, Anthony. "Ethnic Nationalism and Post-Industrialism." *Ethnic and Racial Studies* (January 1984).

_____. "Race Relations and Immigration: A Comparative Perspective." *International Journal of Comparative Sociology* (June 1990).

Rothchild, Donald. "Ethnicity and Conflict Resolution." *World Politics* (July 1970).

Rothermund, Dietmar and John Simon, eds. *Education and the Integration of Ethnic Minorities.* New York: St. Martin's Press, 1986.

Roucek, Joseph. *The Minority Principle as a Problem of Political Science.* Berkeley: University of California Press, 1926.

Schermerhorn, R. A. *Comparative Ethnic Relations.* New York: Random House, 1970.

Segal, Ronald. *The Race War.* London: Jonathan Cape, 1966.

Shils, Edward. *Political Development in New States.* The Hague, Holland: Mouton, 1966.

Sowell, Thomas. *Ethnic America.* New York: Basic Books, 1981.

Spoonley, Paul. *Racism and Ethnicity.* Auckland, New Zealand: Oxford Univ. Press, 1988.

Stone, John, ed. *Race, Ethnicity, and Social Change.* North Scituate, MA: Duxbury Press, 1977.

Suhrke, Astri and Lela Nobel. *Ethnic Conflict in International Relations.* New York: Praeger Publishers, 1977.

UNESCO. *Race, Science and Society.* Paris: The UNESCO Press, 1956.

Van den Berghe, Pierre. *Race and Ethnicity.* New York: Basic Books, 1970.

_____. *Race and Racism.* New York: Wiley, 1967.

Wainhouse, David. *Remnants of Empire.* New York: Harper and Row, 1964.

Weiner, Myron. "Political Integration and Political Development." *The Annals of the American Academy of Political and Social Science* (March 1965).

Young, Crawford. *Ideology of Development in Africa.* New Haven: Yale University Press, 1982.

_____. *The Politics of Cultural Pluralism.* Madison: University of Wisconsin Press, 1976.

Introduction

Apter, David. *The Political Kingdom in Uganda.* New Haven: Yale University Press, 1967.

Barker, Ernest. *The Politics of Aristotle.* New York: Oxford University Press, 1958.

Furnivall, John. *Colonial Policy and Practice.* Cambridge: Cambridge University Press, 1948.

Geertz, Clifford. *Old Societies and New States.* New York: The Free Press, 1963.

Glazer, Nathan. "The Universalisation of Ethnicity: Peoples in the Boiling Pot." *Encounter* (February 1975).

Glazer, Nathan and Daniel Patrick Moynihan. "Why Ethnicity?" *Commentary* (October 1974).

Lijphart, Arend. "Consociational Democracy." *World Politics* (January 1969).

_____. *Democracy in Plural Societies.* New Haven: Yale University Press, 1977.

_____. "Religious vs. Linguistic vs. Class Voting: The Crucial Experiment of Comparing Belgium, Canada, South Africa, and Switzerland." *The American Political Science Review* (June 1979).

Meyer, Marvin, ed. *The Minds of the Founders: Sources of the Political Thought of James Madison.* Hanover, NH: University Press of New England, 1981.

Chapter One: Switzerland
Primary Sources

The Government of Switzerland. *Focus on Switzerland.* Volumes I-IV. New York: Swiss Consulate General, 1991.

Swiss Federal Government. *The Federal Constitution of the Swiss Confederation.* Bern: Switzerland.

_____. *Switzerland: People, State, Economy, Culture.* Bern: Switzerland, 1991.

Swiss Federal Statistical Office. *Population, Language, and Religion Statistics: 1980 Census.* Bern: Switzerland, 1989.

Secondary Sources

Barry, Brian. "Political Accommodation and Consociational Democracy." *British Journal of Political Science* (October 1975).

Bassand, Michel. "The Jura Problem." *Journal of Peace Research* (Spring 1975).

Bohn, David Earle. "Consociational Democracy and the Case of Switzerland." *The Journal of Politics* (February 1980).

_____. "Consociationalism and Accommodation in Switzerland." *The Journal of Politics* (November 1981).

Codding, George. *The Federal Government of Switzerland.* Boston: Houghton Mifflin, 1965.

Crossland, Norman. "A Survey of Switzerland: The Everlasting League." *Economist* (3 February 1979).

Deutsch, Karl. *Politics and Government: How People Decide Their Fate.* Boston: Houghton Mifflin, 1974.

Dunn, James. "Consociational Democracy and Language Conflict: A Comparison of the Belgian and Swiss Experiences." *Comparative Political Studies* (April 1972).

Economist. "Switzerland: Let Each Decide." (29 June 1974).

The Europa Yearbook. London: Europa Publications, 1991.

Freund, Andreas. "Europe's Minorities Are More Vocal, If Not More Violent." *New York Times* (16 September 1975).

Freymond, Jacques. "Can the Confederation Helvetica Be Imitated?—By Way of Conclusion." *Journal of Comparative Politics* (Winter 1988).

Glass, Harold. "Consensus and Opposition in Switzerland." *Comparative Politics* (April 1978).

_____. *Subcultural Segmentation and Consensual Politics: The Swiss Experience.* Ph.D. diss., University of North Carolina, Chapel Hill, 1975.

Hartman, Nicholas. "On Top of the World." *Economist* (30 October 1982).

Henderson, Conway. "Consociational Democracy and the Case of Switzerland." *The Journal of Politics* (November 1981).

Hofmann, Paul. "The Swiss Malaise." *New York Times Magazine* (8 February 1981).

Holt, Peter. "Austrian and Swiss Neutrality." *The World Today* (September 1980).

Keech, William. "Linguistic Diversity and Political Conflict." *Comparative Politics* (April 1972).

Kubly, Herbert. *Switzerland.* New York: Time, 1964.

Lewis, Flora. "Swiss, Stable and Affluent, Facing Problems of Too Much Success." *New York Times* (7 September 1976).

Lijphart, Arend. "Consociational Democracy." *World Politics* (January 1969).

_____. *The Politics of Accommodation.* Berkeley: University of California Press, 1968.

Lipset, Seymour Martin. *Political Man: The Social Basis of Politics.* Garden City, NY: Doubleday, 1960.

Lorwin, Val. "Segmented Pluralism." *Comparative Politics* (January 1971).

Mayer, Kurt. "The Jura Problem: Ethnic Conflict in Switzerland." *Social Research* (Winter 1968).

Rappard, William. *The Government of Switzerland.* New York: Van Nostrand, 1936.

Richardson, Keith. "Swiss Passions Make a Rift in Alps." *London Sunday Times* (24 September 1978).

Schmid, Carol. *Conflict and Consensus.* Berkeley: University of California Press, 1981.

Schmitter, Barbara. "Trade Unions and Immigration in West Germany and Switzerland." *Politics and Society* 10:5 (1981).

Sidjanski, Susan. "The Swiss and Their Politics." *Government and Opposition* (Summer 1976).

Steinberg, Jonathan. *Why Switzerland?* Cambridge: Cambridge University Press, 1976.

Steiner, Jürg. "Research Strategies Beyond Consociational Theory." *The Journal of Politics* (November 1981).

Steiner, Jürg, and Robert Dorff. *A Theory of Political Modes: Intraparty Decision Making in Switzerland.* Chapel Hill: University of North Carolina Press, 1980.

Chapter Two: Britain
Primary Sources

British Nationality Act 1981. London: Central Office of Information, February 1982.

British Nationality Law. London: Her Majesty's Stationery Office (HMSO), 30 July 1980.

British Parliamentary Debates [Hansard], House of Commons, Fifth Series. London: HMSO. Volume 649 (November 1961), Volume 812-814 (February-March 1971), Volume 989 (March-April 1975), and Volume 997 (January 1981).

Central Office of Information. *Immigration into Britain.* London: HMSO, 1981.

First Report from the Select Committee on Race Relations and Immigration: Evidence and Appendices. London: HMSO, 13 March 1978.

Great Britain Home Office. *Commonwealth Citizens: Control after Entry.* London: HMSO, 1969.

_____. *Control of Immigration Statistics.* London: HMSO, April 1978.

Report of the Race Relations Board 1966/1967. London: HMSO, 1968.

Secondary Sources

Apple, R. W. "Labor Is Scornful of Mrs. Thatcher in Debate on Riots." *New York Times* (10 July 1981).

Borders, William. "Britain Debates Immigration and Race." *New York Times* (8 February 1981).

Batson, Thomas. "For All, Britain's Loss of Empire, the Commonwealth Still Matters." *New York Times* (12 June 1977).

Canny, Nicholas. *The Elizabethan Conquest of Ireland: A Pattern Established.* New York: Barnes and Noble, 1976.

_____. "The Ideology of English Colonization: From Ireland to America." *William and Mary Quarterly* (October 1973).

Davison, R. B. *Commonwealth Immigration.* London: Oxford University Press, 1964.

Deakin, Nicholas, ed. *Colour and the British Electorate 1964: Six Case Studies.* New York: Praeger Publishers, 1965.

Gray, M. M. "The Influences of Spenser's Irish Experiences on *The Faerie Queene.*" *Review of English Studies* (October 1930).

Hartley-Brewer, Michael. "Smethwick." In *Colour and the British Electorate 1964: Six Case Studies,* edited by Nicholas Deakin. New York: Praeger, 1965.

Hill, Clifford. *West Indian Migrants and the London Churches.* London: Oxford University Press, 1963.

Hobbes, Thomas. *Leviathan.* Middlesex, England: Pelican Classics, 1968.

Hodgen, Margaret. *Early Anthropology in the Sixteenth and Seventeenth Centuries.* Philadelphia: University of Pennsylvania Press, 1964.

Holmes, Colin, ed. *Immigrants and Minorities in British Society.* London: George Allen and Unwin, 1978.

Jacobs, Brian. *Black Politics and Urban Crisis in Britain.* Cambridge: Cambridge University Press, 1986.

Lambert, Tom. "British Race Relations Worsen." *Los Angeles Times* (23 June 1976).

Lelyveld, Joseph. "Being a Black Bobby Means Hearing I'm Sorry." *New York Times* (14 May 1986).

Locke, John. *Two Treatises of Government.* New York: Mentor Books, 1965.

Madan, Raj. *Colored Minorities in Great Britain: A Comprehensive Bibliography: 1970-1977.* Westport, CT: Greenwood Press, 1979.

Markham, James. "Minorities in Western Europe: Hearing Not Welcome in Several Languages." *New York Times* (5 August 1986).

Mill, John Stuart. *On Liberty.* New York: Norton and Company, 1975.

New York Times. "London Is Seeking to Ease Immigration for Whites." (26 January 1973).

_____. "Lord Butler Dies in Britain at 79; A Longtime Conservative Leader." (10 March 1982).

Nordheimer, Jon. "British Nonwhites Seek Bigger Voice." *New York Times* (8 June 1983).

Patterson, Sheila. *Immigration and Race Relations in Britain 1960-1967.* London: Oxford University Press, 1969.

Rabb, Theodore. *Enterprise and Empire: Merchant and Gentry Investment in the Expansion of England, 1575-1630.* Cambridge: Harvard University Press, 1967.

Economist. "Race in Britain." (27 April 1974).

Race. "Enoch Powell's Speech of 20 April 1968, Roy Jenkins' of 4 May 1968." (July 1968).

Reed, Roy. "The Trouble Began When the Colonies Came Home." *New York Times* (21 August 1977).

Reeves, Frank. *British Racial Discourse.* Cambridge: Cambridge University Press, 1983.

Robinson, Vaughan. *Transients, Settlers, and Refugees: Asians in Britain.* London: Clarendon Press, 1986.

Rose, E. J. B., in association with Nicholas Deakin and others. *Colour and Citizenship.* London: Oxford University Press, 1969.

Shakespeare, William. *The Tempest.* Edited by Frank Kermode. Cambridge: Harvard University Press, 1954.

Spenser, Edmund. *A View of the Present State of Ireland.* Edited by William Lindsay Renwick. London: Eric Partridge, 1934.

Thomas, Jo. "In Riot's Wake, Black Leader's Words Roil Britain." *New York Times* (28 October 1985).

Verney, Douglas. *British Government and Politics: Life Without a Declaration of Independence.* New York: Harper and Row, 1971.

Weinraub, Bernard. "Broad British Laws Proposed to Curb Racial Discrimination." *New York Times* (12 September 1975).

_____. "Poem by Black Annoys London Police." *New York Times* (8 July 1975).

Wills, Garry. "Mrs. Thatcher's Racist Appeal." *Hartford Courant*, Hartford, CT (26 April 1978).

Chapter Three: Northern Ireland
Primary Sources

Disturbances in Northern Ireland: Report of the Commission under the Chairmanship of Lord Cameron, Appointed by the Governor of Northern Ireland. Belfast: HMSO, 1969.

Great Britain. *Constitution of Northern Ireland.* London: HMSO, 1991.

Great Britain. Northern Ireland Department. *The Future of Northern Ireland.* London: HMSO, 1972.

Republic of Ireland. *Agreement between the Government of the United Kingdom of Great Britain and Northern Ireland and the Government of the Republic of Ireland.* London: HMSO, November 1985.

Secondary Sources

Arthur, Paul. "Anglo-Irish Relations since 1968: A Fever Chart Interpretation." *Government and Opposition* (Spring 1983).

_____. "Negotiating the Northern Ireland Problem: Track One or Track Two Diplomacy." *Government and Opposition* (Autumn 1990).

Aughey, Arthur. "Recent Interpretations of Unionism." *Political Quarterly* (April-June 1990).

Barlett, Jonathan. *Northern Ireland.* New York: H. W. Wilson Co., 1983.

Barritt, Denis and Arthur Booth. *Orange and Green: A Quaker Study of Community Relations in Northern Ireland.* Belfast: Northern Friends Peace Board, 1972.

Birch, Anthony. "Minority Nationalist Movements and Theories of Political Integration." *World Politics* (April 1978).

_____. *Political Integration and Disintegration in the British Isles.* London: George Allen and Unwin, 1977.

Birrell, Derek. "A Government of Northern Ireland and the Obstacle of Power-Sharing." *Political Quarterly* (April-June 1981).

Borders, William. "For the British in Northern Ireland, No End in Sight." *New York Times* (14 March 1979).

Bowman, David. *More than the Troubles: A Common Sense View of the Conflict.* Philadelphia: New Society Publishers, 1984.

Boyle, Kevin and Tom Hadden. "How to Read the New Ireland Forum Report." *Political Quarterly* (October-December 1984).

Brendon, Piers. *Eminent Edwardians.* Boston: Houghton Mifflin, 1980.

Buckland, Patrick. *A History of Northern Ireland.* New York: Holmes and Meier, 1981.

_____. "Ireland and the British Government." In *The Cambridge Historical Encyclopedia of Great Britain and Ireland*, Christopher Haigh, ed. Cambridge: Cambridge University Press, 1985.

Burton, Frank. *The Politics of Legitimacy.* London: Routledge and Kegan, 1978.

Cairns, Edward. *Caught in the Crossfire: Children and the Northern Ireland Conflict.* Belfast: Appletree Press, 1987.

Carson, William. *Ulster and the Irish Republic.* Belfast: William Cleland, 1956.

Christian Science Monitor. "New Game in Northern Ireland." Editorial (26 October 1994).

_____. "Peace in Ireland." Editorial (22 November 1994).

_____. "Britain Upgraded Its Northern Ireland Peace Talks." (23 March 1995).

Clarity, James. "Irish Debate How to End Strife in the North." *New York Times* (31 March 1993).

_____. "Irish Ex-Premier Hopeful for Ulster Record." *New York Times* (4 April 1993).

_____. "I.R.A. Welcomes Ulster Plan; Describes It as Basis for Peace." *New York Times* (4 October 1993).

_____. "Initiative on Northern Ireland Stirs Optimism." *New York Times* (6 October 1993).

_____. "Irish Chief Backs Peace Plan and Will See British." *New York Times* (8 October 1993).

_____. "Irish President Backs New Call for Peace in Ulster." *New York Times* (14 October 1993).

_____. "Ireland and Britain Offer Plan for I.R.A. Talks." *New York Times* (30 October 1993).

Clarke, Aidan. *The Old English in Ireland: 1625-1642.* Ithaca, NY: Cornell University Press, 1966.

Connolly, Michael and John Loughlin. "Reflections on the Anglo-Irish Agreement." *Government and Opposition* (Spring 1986).

Cox, Harvey. "Managing Northern Ireland Inter-Governmentally: An Appraisal of the Anglo-Irish Agreement." *Parliamentary Affairs* (January 1987).

_____. "Who Wants a United Ireland?" *Government and Opposition* (Winter 1985).

Conroy, John. *Belfast Diary.* Boston: Beacon Press, 1987.

Cosgrove, Patrick. "The Insoluble Problem of Ulster." *The Round Table* (July 1969).

Crighton, Elizabeth. "Northern Ireland Talks Face Many Pitfalls" *Christian Science Monitor* (19 October 1994).

Crighton, Elizabeth and Martha Abele MacIver, "The Evolution of Protracted Ethnic Conflict," *Comparative Politics* (January, 1991).

Cronin, Sean. *Irish Nationalism: A History of the Roots and Ideology.* New York: Continuum, 1981.

Day, Alan, ed. *Border and Territorial Disputes.* Essex: Longman, 1987.

Devlin, Bernadette. *The Price of My Soul.* New York: Knopf, 1969.

Dutter, Lee. "Northern Ireland and Theories of Ethnic Politics." *The Journal of Conflict Resolution* (December 1980).

Easthope, Gary. "Religious War in Northern Ireland." *Sociology* (September 1987).

Economist. "Ulster's Misery." (11 January 1969).

_____. "So Who Does Rule?" (1 June 1974).

_____. "Fresh Irish Air." (24 February 1979).

_____. "No Such Thing as a Christian Terrorist." (28 July 1979).

_____. "Ulster Devolved in Tears." (22 November 1980).

_____. "A Bridge to Ireland." (23 May 1981).

_____. "Terrorism Equally Evil." (16 January 1993).

_____. "Ireland: St. Patrick's Poor Island." (March 12 1983).

_____. "At Last." (3 September 1993).

_____. "Not Always So Polite." (30 May 1994).

_____. "A Joyful Time, For Some." (10 September, 1994).

_____. "Bipartisan Blair." (10 September 1994).

_____. "Ulster's Tense Peace." (10 September 1994).

_____. "Learning to Batter Walls." (10 October 1994).

_____. "Check Your Bombs at the Door." (24 December 1994, and 6 January 1995).

_____. "A New Dialogue." (25 February 1995).

_____. "Gerry and the Peace-Makers." (18 March 1995).

_____. "When English Eyes are Brimming." (18 March 1995).

Elliot, R. S. P. and John Hickie. *Ulster: A Case Study in Conflict Theory.* London: Longman, 1971.

Fraser, Peter. *Joseph Chamberlain.* London: Cassell, 1966.

Furniss, Norman. "Northern Ireland as a Case Study of Decentralization in Unitary States." *World Politics* (April 1975).

Gallagher, Frank. *The Indivisible Island: The History of the Partition of Ireland.* London: Victor Gollancz, 1957.

Guelke, Adrian. "The Political Impasse in South Africa and Northern Ireland." *Comparative Politics* (January 1991).

Haeger, Robert. "In Ulster, Violence Turns Hope to Despair." *U.S. News and World Report* (2 February 1981).

Haggart, Simon. "The Pleasure of Hate." *The New Republic* (6 and 13 January 1983).

Hastings, Max. *Barricades in Belfast.* New York: Taplinger Publishing, 1970.

Hachey, Thomas. "One People or Two? The Origins of Partition and Prospects for Unification in Ireland." *Journal of International Affairs* (1973).

Heesam, Alan. "Ireland Under the Union." *History Today* (January 1984).

Hodgson, Bryan. "War and Peace in Northern Ireland." *National Geographic* (1981).

Hume, John. "The Irish Question: A British Problem." *Foreign Affairs* (Winter 1979/80).

Inglis, Brian. "No One Wants Ulster." *The Spectator* (22 September 1990).

Jacobsen, John Kurt. "The Republic of Ireland: Perils of Pragmatism." *Dissent* (Winter 1980).

_____. "Stalemate in Northern Ireland." *Dissent* (Summer 1982).

Joffe, Josef. "The New Europe: Yesterday's Ghosts." *Foreign Affairs*, Special Issue, 1993.

Kee, Robert. *Ireland: A History.* Boston: Little, Brown, 1980.

Keesing's Contemporary Archives (December 1985).

Keeton, George and Dennis Lloyd, eds. *The United Kingdom: The Development of Its Laws and Constitutions.* London: Stevens and Sons, 1955.

Kennedy, Carol. "Making of a Martyr." *Maclean's* (18 May 1981).

Kingston, William. "Northern Ireland: The Elements of a Solution." *Political Quarterly* (April-June 1972).

Knight, Robin. "Bombs, Bullets and Fear: Ulster's Agony Flares Anew." *U.S. News and World Report* (22 April 1974).

Larkin, Emmet. *The Roman Catholic Church in Ireland and the Fall of Parnell.* Chapel Hill: University of North Carolina Press, 1979.

Lee, Alfred. "Dynamics of Terrorism in Northern Ireland, 1968-1980." *Social Research* (Spring 1981).

Lijphart, Arend. "The Northern Ireland Problem: Cases, Theories, and Solutions." *British Journal of Political Science* (January 1975).

London *Sunday Times* Insight Team. *Northern Ireland: A Report on the Conflict.* London: Penguin, 1972.

Lynch, John. "The Anglo-Irish Problem." *Foreign Affairs* (July 1972).

McAllister, Jon and Richard Rose. "Can Political Conflict be Resolved by Social Change? Northern Ireland as a Test Case." *Journal of Conflict Resolution* (September 1983).

MacDonald, Michael. *Children of Wrath*. Cambridge: Polity Press, 1986.

MacLeod, Alexander. "Protestant Cease-Fire Puts Peace on Ulster's Horizon." *Christian Science Monitor* (14 October 1994).

_____. "Peacemaker Abroad, Irish Premier Ousted" *Christian Science Monitor* (18 November 1994).

_____. "US Muscles Britain to Speed Up Northern Ireland Peace Talks." *Christian Science Monitor* (2 December 1994).

McGarry, John. "The Anglo-Irish Agreement and the Prospects for Power-Sharing in Northern Ireland." *Political Quarterly* (April-June 1988).

Mansergh, Nicholas. *The Government of Northern Ireland: A Study in Devolution*. London: George Allen and Unwin, 1936.

_____. *The Irish Question: 1840-1921*. London: George Allen and Unwin, 1965.

_____. "Northern Ireland: The Past." *Race* (1972).

Menendez, Albert. "Northern Ireland: Is There Any Hope?" *Church and State* (June 1973).

_____. "Ulster's Educational Apartheid." *Church and State* (June 1973).

Moody, Theodore. *The Londonderry Plantation 1609-1641*. Belfast: Mullan and Son, 1939.

Moody, Theodore and F. X. Martin. *The Course of Irish History*. Cork, Ireland: The Mercier Press, 1967.

Moore, Robert. "Race Relations in the Six Counties: Colonialism, Industrialization and Stratification in Ireland." *Race* (1972).

New Statesman and Society. "Ireland's Fragile Peace." Editorial (18 November 1994).

O'Brien, Conor Cruise. "Introductory Remarks." *Proceedings of the Irish Question*, Patricia Slattery, ed. Winooski, VT: St. Michael's College Press, 1982.

_____. Review of *The Wrath of a Nation: Civilization and Furies of Nationalism*, by William Praff, Foreign Affairs (November-December, 1993).

_____. "Northern Ireland: The Future." *Race* (1972).

_____. *Parnell and His Party*. Oxford: Clarendon Press, 1957.

_____. *States of Ireland*. New York: Vintage Press, 1972.

O'Neil, Daniel. *Three Perennial Themes of Anti-Colonialism: The Irish Case*. Denver: University of Denver Press, 1976.

O'Neill, Shane. "Pluralistic Justice and Its Limits: The Case of Northern Ireland." *Political Studies* (September 1994).

Paisley, Jon. *United Ireland—Never!* Belfast: Puritan Press, 1972.

Parker, Tony. "From Bloody Sunday to the Bitter End." *New Statesman* (June 1993).

Porter, A. N., ed. *Atlas of British Overseas Expansion*. New York: Simon and Schuster, 1991.

Prager, Jeffrey. *Building Democracy in Ireland: Political and Cultural Integration in a Newly Independent Nation*. Cambridge: Cambridge University Press, 1986.

Quinn, David Beers. *The Elizabethans and the Irish*. Ithaca: Cornell University Press, 1966.

Reik, Miriam. "Ireland: Religious War or Class Struggle." *Saturday Review* (18 March 1972).

Rooke, Donal. "Nationalism in Northern Ireland." *The Valley Advocate* (7 April 1986).

Rose, Richard. "The Dynamics of a Divided Regime." *Government and Opposition* (Spring 1970).

_____. *Governing Without Consensus: An Irish Perspective*. Boston: Beacon Press, 1971.

Rowse, A. L. "Tudor Expansion: The Transition from Medieval to Modern History." *William and Mary Quarterly* (July 1957).

Rowthorn, Bob. "Northern Ireland: An Economy in Crisis." *Cambridge Journal of Economics* (March 1973).

Rumpf, E. and A. C. Hepburn. *Nationalism and Socialism in Twentieth Century Ireland*. New York: Barnes and Noble, 1977.

Rutherford, Ward. "Options for Ulster." *World Today* (August 1980).

Seton-Watson, Hugh. *Nations and States: An Enquiry into the Origins of Nations and the Politics of Nationalism*. Boulder, CO: Westview Press, 1977.

Shannon, William. "The Anglo-Irish Agreement." *Foreign Affairs* (Spring 1986).

Smith, Scott S. "Nationalist vs. Unionist: Two Views of Northern Ireland. Misconceptions of Nationalism Prevent Peace." *Christian Science Monitor* (2 April 1987).

Smooha, Sammy. "Control of Minorities in Israel and Northern Ireland." *Comparative Studies in Society and History* (April 1980).

Smythe, Clifford. *The IRA, Eire, and the Church of Rome: The Axis against Ulster.* Belfast: Puritan Press, 1972.

Strauss, E. *Irish Nationalism and British Democracy.* London: Methuen, 1951.

Terchek, Ronald. "Conflict and Cleavage in Northern Ireland." *Annals of the American Academy of Political and Social Sciences* (September 1977).

Terry, Sara. "Bearing the Burden of Grown Ups' Hatred." *Christian Science Monitor* (13 April 1988).

Thompson, David. "Ulster: Rebellion and Realignment." *The Progressive* (November 1973).

Thompson, J. L. P. "Deprivation and Political Violence in Northern Ireland, 1922-1985." *Journal of Conflict Resolution* (December 1989).

U.S. News and World Report. "ABC's of Ireland's Endless Strife." (31 July 1972).

U.S. News and World Report. "Ulster's Civil War: Agony without End." (10 September 1979).

Van Voris, William. *Violence in Ulster.* Amherst, MA: University of Massachusetts Press, 1975.

Weinraub, Bernard. "Free Derry, run by IRA, is a state within a state." *New York Times* (27 April 1972).

Wheatcroft, Geoffrey. "The Party Line." *New Statesman* (9 December, 1994).

Whyte, John. "How is the Boundary Maintained Between the Two Communities in Northern Ireland?" *Ethnic and Racial Studies*, (April, 1986).

Winder, David. "Anglo-Irish Agreement: A Modest Beginning." *Christian Science Monitor* (14 November 1985).

Chapter Four: Canada
Primary Sources

Canada Parliament, House of Commons. *Multiculturalism: Building the Canadian Mosaic*. Ottawa: Queen's Printer of Canada, June 1987.

Canadian Department of Indian Affairs and Northern Development. *Indians of British Columbia: A Historical Review*. Ottawa: Queen's Printer, March 1967.

Canadian Ministry of Indian and Northern Affairs. *A Survey of Indian Conditions*. Ottawa: Queen's Printer, June 1980.

Office of the Canadian Prime Minister. "Meeting of the First Ministers on the Constitution: 1987 Constitution Accord." 3 June 1987.

Secondary Sources

Baugh, David. "Affirmative Action and the Sign Law." *Options Politiques* (May 1992).

Beek, Stanley and Ivan Bernier, eds. *Canada and the New Constitution: The Unfinished Agenda.* Montreal: The Institute for Research on Public Policy, 1983.

Borders, William. "Deportation Plan Rouses Canadians." *New York Times* (29 October 1974).

_____. "Racial Trend in Immigration Troubling Canadians." *New York Times* (25 November 1974).

_____. "Oil, the Big Issue in Alberta Voting." *New York Times* (14 March 1975).

_____. "A Vein of Bias Exposed in Vancouver by Immigration from India." *New York Times* (12 April 1975).

Burns, John. "Accord to Give the Eskimos Control of a Fifth of Canada." *New York Times* (17 December 1991).

Burns, John. "Fury Rising in Quebec over Mohawk Standoff." *New York Times* (22 July 1990).

_____. "Quebec Isn't Feeling Especially Canadian." *New York Times* (8 December 1991).

_____. "A Sovereign Quebec, He Says, Needn't Be Séparé." *New York Times* (21 February 1992).

_____. "With Canada's Future in Question, Newfoundland Ponders a Vital Vote." *New York Times* (18 June 1990).

Daily Hampshire Gazette. "Trudeau's Statement after the Defeat of the 1980 Referendum in Quebec." Northampton, MA (21 May 1980).

Deutsch, Karl. "The Growth of Nations: Some Recurrent Patterns of Political and Social Integration." *World Politics* (January 1953).

_____. *Politics and Government: How People Decide Their Fate.* Boston: Houghton Mifflin, 1970.

Deutsch, Karl and William Foltz, eds. *Nation-Building.* New York: Atherton Press, 1966.

Dyck, Rand. *Provincial Politics in Canada.* Scarborough, Ontario: Prentice-Hall, 1986.

Farnsworth, Clyde H. "Mulroney Proposes New Canadian Framework to Stall Separation." *New York Times* (25 September 1991).

_____. "Ottawa Plan Gets Wary Responses." *New York Times* (29 September 1991).

_____. "In a Language Minefield, Enforcer Treads Softly." *New York Times* (9 October 1991).

_____. "A Canada Now Beyond Secessionism?" *New York Times* (24 February 1992).

Freed, Kenneth. "Dream of Independence Fades for Quebec Residents." *Los Angeles Times* (21 December 1984).

Gibbins, Roger. *Regionalism: Territorial Politics in Canada and the United States.* Toronto: Buttersworth Companies, 1982.

Giniger, Henry. "Canada Says Gap Persists between Indians and Whites." *New York Times* (29 June 1980).

_____. "Canadian Leaders Agree on Charter: Quebec is Opposed." *New York Times* (6 November 1981).

_____. "Trudeau Preaches His Own New Federalism." *New York Times* (1 March 1982).

Hempstone, Smith. "Canadian West Gaining Attention—At Last." *Daily Hampshire Gazette*, Northampton, MA (30 September 1977).

Jackson, Robert, Doreen Jackson, and Nicolas Barter-Moore. *Politics in Canada: Culture, Institutions, Behaviour and Public Policy*. Scarborough, Ontario: Prentice-Hall, 1986.

Janigan, Mary. "Drumbeats of Rage: Native Canadians Prepare for a Showdown on Self-Government." *Maclean's* (16 March 1992).

Kelly, Brendan. "Repatriating Cultural Power." *The Financial Times* (9 January 1993).

Kornberg, Allan and Harold Clarke, eds. *Political Support in Canada: The Crisis Years*. Durham, NC: Duke University Press, 1983.

Lipset, Seymour Martin. *Continental Divide: The Values and Institutions of the United States and Canada*. London: Routledge, 1990.

Lévesque, René. "For an Independent Quebec." *Foreign Affairs* (July 1976).

Malcolm, Andrew. "Language Again Threatening to Split Canadian Federation." *New York Times* (24 March 1990).

_____. "Pleasing Both Sides, Court Just Sharpens Canada Crisis." *New York Times* (4 October 1981).

_____. "Trudeau Calls for National Healing and Prompt Effort on New Charter." *New York Times* (22 May 1980).

Martin, Douglas. "Quebec Independence: The Vision Has Faded." *New York Times* (26 January 1984).

Mayo, Henry. *An Introduction to Democratic Theory*. New York: Oxford University Press, 1960.

McWhinney, Edward. *Canada and the Constitution 1979-1982: Patriation and the Charter of Rights.* Toronto: University of Toronto Press, 1982.

Morf, Gustav. "Ethnic Groups and Developmental Models: The Case of Quebec." In *Ethnicity in an International Context: The Politics of Disassociation*, edited by Abdul Said and Luis Simmons. New Brunswick, NJ: Transaction Books, 1976.

New York Times. "Indians Ask Canada for a Province." (26 October 1976).

_____. "Referendum Question for Quebec Province." (21 May 1980).

_____. "Quebec Votes for Canada." Editorial (22 May 1980).

_____. "Trudeau Resigns as Leader of His Party." (1 March 1984).

Said, Abdul and Luis Simmons, eds. *Ethnicity in an International Context: The Politics of Disassociation.* New Brunswick, NJ: Transaction Books, 1976.

Sheppard, Robert and Michael Valpy. *The National Deal: The Fight for a Canadian Constitution.* Toronto: Fleet Books, 1982.

Stockton, William. "René Lévesque and the Divided House of Canada." *New York Times* (20 May 1979).

Trumbull, Robert. "Canada Tightens Rules Covering Immigration Flow." *New York Times* (23 October 1974).

Vano, Gerard. *Neo-Feudalism: The Canadian Dilemma.* Toronto: Anansi Press, 1981.

Vidal, David. "Canadian Tribes Drop Land Claims." *New York Times* (7 December 1975).

Walsh, Mary. "Charges of Prejudice Rattle Canadians." *Los Angeles Times* (13 June 1992).

_____. "A Lamp to the Nations Flickers." *Los Angeles Times* (18 June 1992).

_____. "Proposals for Canadian Unity Prove Divisive." *Los Angeles Times* (27 June 1992).

Wren, Christopher. "Canada Supreme Court Rules Solely English Law Invalid." *New York Times* (14 June 1985).

_____. "Quebecers Seem Interested in Success, Not Secession." *New York Times* (27 January 1985).

Chapter Five: Malaysia
Primary Sources

British Colonial Office and Central Office of Information. *Introducing the Eastern Dependencies.* London: HMSO, 1955.

Great Britain Colonial Office. *British Dependencies in the Far East, 1945-1949.* London: HMSO, May 1949.

_____. *Constitution Proposals for the Federation of Malaya.* London: HMSO, June 1957.

_____. *Malayan Union and Singapore: Statement of Policy on Future Constitution.* London: HMSO, 1946.

_____. *Federation of Malaya: Summary of Revised Constitutional Proposals.* London: HMSO, July 1947.

Malayan Constitutional Documents. Kuala Lumpur: Government Press, 1962.

Malaysian Government. *The Federal Constitution.* Kuala Lumpur: Government Press, 1964.

Secondary Sources

Bedlington, Stanley. *Malaysia and Singapore: The Building of New States.* Ithaca, NY: Cornell University Press, 1978.

Brown, David. "The State of Ethnicity and the Ethnicity of the State: Ethnic Politics in Southeast Asia." *Ethnic and Racial Studies* (January 1989).

Deutsch, Karl. *Political Community and the North Atlantic Area.* Princeton: Princeton University Press, 1957.

_____. *Political Community at the International Level.* Garden City, NY: Doubleday, 1954.

Fletcher, Nancy. *The Separation of Singapore from Malaysia.* Ithaca, NY: Cornell University, 1969.

Glaser, Kurt and Stefan Possony. *Victims of Politics.* New York: Columbia University Press, 1979.

Groves, Harry. *The Constitution of Malaysia.* Singapore: Malaysia Publications, 1964.

Kessler, Clive. *Islam and Politics in a Malay State: Kelantan 1838-1969.* Ithaca, NY: Cornell University Press, 1978.

Lapping, Brian. *End of Empire.* New York: St. Martin's Press, 1985.

Lijphart, Arend. *Democracies: Patterns of Majoritarian and Consensus Government in Twenty-one Countries.* New Haven: Yale University Press, 1984.

Mahajani, Usha. *The Role of Indian Minorities in Burma and Malaya.* Bombay, India: Vora and Company, 1960.

Means, Gordon. *Malaysian Politics.* London: University of London Press, 1970.

Milne, R. S. *Government and Politics in Malaysia.* Boston: Houghton Mifflin, 1967.

Milne, R. S. "Malaysia: A Federation in the Making." *Asian Survey* (February 1963).

Milne, R. S. *Politics in Ethnically Bipolar States.* Vancouver, Canada: University of British Columbia Press, 1981.

Milne, R. S. and K. J. Ratnam. *Malaysia—New States in a New Nation: Political Development of Sarawak and Sabah in Malaysia.* London: Frank Cass, 1974.

Newman, Barry. "Ethnic Upheaval: Malaysia Torn by Drive for More Malay Rights at Expense of Chinese." *Wall Street Journal* (8 May 1978).

New York Times. "Sought Aid for Refugees." (11 January 1982).

Osborne, Milton. *Singapore and Malaysia.* Ithaca, NY: Cornell University, 1964.

Purcell, Victor. *The Chinese in Southeast Asia.* London: Oxford University Press, 1965.

Ratnam, K. J. *Communalism and the Political Process in Malaya.* Kuala Lumpur: University of Malaya Press, 1965.

Renan, Ernest. "What Is a Nation?" In *Modern Political Doctrine,* edited by Alfred Zimmern. London: Oxford University Press, 1939.

Sandhu, Kernial Singh. *Indians in Malaya.* Cambridge: Cambridge University Press, 1969.

Schoenberger, Karl. "Malaysia's Trade Minister Exhibits a True Grit." *Los Angeles Times* (15 June 1992).

Scott, Margaret. "Where the Quota Is King." *New York Times Magazine* (17 November 1991).

Sheridan, L. A. *The Federation of Malaya Constitution.* Singapore: University of Malaya, 1961.

Simandjuntak, B. *Malayan Federalism 1945-1963: A Study of Federal Problems in a Plural Society.* London: Oxford University Press, 1969.

Snodgrass, Donald. *Inequality and Economic Development in Malaysia.* New York: Oxford University Press, 1980.

Steinberg, David Joel. *In Search of Southeast Asia.* Honolulu: University of Hawaii Press, 1986.

Sterba, James. "Malaysia Is About to Amend Constitution to Declare Discussion of Racial Issues a Crime." *New York Times* (2 March 1971).

Strauch, Judith. *Chinese Village Politics in the Malaysian State.* Cambridge: Harvard University Press, 1981.

The World Almanac. New York: Pharos Books, 1991.

Chapter Six: Nigeria
Primary Sources

British Colonial Office. *Nigeria: Report of the Commission Appointed to Inquire into the Fears of Minorities and the Means of Allaying Them.* London: HMSO, July 1958.

Morris-Hale, Walter. *British Administration in Tanganyika from 1920 to 1945: With Special Reference to the Preparation of Africans for Administrative Positions.* Geneva, Switzerland: Imprimo, 1969.

United States State Department. "Memorandum from the Vice President [Nixon] to the President [Eisenhower] of the United States." *State Department Bulletin* (22 April 1957).

Secondary Sources

Africa Magazine. "Nigeria: Special Report." (April 1979).

Africa Newsfile. "Nigeria: Disinformation." (19 June 1989).

Aluko, Olajide. *Ghana and Nigeria 1957-1970: A Study in Inter-African Discord.* London: Collings, 1976.

Arikpo, Okoi. *The Development of Modern Nigeria.* Middlesex, England: Penguin Books, 1967.

Arnold, Guy. *Modern Nigeria.* London: Longman, 1977.

Awolowo, Obafemi. *Path to Nigerian Freedom.* London: Faber and Faber, 1947.

Bienen, Henry. *Armies and Parties in Africa.* New York: Africana Publishing, 1978.

Carter, Gwendolen, ed. *National Unity and Regionalism in Eight African States*. Ithaca, NY: Cornell University Press, 1966.

Carter, Gwendolen and Patrick O'Meara, eds. *African Independence: The First Twenty-Five Years*. Bloomington: Indiana University Press, 1986.

Coleman, James. *Nigeria: Background to Nationalism*. Berkeley: University of California Press, 1958.

Cowell, Alan. "Nigeria, Rich with Oil, Is Dependent on U.S. and Other Nations for Food." *New York Times* (15 August 1981).

_____. "Nigeria's Oil Exports to the US: World Oil Glut Cramps Nigeria's Development." *New York Times* (26 November 1982).

Crowder, Michael. *The Story of Nigeria*. London: Faber and Faber, 1978.

de St. Jorre, John. *The Nigerian Civil War*. London: Hodder and Stoughton, 1972.

_____. "Nigeria's Unhappy Prospects." *New York Times* (7 January 1984).

de Tocqueville, Alexis. *L'ancien regime et la revolution*. Translated by Stuart Gilbert [The old regime and the French Revolution]. Garden City, NY: Doubleday, Anchor Books, 1955.

Diamond, Larry. *Class, Ethnicity and Democracy in Nigeria*. Syracuse: Syracuse University Press, 1988.

_____. "Nigeria in Search of Democracy." *Foreign Affairs*, Spring 1984.

Diamond, Larry, Juan Linz, and Seymour Martin Lipset. *Democracy in Developing Countries: Africa.* Boulder, CO: Lynne Rienner Publishers, 1988.

Emerson, Rupert. "Nation-Building in Africa." In *Nation-Building*, edited by Karl Deutsch and William Foltz. New York: Atherton Press, 1963.

Fetter, Bruce. *Colonial Rule in Africa.* Madison: University of Wisconsin Press, 1979.

Freund, Bill. *The Making of Contemporary Africa: The Development of African Society since 1800.* Bloomington: Indiana University Press, 1984.

Gupte, Pranaye. "Civilian Leader Quietly Puts His Stamp on Nigeria." *New York Times* (19 August 1980).

_____. "Nigeria, a Year Away from Military Rule, Struggles to Build a U.S.-Style Democracy." *New York Times* (17 August 1980).

Herskovits, Jean. "Democracy in Nigeria." *Foreign Affairs* (Winter 1979/1980).

_____. "One Nigeria." *Foreign Affairs* (January 1973).

_____. "Nigeria: Africa's New Power." *Foreign Affairs* (January 1975).

Jackson, Robert and Carl Rosberg. *Personal Rule in Black Africa: Prince, Autocrat, Prophet, Tyrant.* Berkeley: University of California Press, 1982.

Kaufman, Michael. "In Africa, When Lagos Speaks Everybody Else Listens." *New York Times* (2 July 1978).

Legum, Colin, ed. "Nigeria: Bold Initiatives for the Future, Military Rule until 1992." In *Africa Contemporary Record 1986-1987*. London: Africana Publishing, 1988.

Liebenow, Gus. *African Politics: Crises and Challenges*. Bloomington: Indiana University Press, 1986.

Los Angeles Times. "Army Seizes Control of Nigeria Coup." (1 January 1984).

Lubeck, Paul. *The African Bourgeoisie: Capitalist Development in Nigeria, Kenya, and the Ivory Coast*. Boulder, CO: Lynne Rienner Publishers, 1987.

Maitland-Jones, J. F. *Politics in Africa: The Former British Territories*. New York: Norton and Company, 1973.

May, Clifford. "Africa's Men In Khaki Are Often A Law Unto Themselves." *New York Times* (6 October 1985).

_____. "Nigeria's Oil Export Earnings." *New York Times* (8 January 1984).

Miles, William. *Elections in Nigeria: A Grassroots Perspective*. Boulder, CO: Lynne Rienner Publishers, 1988.

Mok, Michael. *Biafra Journal: A Personal Report on a People in Agony*. New York: Time-Life Books, 1969.

New York Times. "Moving Misery in Africa." (3 February 1983).

New York Times. "Nigeria Says 1.2 Million Have Been Expelled." (15 February 1983).

New York Times. "Muslims Rioting Against Christians Continues in North Nigerian City." (17 October 1991).

Nixon, Charles. "Self-Determination: The Nigeria-Biafra Case." *World Politics* (July 1972).

Nkrumah, Kwame. *Class Struggle in Africa.* New York: International Publishers, 1970.

Nnoli, Okwudiba. *Ethnic Politics in Nigeria.* Enugu, Nigeria: Fourth Dimension Publishers, 1978.

Noble, Kenneth. "Nigeria Reveals Census' Total, 88.5 Million, and Little More." *New York Times* (25 March 1992).

Nordlinger, Eric. *Soldiers in Politics: Military Coups and Governments.* Englewood Cliffs, NJ: Prentice-Hall, 1977.

Nwankwo, Arthur and Samuel Ifejika. *The Making of a Nation: Biafra.* London: C. Hurst Company, 1969.

Olorunsola, Victor, ed. *The Politics of Cultural Sub-Nationalism in Africa: Africa and Problem of "One State, Many Nationalisms."* Garden City, NY: Anchor Books, 1972.

Ostheimer, John. *Nigerian Politics.* New York: Harper and Row, 1973.

Pakenham, Valerie. *The Noonday Sun: Edwardians in the Tropics.* London: Methuen, 1985.

Rivkin, Arnold. *Nation-Building in Africa: Problems and Prospects.* New Brunswick, NJ: Rutgers University Press, 1969.

Rodney, Walter. *How Europe Underdeveloped Africa.* Dar es Salaam, Tanzania: Tanzania Publishing House, 1972.

Schwarz, Frederick. *Nigeria: The Tribes, the Nation, or the Race—The Politics of Independence.* Cambridge, MA: M.I.T. Press, 1965.

Shingler, John and F. Seth Singleton. *Africa in Perspective.* New York: Hayden Books, 1967.

The Hammond Almanac, 1982. Maplewood, NJ: Hammond Almanac, 1981.

Whitaker, Jennifer Seymour. *How Can Africa Survive?* New York: Council of Foreign Relations Press, 1988.

Winfrey, Carey. "Oil and Nigeria's Economy." *New York Times* (8 July 1979).

Wiseman, John. *Democracy in Black Africa: Survival and Revival.* New York: Paragon House Publishers, 1990.

Chapter Seven: South Africa
Primary Sources

South African Bureau of Information. "Address by the State President, Mr. F. W. de Klerk, at the Opening of the Third Session of the Ninth Parliament of the Republic of South Africa." Cape Town, 1 February 1991.

South African Department of Information. *This is South Africa.* Pretoria: Department of Information, 1971.

Secondary Sources

Adam, Heribert. *Modernizing Racial Domination.* Berkeley: University of California Press, 1972.

Adams, James. *The Unnatural Alliance.* London: Quartet Books, 1984.

Barker, Ernest. *Church, State, and Education.* Ann Arbor: University of Michigan Paperbacks Press, 1957.

Barton, Frank. *The Press of Africa.* New York: Holmes and Meier, 1979.

Benson, Mary. *South Africa: The Struggle for a Birthright.* New York: Funk and Wagnalls, 1969.

Bradford, Helen. *A Taste of Freedom: The Industrial and Commercial Workers' Union in Rural South Africa 1924-1930.* New Haven: Yale University Press, 1987.

Branford, Jean. *A Dictionary of South African English.* Cape Town: Oxford University Press, 1980.

Bunting, Brian. *The Rise of the South African Reich.* London: Penguin Books, 1964.

Burns, John. "Mandela, Inspiration and Legend, Faces Real Politics." *New York Times* (4 February 1990).

Butler, Jeffrey, Robert I. Rotberg, and John Adams. *The Black Homelands of South Africa.* Berkeley: University of California Press, 1978.

Calpin, G. H. *Indians in South Africa.* Pietermaritzburg: Shuter and Shooter, 1949.

Carter, Gwendolen. *Which Way is South Africa Going?* Bloomington: Indiana University Press, 1980.

Carter, Gwendolen and Patrick O'Meara. *Southern Africa: The Continuing Crisis.* Bloomington: Indiana University Press, 1979.

Clough, Michael and Jeffrey Herbst. *South Africa's Changing Regional Strategy: Beyond Destabilization.* New York: Council of Foreign Relations Press, 1989.

Cowell, Alan. "To the Far Right of Apartheid." *New York Times Magazine* (23 November 1986).

Davenport, T. R. H. *South Africa: A Modern History.* Toronto: University of Toronto Press, 1977.

de St. Jorre, John. *A House Divided: South Africa's Uncertain Future.* New York: Carnegie Endowment for International Peace, 1977.

de Villiers, Les. *South Africa: A Skunk Among Nations.* London: Universal-Tandem, 1975.

Dillenberger, John. *John Calvin: Selections from His Writings.* New York: Anchor Books, 1971.

Elphick, Richard. *Khoikhoi and the Founding of White South Africa.* Johannesburg: Ravan Press, 1985.

Elphick, Richard and Hermann Gibiomee, eds. *The Shaping of South African Society 1652-1820.* London: Longman, 1979.

Fatton, Robert. *Black Consciousness in South Africa: The Dialectics of Ideological Resistance to White Supremacy.* Albany: State University of New York Press, 1986.

Frankel, Philip. *Pretoria's Praetorians.* Cambridge: Cambridge University Press, 1984.

Fredrickson, George. *White Supremacy: A Comparative Study in America and South African History.* New York: Oxford University Press, 1981.

Gann, L. H. and P. Duignan. *White Settlers in Tropical Africa*. London: Penguin Books, 1962.

Gerhart, Gail. *Black Power in South Africa: The Evolution of an Ideology*. Berkeley: University of California Press, 1978.

Grundy, Kenneth. *The Militarization of South African Politics*. Bloomington: Indiana University Press, 1986.

Hanf, Theodor, Heribert Weiland, Gerda Vierdag, Lawrence Schlemmer, Rainer Hampel, and Burkhard Krupp. *South Africa: The Prospects of Peaceful Change*. Bloomington: Indiana University Press, 1981.

Harrison, David. *The White Tribe of Africa*. Berkeley: University of California Press, 1981.

Houghton, D. Hobart. *The Tomlinson Report: A Summary of the Findings of the Recommendations in the Tomlinson Commission Report*. Johannesburg: The South African Institute of Race Relations, 1956.

Huddleston, Trevor. *Naught for Your Comfort*. London: Fortana Books, 1957.

Human Sciences Research Council. *The South African Society: Realities and Future Prospects*. Westport, CT: Greenwood Press, 1987.

Hund, John and Hendrik van der Merwe. *Legal Ideology and Politics in South Africa*. Lanham, MD: University Press of America, 1986.

James, Wilmot. *The State of Apartheid*. Boulder, CO: Lynne Rienner Publishers, 1987.

Jenkins, Simon. "The Great Evasion: South Africa: A Survey." *Economist* (21 June 1980).

Johns, Sheridan and R. Hunt Davis, eds. *Mandela, Tambo, and the African National Congress: The Struggle Against Apartheid, 1948-1990*. New York: Oxford University Press, 1991.

Jooma, Ahmed. *Migrancy: After Influx Control*. Johannesburg: South African Institute of Race Relations, 1991.

Keller, Bill. "Mandela Shares Nobel Accolade with de Klerk." *New York Times* (16 October 1993).

_____. "Party's Split Casts Shadow on a Dream." *New York Times* (16 August 1992).

_____. "South African Rightists Rally behind Ex-Generals." *New York Times* (6 May 1993).

Lambert, Bruce. "Andries Treurnicht, 72, Leader of Hard-Line Pro-Apartheid Party." *New York Times Obituary* (23 April 1993).

Laurence, John. *The Seeds of Disaster: A Guide to the Realities, Race Politics and World-wide Propaganda Campaigns of the Republic of South Africa*. London: Victor Gollancz, 1968.

Le May, G. H. *Black and White in South Africa: The Politics of Survival*. New York: American Heritage Press, 1971.

Lewis, Gavin. *Between the Wire and the Wall: A History of South African Coloured Politics*. New York: St. Martin's Press, 1987.

Lodge, Tom. *Black Politics in South Africa since 1945*. London: Longman, 1983.

Mackler, Ian. *Pattern for Profit in Southern Africa*. New York: Atheneum, 1975.

Mansergh, Nicholas. *South Africa 1906-1961: The Price of Magnanimity.*
New York: Praeger, 1962.

Marks, Shula and Stanley Trapido. *The Politics of Race, Class and
Nationalism in Twentieth-Century South Africa.* London: Longman,
1987.

Marquard, Leo. *The Peoples and Policies of South Africa.* London:
Oxford University Press, 1969.

Mason, Philip. *Patterns of Dominance.* London: Oxford University
Press, 1971.

McCallum, R. B. *The Liberal Party from Earl Grey to Asquith.* London:
Victor Gollancz, 1963.

Mzimela, Sipo. *Apartheid: South African Naziism.* New York: Vantage
Press, 1983.

New York Times. "Rival Black Group Offers to Join with Mandela" (25
November 1990).

Özgur Özdemir. *Apartheid: The United Nations and Peaceful Change in
South Africa.* Dobbs Ferry, NY: Transnational Publishers, 1982.

Platzky, Laurine and Cherryl Walker. *The Surplus People: Forced
Removals in South Africa.* Johannesburg: Ravan Press, 1985.

Price, Robert. *The Apartheid State in Crisis: Political Transformation in
South Africa 1975-1990.* New York: Oxford University Press, 1991.

Price, Robert and Carl Rosberg, eds. *The Apartheid Regime: Political
Power and Racial Domination.* Berkeley: University of California
Press, 1980.

Rogers, Barbara. "South Africa's Fifth Column in the United States." *Africa Report* (November-December 1977).

_____. "Sunny South Africa: A Worldwide Propaganda Machine." *Africa Report* (September-October 1977).

Salvadori, Massimo. *European Liberalism.* New York: John Wiley and Sons, 1972.

Sampson, Anthony. *Black and Gold.* New York: Pantheon Books, 1987.

South Africa 1992. Johannesburg: The South Africa Foundation, 1992.

South African Scope. "Separate Development: South Africa and the European Example." (September 1975/January 1976).

Suzman, Helen. *Holding the High Ground.* Johannesburg: South African Institute of Race Relations, 1991.

Tatum, Lyle, ed. *South Africa: Challenge and Hope.* New York: Hill and Wang, 1987.

The Study Commission on U.S. Policy toward Southern Africa. *South Africa: Time Running Out.* Berkeley: University of California Press, 1981.

Thompson, Leonard. *The Political Mythology of Apartheid.* New Haven: Yale University Press, 1985.

Thompson, Leonard and Andrew Prior. *South African Politics.* New Haven: Yale University Press, 1982.

Treverton, Gregory, ed. *Europe, America and South Africa.* New York: Council of Foreign Relations Press, 1988.

Van den Berghe, Pierre. *South Africa: A Study in Conflict.* Berkeley: University of California Press, 1967.

South African Digest. "Watershed Years for South Africa." Extract from an address by Dr. C. D. Mulder, Minister of Information, to the Johannesburg Afrikaanse Sakakamer, 10 September 1976.

Wren, Christopher. "Afrikaner Cohesion: A Myth System Blown Apart." *New York Times* (14 August 1991).

_____. "A.N.C. Figure to Lead Communists." *New York Times* (8 December 1991).

_____. "Fewer Options for South Africa's Rightists." *New York Times* (1 March 1992).

_____. "South Africa's Buthelezi: The Chief Steps Forward." *New York Times Magazine* (17 February 1991).

_____. "Zephania Mathopeng, 77, Dies; Headed South African Movement." *New York Times Obituary* (24 October 1990).

_____. "Zulu Chief Turning Movement into Political Party." *New York Times* (15 July 1990).

Conclusion

Butterfield, Herbert. *The Statescraft of Machiavelli.* New York: Collier Books, 1967.

Dahl, Robert. *Dilemmas of Pluralist Democracy: Autonomy vs. Control.* New Haven: Yale University Press, 1982.

Germino, Dante. "Second Thoughts on Leo Strauss's Machiavelli." *The Journal of Politics* (November 1966).

Gurr, Ted Robert. "Speaking about Democracy and Peace." *Journal of the United States Institute of Peace* (June 1990).

Machiavelli, Niccolo. *The Prince and The Discourses.* New York: Random House, 1950.

Morris-Hale, Walter. "Review Article: Machiavelli's *The Prince* in Unstable Times; Machiavelli's *The Discourses* in Stable Times." *The Journal of Politics* (February 1977).

Nicholls, David. *Three Varieties of Pluralism.* New York: The New American Library, 1956.

Pocock, J. G. A. "Machiavelli, Harrington and English Political Ideologies in the Eighteenth Century." In *Politics, Language and Time.* London: Atheneum, 1971.

Strauss, Leo. *Thoughts of Machiavelli.* Chicago: University of Chicago Press, 1958.

Tsurutani, Taketsugu. "Machiavelli and the Problem of Political Development." *Review of Politics* (July 1968).

Index

MAJOR CONCEPTS IN POLITICS AND POLITICAL THEORY

This series invites book manuscripts and proposals on major concepts in politics and political theory—justice, equality, virtue, rights, citizenship, power, sovereignty, property, liberty, etc.—in prominent traditions, periods, and thinkers.

Send manuscripts or proposals, with author's vitae to:

Garrett Ward Sheldon
General Editor
College Avenue
Clinch Valley College
University Virginia
Wise, VA 24293